electric ufos

electric ufos

fireballs, electromagnetics and abnormal states

Albert Budden

BLANDFORD

Dedicated to my dear daughter Verity Victoria

A BLANDFORD BOOK

First published in the UK 1998 by Blandford
A Cassell imprint, Wellington House, 125 Strand
LONDON WC2R 0BB

Distributed in the United States by Sterling Publishing Co., Inc.
387 Park Avenue South, New York, NY 10016–8810

British Library Cataloguing-in-Publication Data
A catalogue record for this book is available from the British Library.

ISBN 0 7137 2730 6 (hardback)
ISBN 0 7137 2685 7 (paperback)

Text design by Richard Carr
Illustrations on pages 6, 36, 39 and 204 by Ethan Danielson
Printed and bound in Great Britain by Creative Print and Design Wales,
Ebbw Vale

Contents

INTEGRATED ELEMENTS OF THE ELECTROMAGNETIC POLLUTION APPROACH

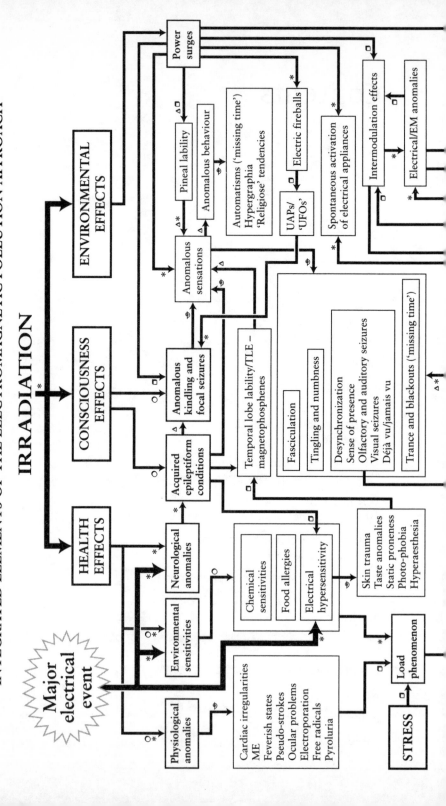

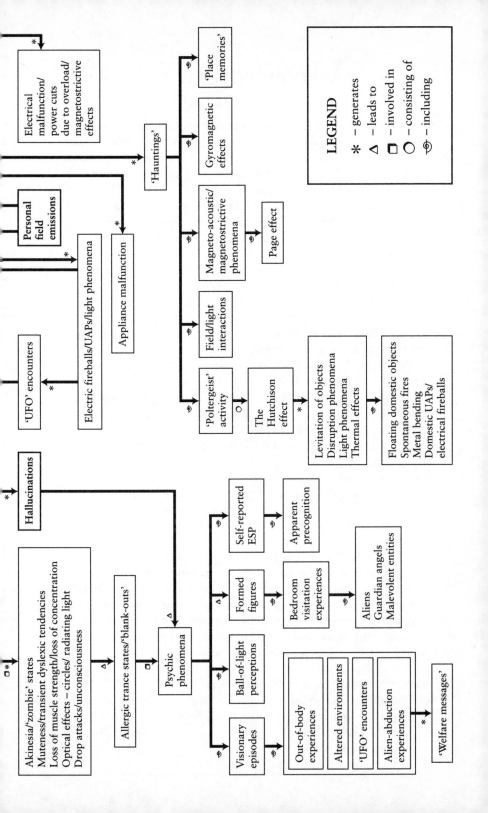

Acknowledgements

Many people who are specialists within their own field have contributed directly or indirectly to this work. Firstly, I must thank optician Anne Silk, of Buckinghamshire, UK – without whom none of this would have been possible – for her continued support and erudite knowledge on health effects and medical matters.

My heartfelt thanks also go to Dr Jean Monro and Dr Andrew Fountain of the Breakspear Hospital, Hertfordshire, UK, who generously provided their time, insights and references. My thanks also to:

Nicholas Reiter, of Gibsonburg, Ohio, USA, for allowing me to include his pioneering investigations, and for opening so many doors I never knew existed.

John Hutchison, of British Columbia, Canada, without whose ground-breaking work I could not have been so spectacularly vindicated in my claims about the electromagnetic nature of the physical phenomena of 'poltergeist' outbreaks.

George Hathaway, of Ontario, Canada, for all his first-hand observations and authoritative information.

James F. Corum, of West Virginia, USA, for his spontaneous generosity in his donations of information and photographs of laboratory-produced electric fireballs.

Professor Kenneth Ring, of the University of Connecticut, USA, for recognizing the value of my work in the early months and for his endorsement and insightful advice.

Dr Jacques Vallée, of San Francisco, USA, for recognizing and endorsing my approach, and for providing additional case examples.

Dr Michael Persinger, of Laurentian University (Neuroscience), Canada, for his encouraging compliments.

Dr David Gotlib, of Ontario, Canada, for his enthusiasm towards my new approach, and recognition that 'you are onto something'.

Dr Eddie Bullard, of Indiana, USA, for his definitive statements, encouragement and recognizing that the electromagnetic approach presents a significant challenge to the extraterrestrial hypothesis (ETH).

British earth-lights pioneer Paul Devereux, for his advice and warnings, as he has trodden a similar iconoclastic path.

Jean Phillips of the environmental group 'Powerwatch', Cambridgeshire, UK, for her interest and encouragement.

I would also like to thank all the experiencers in the UK, Australia and the USA who have contributed to this book.

Lastly, my special thanks to artists Michael Buhler, Graham Fletcher and Poppy Palin.

Preface

A new scientific truth does not triumph by convincing its opponents and making them see the light, but rather because its opponents eventually die, and a new generation grows up that is familiar with it.

Max Planck

WHILE THERE has been considerable research into the effects of electromagnetic (EM) fields within many types of systems in the physics laboratory or engineering workshop, the literature on their effects upon the environments in which we live is sparse. Further, it could be said that research into their effects upon the human system is in its infancy, and because such empirical investigations within the last few decades have taken place within the context of their unintentional side-effects on health, where the stability of power and communication industries is potentially at risk, it has not seemed possible for unbiased information to be established.

Authorities are concerned that the floodgates of litigation will be opened, if not the Pandora's box of property devaluation, and they will be financially ruined. It is not an exaggeration to suggest that whole economies would be at risk. Potentially, the issue of EM pollution is dynamite. In fact, so sensitive an issue is it, and so far-reaching, that protest has been minimal and localized. Many people are wary of undermining that very aspect on which our survival in towns and cities rests: the supply of electricity.

Likewise, the mass dependency on the telecommunication industry causes many researchers to think hard before they deliver to the public domain any indictments relating to adverse health effects. Many think, I suspect, that it is a small price to pay for the services which the industry provides. Therefore, there is no doubt that the issue is potentially explosive politically, and there is evidence to suggest that a nervous telecommunications sector periodically organizes international conferences where papers are presented by experts to show that the whole EM-pollution approach is a mythology perpetrated by cranks and the misguided.

To my mind, this does their defence more harm than good, as many of the methodologies of the experiments presented are so transparently weak that they serve only to deepen the suspicion of anyone entering the field for the first time, if you will pardon the pun. Similarly, however, counterconferences take place which paint a reversed picture, and one may feel that the truth lies somewhere in between. To my mind, this is a mistake, as I can state unequivocally, as someone who goes out into the field (literally!) and investigates, that prolonged exposure to EM fields *does* produce adverse effects on the health of individuals. However, it is not generally realized that this includes mental health and, in many cases, sufferers undergo disturbing visions that were previously thought to be the material for psychical research or studies of unidentified flying objects (UFOs).

There is plenty of material for conspiracy theorists to construct a very sinister scenario within the EM-pollution issue. Because whole economies are potentially at risk from revelations concerning adverse health effects, and even mortalities, it is not outside the bounds of feasibility for authorities to initiate the liquidation of the originators of such information, depending on the effects which it is having on the hearts and minds of the populace. At the very least, we could certainly conceive of covert surveillance, telephone-tapping and the keeping of secret files.

There is even a case to answer, in one instance, for EM harassment having taken place, although this was said to have been in connection with the testing of an EM weapons system by the British Ministry of Defence, during which UFOs were observed by the inhabitants of a small Kentish town in the UK. Extending this, I have received several reports, originating in the USA, of secret government projects concerned with testing psychotronic weaponry on an unsuspecting population. It has proved impossible to check upon such claims and, in the end, they have smacked of being just another marketable item in the process of creation. However, it is entirely unnecessary to evoke such conspiratorial scenarios because the conditions already exist as accidental EM configurations in the environment, and these are able to induce a range of bizarre consciousness and adverse health effects.

Before the complexities of EM pollution, and as an introduction, let us stand back from the collections of specific detail for a more panoramic vista of this strange area of study. This viewpoint – to see these energies abroad in the environment as a whole complex enigmatic phenomenon in itself – is revealing because it shows how traditional aspects of the unknown have really just been redirected, as opposed to the reductionist view, which says that there is nothing to get excited about – all mysteries are only field effects of one kind or another. We cannot all pack up and go home – mysteries solved – which is how many have mistakenly regarded my approach. Instead, we can stay in the field, but with a new sense of awareness, whereby the knowledge embodied in the EM-pollution approach gives us a sense of being the conjurer rather than the mystified audience.

Knowing how the tricks are done may spoil it for some, but for those who can see past this, it is *empowering*, as they will realize that we are dealing with something very strange indeed and will want to become members of the magic circle. This may mean accepting that the Chinese linking rings do not really dematerialize in order to link, but such super-natural 'miracles' are now being superseded by the weird events in the EM laboratory of John Hutchison, for example, where phenomena have occurred, and continue to occur, which outstrip any conjuring trick for presenting 'impossible' realities. In fact, so genuinely strange and anom-alous is the Hutchison effect that many just refuse to accept it; in their eyes, whatever evidence is presented, from whatever respected scientific establishment, it remains a hoax or trick.

So dear reader, take note. This is an extremely rare event. I will be describing a cluster of physical effects that are genuine anomalies and really *do* press against the known laws of physics. However, as mentioned, these effects are so strange and unlikely, and apparently so simply generated, that there is a strong chance that you just will not believe them. They are all the result of the Hutchison effect (see chapter 2), which is generated at low power and at a distance, but it is so odd that many eminent and sensible scientists will just refuse to believe in it. It is the cluster of phenomena that psychical researchers have been calling 'poltergeists' for many decades.

So, apart from the Hutchison effect, what is it that this 'standing back to look' perspective will show us that is so strange and fascinating but not already self-evident? It is not only the unintended but also the completely *unimagined* outcomes of installing electricity and EM fields, for whatever reasons, within the environment in which we all live. It was a gradual realization that I found completely stunning, as it dawned upon me what the weird long-term consequences were of taking field-emitting devices constructed in a laboratory workshop and placing them in rural, urban and residential environments, there to constantly pour out EM energy. This surely seems like a fundamental act against nature that we have all accepted, if not taken for granted. Such devices have become like wallpaper in that we just do not notice them anymore, assuming that we did in the first place. However, it is in such 'hot spots' that rogue fields interact with each other, as well as with the existing natural earth energies, causing havoc with the functioning of the human biological system. I am not just referring to the adverse health effects of living near power lines, but the fact, which has become evident to me, that such mundane developments of electrical engineering could translate into the utterly bizarre consciousness effects of alien abductions, out-of-body experiences (OBEs), ghostly visitations and the physical phenomena of 'hauntings', poltergeists and UFOs.

The wide range of enigmas which are stimulated into being by EM energies reflects the same versatility of electricity which is evident from its uses in the systems and devices that are so familiar to us. Just as these energies, when processed through electronic systems, can become the moving/talking imagery of television and video, so too can they simulate the vivid reality of the field-driven vision when processed by the brain. And, for the technically minded, just as Lenz's law allows the non-ferrous wheel of a car's speedometer to be manipulated by magnetic fields, so too can the Hutchison effect levitate an 8.6kg (19lb) bronze cylinder or induce a plank of wood to hover using fields in the microvolt range. Who would have thought that such a thing was possible? It is therefore entirely understandable for past researchers, knowing that magnetic fields only affect objects made of iron, to have thought that a mysterious mind-energy, called 'psychokinesis', was involved in poltergeist activity. Established psychical researchers in particular will have to take account of the new perspectives I have to offer and radically alter their thinking. It has become increasingly obvious that their past investigations into the EM option for understanding physical phenomena have been inadequate and dismissed with an ignorance that is quite worrying.

The fascinating picture and area of study which I am presenting is that the phenomena of aliens from outer space, spirits of the dead, or destructive entities from the astral plane, are instead the completely unexpected, unimaginable and bizarre outcomes of exposure to EM fields, including the natural EM energies from the earth and skies which have always been with us. It is the study of how the human organism responds to an accelerated EM environment, which, in evolutionary terms, has arrived so recently that the body has not had time to adapt. That is to say, to a large degree, this area is the study of the body and mind's maladaptation to these newly arrived electric skies.

Albert Budden
Brentford, 1998

Introduction
Electromagnetics: the psychical connection and close encounters

THE ISSUE OF EVIDENCE

In the past, researchers have not associated the paranormal with electromagnetic (EM) pollution, but investigations have shown that it is centrally implicated within it (see Budden, 1995).

One of the ground rules that have developed out of my investigations of psychic experiences involving apparent confrontation with otherworldly beings is that they have the same cause and are basically just different versions of the same effect. That is to say, certain sensitive people hallucinate spacemen and aliens, guardian angels, men in black, robots, exotic animals, religious icons and many other formed figures, and any division of these into separate categories is a spurious activity. One television researcher who examined my work simply said that I regarded aliens and ghosts as basically the same phenomenon, although this is a somewhat oversimplified and extreme interpretation of my approach. Anyone who has read my work to any extent will be aware that I maintain that such hallucinatory/visionary perceptions are caused ultimately by the action of EM fields in the environment on the human system, although physiological factors that are involved point to synergistic mechanisms.

However, I am equally aware that there are other causes of perceptions of ghosts; i.e. there is a mixture of causes. For example, it would seem evident that some, such as the apparitions of relatives seen by the bereaved in the weeks after death, are induced by purely psychological factors and are a not uncommon phenomenon. One woman regularly glimpsed her recently deceased mother in the shopping mall which they once used together. This has no apparent EM undertones. Equally, there are reliable accounts of two or more witnesses who briefly encounter someone at a time which they later learn was the time of his/her death. Again, there are no obvious EM fields involved, and such accounts are the staple material of the annals of psychical research. One of my favourite examples of this comes from a fireman who was active during World War Two:

> *After the war, Henry took his small son on a visit to the city area where he and his mates had endured their agony. Although he was unable to identify the streets amid the desert of rubble, he told the little lad how he had appeared as a vision which had guided his dad and brought him to safety.*
>
> *Henry Burrow, with his face scorched and hands badly burned, became confused, lost his sense of direction and his ability to think clearly. Suddenly, as he later related to his wife from his hospital bed, amid all the turmoil and din, flame and smoke, he had a vision of their small son beckoning from the doorway of a blazing building. He ran over and discovered stairs leading to the basement, which he descended, finding relief from his immediate peril. He was unable to recall his movements after that but eventually he was discovered wandering in a street party of soldiers. [Demarne, 1991.]*

This story is charming, but how scientific are such accounts? That is to say, while such anecdotal evidence is intriguing, can it be regarded as data in the sense of its testability? For example, are there any tangible factors, regularly associated with these reports, that will always be found and which will act as a hallmark of their authenticity? The consistency of the stories themselves would certainly seem to be a reliable aspect, except that we can find just such dogged consistency in a variety of the urban myths that people love to repeat and that folklorists assure us have no basis in reality; one cannot help wondering how many tales similar to the fireman's were told during and after the war, witnessed by a friend of a friend. Perhaps we may safely assume that the blitzed streets were thick with such visionary children! Furthermore, how can we be sure that investigators are not just spreading the 'phenomenon' of bereavement apparitions, e.g. by collecting and publicizing these stories? Personally, I find such accounts entirely convincing for a number of subtle reasons, but that is probably because I am an investigator who goes out into the field and explores such cases firsthand.

THE PSYCHOSOCIAL FALLACY

Most people get their information about alien encounters or apparitional confrontations, etc. from written accounts in books or the specialist literature, which is very much like looking at a picture of a portrait, as opposed to looking directly upon the person themselves. The school of thought known as the *psychosocial approach* is particularly guilty of this, as it is this approach which maintains that there are no physical stimuli behind unidentified flying objects (UFOs), alien-abduction experiences, hauntings, poltergeists, etc., but that such phenomena are created and maintained by belief systems, urban myth, rumour, group cohesion and other sociological constructs. In the UK, for example, such an approach certainly appears to be the main thrust of the periodical *Magonia* (see Note 1). The raw material for this approach rests mainly on written accounts, especially in the specialist literature of the subcultures which are preoccupied with such subjects, and its proponents do not appear to carry out any firsthand investigations, as it is their *a priori* assumption that there is nothing to investigate! Instead they gather material from historical texts and trace the development of mythologies, never realizing the severe limitations inherent in this scholarly activity. As American folklorist Dr T.E. Bullard explains in the introduction to his epic study of alien-abduction experiences, *UFO Abductions: The Measure of a Mystery*, even firsthand accounts, let alone historical texts, are far removed from the true reality of such experiences:

> *In a final analysis, the subject matter of this study is not really abductions or, properly speaking, even eyewitness reports. It is something less than either one. All we have to work with are texts of those reports – dead texts, with all the juice of human emotion dried out of them, cut off from the investigator's one-to-one relationship with the witness, and separated from any physical traces the event may have inscribed on the human body or landscape. An investigator can cross-examine a live witness, delve into his feelings and weigh his responses, check for physical traces and evaluate the case from several perspectives. No such dialogue is possible with texts. They are mute beyond their literal affirmation. Any conclusions reached here must be conclusions about texts. All evaluations, all comparisons, all consistencies apply to texts alone and not necessarily to any truth underlying them. Final answers lie outside these bounds among those very dimensions a text excludes. [Bullard, 1987.]*

This damning indictment of the psychosocial approach is further compounded by the fact that its main proponents appear to carry out no sociological experiments themselves, despite the fact that the sociological literature provides the methodology and conclusions of field studies on many subcultures comparable to the UFO/paranormal groups. It is fair to say, in the UK at least, that its main proponents (e.g. writer Kevin McClure and editor John Rimmer) are non-scientists attempting to comment on scientific/ medical approaches, the EM-pollution/environmental health approach being one of them.

If anyone is in the position to make a definitive judgement on the psychosocial status of abduction reports, Dr Bullard certainly has the background to do so, having explored the generation of folklore/urban myths at academic levels and alien-abduction accounts as a unique study. However, he is not at all convinced:

> *Abduction reports do not act like narratives under the influence of cultural forces. The dynamics are not there … One way or another, there's no escape from the mystery of consistency in abduction reports. It suggests an underpinning more substantial than fantasy, an experience of some sort that happens to diverse people and happens to them in a similar way. Whether the experience is subjective or objective remains to be seen, but something more than sociocultural forces or personal needs appears to underlie the abduction phenomenon. (Bullard, 1987)*

No further knock-out blows to the ethos of the psychosocial approach are needed, as this debate is surely at an end. I read sociology at university and am aware that, while these unusual consciousness effects generate sociological implications, because they involve human groups, they are not sociological in themselves, but bioelectromagnetic in nature.

THE VALIDITY OF REPORTS

The same non-scientific status could be said of most UFO-related events. The people who relate such accounts do not usually share the same concern for establishing any form of objective truth about these events as investigators into this kind of phenomenon. That is to say, while it should be the concern of investigators to discern truth from falsity, the people who relate these accounts are usually much more preoccupied with simply being believed and, from my experience, there is a distinct trend to add confirming aspects. For example, other witnesses with professional status will appear, and even crowds of people evoked. Such embellishments are added with a certain feeling of justified licence by witnesses, as they cannot usually offer anything to substantiate their experience other than their sincerity. Consider the following:

> *A case I examined in my early years as an investigator was related to me by someone who I took to be a seasoned investigator themselves. This investigator described her circumstances when she was much younger, with two small children, living in a suburb of London. It transpired, she explained, that one hot summer's day one of the children was overcome with heatstroke and the doctor was called. When the doctor arrived he found that he had left behind some essential medicine and invited mother and children to ride back with him to his surgery. However, on the way through the quiet leafy avenues, the car began to malfunction and eventually ground to a halt. They then became aware of a huge shadow which*

*loomed above them. On looking up they saw a vast saucer-shaped craft
which slowly descended and came to a stop a mere 6m (20ft) above the
car, spanning the width of the road and overlapping the front gardens
either side. Dumbfounded, they became frightened that this heavy-
looking, gun-metal-coloured machine would drop down even further and
crush them. The mother then recovered enough to examine the underside,
which she described as having three spheres mounted equidistantly at the
points of a triangle, apparently serving as some kind of landing gear. She
looked round and called to some children playing in the street to look up
at the saucer, which they did and were duly amazed. After a few bemused
minutes they became aware of a low humming noise ('You know, that
deep powerful diesel-like sound that a saucer's engine would make') and,
with no other warning, the whole craft rose up about 15m (50ft), tilted
at an angle and shot into the sky and was a small dot 'in seven seconds'.*

Working in my first year as an investigator, I was greatly impressed with
this account of events purported to have taken place 30 years previously.
However, a thorough examination of standard reference material found
that the doctor cited was not on any medical register for the year in
question, nor on any official listing for the 2 years before or after. The
children in the street could not be traced and I could find no other
witnesses whatsoever living in the surrounding houses. The children in
the car, as young adults, did seem to confirm the mother's story, but
their written accounts did not match up in many details with each
other's or their mother's account. There were also small annotations in
the margins of their reports in their mother's distinctive handwriting.
On balance, I decided that the whole story was fabricated. However, I
was aware that the sort of balancing I was doing was the sort of activity
that a juror would do after listening to the pros and cons of a case in a
court of law. There was nothing directly tangible or testable about this
case, and certainly nothing about it could be translated into an experiment of any kind. It served as a salutary lesson to me as an inexperienced
investigator that we are not studying UFOs at all, but *reports* of UFOs.

One of the quite legitimate criticisms that scientists could level
against reports of alien abductions is that there is no way of telling the
difference between a genuine experience, whatever that may mean, and
a fabricated one. A doctor called Lawson asked several subjects to
describe an imaginary alien-encounter experience and found that the
same details cropped up in these accounts as in those which had been
collected by investigators in the field and deemed to be genuine.

So this fundamental problem of how to tell the difference between a
genuine case and a fabricated one is an aspect that has not been satisfac-
torily overcome by ufologists, although the better ones are working on it.

Consistency has again been offered as an objective criterion but, as details of well-known cases are presented in best-selling books, this factor has been destroyed, i.e. the hallmarks of authenticity can be learned and woven into a false account. Once again, we are dealing with reports on the level of a court-room argument rather than using any scientific criteria. However, it is true to say that many investigators who are truly concerned with distinguishing authentic accounts from false ones build up their own idiosyncratic criteria to rely on, which often include 'little details' or a 'gut feeling'. Neither however, is scientific.

So what would we need to be able to identify cases scientifically? Faced with an individual who relates the spontaneous appearance of 8-foot tall humanoids made of dazzling golden light, who slowly emerge through the walls of his bedsitting room, how would the scientist or even physician be able to make an informed decision on the authenticity of such a report? Before I answer this question, let us not be confused about what would be regarded as an authentic or genuine case. Let us take a purely phenomenological approach. That is to say, without making any assumptions about whether such beings exist objectively, or are autonomous in any sense of the word, let us consider the issue of whether or not the individual really perceives such things or is merely making it all up. In fact, the description given is from an actual case (Ian of Peckham), which is explored in more detail on p.204. After I had listened to Ian for some time, while sitting in his room, he suddenly turned, looked me in the eye and simply asked, 'Well, do you believe me?' To his intense and visible relief I told him that I did. Why?

THE MEDICAL/ENVIRONMENTAL HEALTH MODEL

The scientific method involves the construction of a hypothesis and then setting up criteria to test its validity. In actuality, we can, at best, only arrive at a position of strong circumstantial evidence; only in the fields of logic and pure mathematics do we get absolute proof. But, with the parameters identified in the case studies of the phenomena that are the topic of this book, the evidence is so consistent (if not monotonous) that it soon becomes clear that we are looking at an extremely robust effect across populations of experiencers. However, note well that I will not be offering the consistency of the accounts *per se* as evidence of their objective status, for we have already seen how these can be manipulated by psychosocial factors. Instead, I offer parameters that include a set of signs and symptoms which would be used by any general practitioner as part of a diagnostic process. Reports of these signs and symptoms would not have been passed on via psychosocial processes mainly because both experiencer and investigator are unaware of their existence and significance in the context of these consciousness effects, i.e. alien-contact/abduction experiences. That is to say, the areas of potential urban myth have been completely side-stepped. Instead we will be considering the identification of a *clinical syndrome,* one symptom of which involves the propensity to experience vivid hallucinatory realities that, at times, appear to the experiencer to be virtually identical to their everyday reality. In fact, this is not quite accurate, as the experiences of alien contact and abduction are repeatedly reported as having a vivid super-real quality about them. This unusual subsidiary aspect is entirely consistent with the stimulus identified as being the cause of these perceptions, i.e. EM pollution, and reasons for the appearance of this super-real quality will be outlined. However, in order to provoke the interest of the reader, it can be mentioned that this hallucinatory vividness is due to the fact that, frequently, these electrically driven visions are the result of induced body currents being translated into imagery in the visual cortex of the brain. So what are these environmental/medical parameters that occur with such robustness across populations of experiencers?

The following is a 'blueprint' summary of my approach; it may strike the reader as being somewhat dense but it will be broken down and simplified as it is applied to the cases presented. It is included for those readers who are interested in the more specialized medical/technical aspects; and will be expanded upon in Chapter 3, which concerns holistic medicine. It is also outlined here in order to release me from having to explain many new concepts later, at points when the intended emphasis is elsewhere. However, I will show how the same basic parameters in the individual and in the environment can be found over and over again, in case after case, with monotonous regularity. This is an extremely robust approach and any failure to adopt it as the primary way of understanding the phenomena it encompasses lies in factors which originate within individuals and/or groups, and not in the environmental health approach itself. In fact, the primary reason for such a 'blueprint' is to familiarize the reader with the natural history of these bioelectromagnetic consciousness effects.

THE ENVIRONMENTAL HEALTH APPROACH: a preliminary blueprint

In the course of my investigations over the past 4 years I have discovered that contactees, or 'abductees' as they have come to be known, have developed an environmental sensitivity syndrome which includes food allergies, chemical sensitivities, electromagnetic hypersensitivity (EH) (Smith & Best, 1989) and symptoms of epileptiform conditions, their subsequent hallucinatory/visionary experiences being a symptom of this syndrome.

Many experiencers were quite unaware of their nutritional maladaptations, although, with some, it was evident from their physical appearance, which was due to the incidence of *masked food allergies*. In such allergies, a food is taken which induces adverse symptoms but, paradoxically, it is also craved by the sufferer as a sort of food addiction. This frequent intake of an allergen induces a characteristic double wrinkle under the eyes, known as *Dennie's sign*, and is often accompanied by dark crescents and a pale complexion, giving the subject the 'allergic look' (Rapp, 1979). However, while certain experiencers displayed this, many did not, and it was found that chemical sensitivities were more typically associated with the condition primarily responsible for their hallucinatory experiences, i.e. EH, and this sensitivity to common substances (e.g. domestic gas, make-up, aerosols) does not seem to register physically in the way that food allergies evidently do.

Apart from their bizarre experiences, which include apparitions and alien-encounter experiences, most experiencers knew that there was something unusual about them by the way that electrical equipment regularly malfunctioned in their presence. This is something that many investigators have found and is a sign of EH; the subject, as an allergic reaction when exposed to fields, actually emits coherent (i.e. beam-like) magnetic fields as a whole-body effect (Smith & Best, 1989). Investigators have found that this can cause malfunction of the tape-recorders which they use to record interviews; the microscopic ferrite elements in the electronics of the tape-recorder change shape (i.e deform) in response to a magnetic field, so that critical contacts are lost, causing a temporary malfunction. This physical effect is known as *magnetostriction* (Burke, 1986). When the subject's personal magnetic emissions cease, the minute electronic structures return to their normal shape, contacts are regained and the appliance resumes working. Of course, many experiencers have been encouraged by the extraterrestrial hypothesis (ETH) enthusiasts to regard this as the covert activity of aliens in order to prevent evidence of their existence on Earth spreading, or as the malevolent wishes of a spirit of a haunting, depending on current beliefs.

EFFECTS OF EXPOSURE TO ELECTROMAGNETIC FIELDS

Case-file studies have indicated that there exists in the population the propensity to undergo realistic and vivid hallucinatory/visionary experiences associated with specific clinical parameters primarily as a result of exposure to fields from a variety of sources of electrical and EM pollution in the environment, frequently in combination with natural geoelectromagnetic emissions at locations over fault lines. These consciousness effects, which are intrinsically associated with a range of physiological dysfunctions, are an indicator that the body is failing to adapt to EM stressors in the environment, leading to a breakdown of the regulatory systems of the body. Artificial fields, classified as electronic and electrical pollution, are emitted from communication and power-line systems. These produce raised ambient field levels at geographically located EM hot spots, e.g. calculated power-line and/or radio-transmitter proximity. It is in these hot-spot locations that individuals who are subjected to prolonged irradiation develop sensitivities to EM fields generally.

MAJOR ELECTRICAL EVENTS

It has been found that EH is especially enhanced in individuals who, earlier in their lives, have been in close proximity to such events as a lightning strike, ball lightning, earth lights (Devereux & McCartney, 1982), corona discharges and aerial light phenomena, or have suffered major electrocution. Such extreme and sudden exposure to massive EM-field strengths and/or currents is known as a *major electrical event* (MEE) and it is this electrical initiation which kick-starts the body into field sensitivity.

Individuals thus affected frequently become sensitive to general environmental stimuli, e.g. noise, light and vibration (*hyperaesthesia*), and, as an extension of this, begin to report psychic effects such as extrasensory perception (ESP), or precognition. Double-blind tests have not been carried out on such predictions and it is not known to what extent they are valid. It would appear that this acquired faculty is facilitated by the individuals' ability to detect weak electrical ambiences in the environment and from the physiology of others, although research into this is in its infancy. However, researchers such as Dr C. W. Smith and Dr Jean Monro of the Breakspear Hospital, Hertfordshire, UK, where EH is treated, regard the perceptions of ghosts as *place memories*, whereby the EH individual is able to scan his/her immediate environment (rather like an electric fish detects prey) and perceive 'recordings' of events retained in the environmental water inherent in the fabric of buildings, roads, etc. In fact, this is consistent with my own findings where 'abductees' typically have a history of ghostly encounters and/or visionary experiences. However, it must be clarified that EH subjects sometimes have the *dual ability* to detect such place memories, which can be regarded as objective phenomena, and hallucinate in response to exposure to EM radiation, perceiving imagery which is endogenous in origin, i.e. from their own unconscious 'image bank'.

THE LOAD PHENOMENON: synergistic mechanisms

The condition of EH consists of a range of clinically detectable signs and symptoms and is frequently linked to other sensitivities, such as food allergies and chemical intolerances (e.g. to aerosols, cleaning products, perfume, cigarette smoke, domestic gas). Frequently in combination with psychological stress, which also induces adverse chemical changes in the body, it is instrumental in producing a breakdown of the body's regulatory systems. This physiological dysfunction can lead to an intolerance threshold in nutritional, chemical and EM terms which is known as the *load phenomenon* (Breakspear Hospital, 1994).

It is during such high physiological load levels that hallucinatory states are precipitated if the hypersensitive individual is then exposed to environmental fields; these additional stressors cause the body's systems to exceed tolerance thresholds. Such hypersensitive field-triggered individuals perceive hallucinations as formed figures, altered environments, out-of-body experiences (OBEs), alien-contact/abduction experiences and other perceptual anomalies.

EPILEPTIFORM STATES

The mechanisms instrumental in precipitating such hallucinatory states are consistent with epileptiform focal seizures, or *syncopes*, in which an electrical destabilization of the brain occurs due to frequent and prolonged irradiation by EM fields from the environmental sources mentioned, the skull being entirely transparent to this irradiation. Therefore, EH percipients, in addition to experiencing hallucinations as visual seizures, display signs and symptoms typical of general epileptiform states, although *grand mal* seizures have not been found. These symptoms are described below.

1. Automatism
Individuals have periods of time for which they cannot account, i.e. 'missing time'. During these periods they carry out routine behaviour, such as walking or even driving, but have no memory of their actions (amnesic periods, transient global amnesia). Subjects may return with minor physical injuries or other evidence of automatic behaviour, e.g. one subject awoke to find that he was the wrong way round in bed and had dirty feet due to his amnesic 'walkabout'. [See Nathan, 1988.]

2. Trance states, or 'blank-outs'

During such disassociated periods subjects become 'zombie-like' and may be mute. Vivid visual hallucinatory realities may be experienced of a fantastic/symbolic nature.

3. Periods of unconsciousness or black-outs

These frequently occur during nocturnal hours and individuals have reported as being 'deeply asleep' or 'in a coma' by family members. During waking activities they may exhibit *drop attacks*.

4. Paralysis (*akinesia*)

Individuals experience transient periods of immobility, frequently although not exclusively on awakening.

5. Tingling (*somesthesia*) and numbness (*paresthesia*)

Bodily tingling and painful electrical sensations rippling in the muscles just below the skin (*fasciculation*) may occur on exposure to elevated ambient fields. Also, neuralgia-like sensations may be felt in the face. Sensations typically occur in the extremities and eyelids.

6. Visual seizures/hallucinations

These may be experienced as balls of light or formed figures, e.g. apparitions/aliens, altered/distorted environments, non-existent objects, UFOs. [See Gilroy, 1990, pp. 71–72.]

7. Sense of presence

Individuals feel that someone or something is in the room with them although they cannot see anything. This may be accompanied by a strong feeling of being watched. [See Ruttan *et al.*, 1990.]

8. *Déjà vu*

This common sensation is distinguished in EH subjects by its frequency and intensity. [See Halgren *et al.*, 1978.]

9. *Jamais vu*

Familiar surroundings are experienced as being strange. [See Gilroy, 1990.]

10. *Magnetophosphenes*

Stimulation and focal seizures in the temporal lobes produce this visual effect as swarms of light-flecks, dancing lights or sparkling aspects in the environment. They are seen in the upper left quadrant of the visual field. [See Ruttan *et al.*, 1990.]

11. *Sudden and intense fear*

Subjects may experience this emotional response as a physical state, with no apparent stimulus. It can be induced by electrical stimulation of the amygdala of the brain. [See Halgren *et al.*, 1978.]

SOURCES OF ELECTROMAGNETIC POLLUTION

Sources of EM fields in the environment include: radio-frequency (RF) transmitters (radio and TV stations, police stations, hospitals, fire services, transport-control centres, taxi-cab offices, diplomatic wavebands, radio hams, Citizens' Band (CB) radio networks, telecommunication towers, telephone exchanges, mobile-phone systems, airports, aircraft homing beacons, military and civil radar, military communication networks, microwave repeaters, etc.), power lines, high-tension cables, transformers, substations, junction boxes.

As well as these man-made sources of EM pollution, geomagnetic and geoelectrical fields produced during tectonic activity from faults in geological strata have always irradiated the interiors, and therefore the occupants, of dwellings built over them. Also, underground water conducts subterranean currents to and from strata. It is these natural sources of EM fields in the environment which have, in pre-electrical eras, been actively instrumental in the production of such historical and culture-bound antecedents to the alien mythology as demonic, angelic and other 'visitations' by entities thought to originate from non-corporeal realms, and they continue to provide objective imagery as place memories at 'haunted' locations. Today, these natural fields interact with their artificial counterparts, and add to the total EM environment.

ALIEN-ABDUCTION
EXPERIENCES/CONSCIOUSNESS EFFECTS

Analysis of the content of these experiences as an internal drama involving the captive examination of the percipient, or confrontation by a variety of 'aliens', frequently reveals the expression of a systemic dysfunction, i.e. illness induced by field exposure, in symbolic form. These have been termed *welfare messages*. This subjective imagery is actually highly personal in that it reflects the experiencers' physiological dysfunction and is a comment on the state of their health, ie. the content of these visions can be traced to the background and state of health of the experiencers.

EM-field-stimulated somatic sensations induce the recurring visionary depiction of an intrusive bodily examination by alien forms as a direct reflection of the effects that the fields are having on the body/nervous system. As stated, in the language of the human biological system, the external, artificial, foreign and intrusive EM fields comprise the physical 'alien' activity, which is depicted accordingly in symbolic form. For example, stimulation of the language centres of the brain – Broca's and Werninke's areas – produces apparent telepathic communication whereby the experiencer hears voices intruding into his thoughts.

CONCLUSION

Case-file studies indicate that a significant minority of the population is adversely affected by EM pollution to a greater extent than is generally recognized. Acute end-states of such systemic dysfunction (i.e. EH and multiple allergies/sensitivities) are intrinsically associated with a number of discrete consciousness effects which involve hallucinatory imagery triggered by exposure to fields during states where a physiological load threshold is exceeded. These subjects typically have a history of 'paranormal' experiences, sometimes reaching back to childhood, e.g. visual perceptions of formed figures, surreal environments, visionary episodes, self-reported ESP, OBEs, which have been associated with EH in clinical contexts (See Note 2); their alien-contact/abduction experiences are a further manifestation of this psychic activity.

INVESTIGATION GUIDELINES

PRIMARY PARAMETERS

In conclusion, investigators in the field should search for the primary parameters which are associated with these EM induced consciousness effects. They include the parameters of EH and hot-spot exposure, and are embodied in an investigative questionnaire known as 'The 25 Questions' (see p. 28). The following is a list of primary parameters.

1. Subjects report a history of psychic experiences, e.g. apparitions, formed figures, self-reported extrasensory perception (ESP), OBEs.

2. Subjects live in EM hot spots (and have exposure opportunity), e.g. near power lines, in the near-field of radio-frequency (RF) transmitters, close to a radio ham or CB radio, etc., beside substations, transformers, junction boxes, etc. (This should, of course, be verified by field surveys, using meters to measure the magnetic, electric and RF/microwave fields separately.)

3. Subjects have been exposed to an MEE, often in their formative years. (This is especially associated with alien-abduction experiences.) Examples of

MEEs include: proximity to a lightning strike, ball lightning (BL), unclassified atmospheric phenomena (UAPs), corona discharges, major electrocution, electroconvulsive therapy (ECT), defibrillation.

4. Subjects suffer from food allergies and/or chemical sensitivities, often without being aware of this, i.e. at subclinical levels (masked allergies). These include allergies to milk and wheat products, E-rated additives, aerosols, cleaning products, tobacco smoke, domestic gas, perfume, after-shave, spirits and other volatile substances.

5. Subjects are hypersensitive to bright light (*photophobia*), e.g. sunlight. They cannot tolerate fluorescent light (full-spectrum is tolerated better), which produces headaches, tiredness, etc. Also strobing/flickering lights are contra-indicated.

6. Subjects report sensitivity to electrical equipment, which often malfunctions in their presence, especially electronically sophisticated appliances, e.g. computers, check-out tills, photocopiers, tape-recorders, quartz watches, etc. Often watches do not work when worn. Also, electrical equipment behaves oddly in their home, e.g. TV comes on spontaneously, light-bulbs last for very short periods of time, other appliances activate spontaneously.

7. Subjects report a metallic taste in the mouth due to an electrolyte effect between saliva and the amalgam of tooth fillings induced by the presence of an electrical field.

8. Subjects report an overwhelming feeling that someone or something is in the room with them, and that they are being watched, although they cannot see anyone (*sense of presence*).

9. Subjects have periods of time for which they cannot account. This is due to automatic behaviour, drop attacks or allergic/EH trance states ('blank-outs'). They also experience time distortions, where time seems to stand still or pass in a flash (*desynchronization*), and repeated periods of intense *déjà vu,* or conversely, *jamais vu.* Another very distinctive neurological effect, in addition to a sense of timelessness, is a strange eerie silence, during which all ambient sound is lost. This is due to the stimulation of the reticular portions of the mid- and forebrain.

10. Subjects display profuse writing activity, often on subjects of cosmological/philosophical significance (*hypergraphia*). Poetry and stream of consciousness/creative compilations are typical. Often writing takes place at night during periods of intense meaningfulness. Lunar/night sky fascination is typical.

11. Subjects experience tingling, 'pins and needles' and/or numbness (*somesthesia* and *paresthesia*). They also experience painful electrical rippling sensations in the muscles just under the skin (*fasciculation*).

12. Subjects report generalized sensitivity to noise, vibration and crowds (hyperaesthesia). A homebound life-style is typical. Also, subjects may hear Morse-code-like signalling, buzzing, whines, clicking, etc. (*microwave hearing*).

13. Subjects experience highly enhanced static build-up and painful electric shocks on contact with metal bodies, e.g. car bodywork, door handles.

14. Subjects display Reiter's magnetic response (MR) when strong magnets on the 1000–2000 Gs range are placed at various positions on the skull (see p.88).

15. Subjects commonly have a history of childhood abuse.

USE OF CONTROLS

Over 50 control subjects were selected on the basis of the *exclusion* of identified hot-spot locations, i.e. they were *not* subject to EM pollution and did *not* live in locations with raised levels of time-varying fields. Also, none had experienced an MEE. Such subjects were chosen for comparisons with the study group of experiencers, which also consisted of over 50 people. Results showed that EH had not developed in the control group, who did not experience formed figures or alien-abduction experiences or exhibit primary parameters to any significant extent.

ELABORATION AND GENERAL COMMENTS

All of the aspects outlined in this preliminary blueprint will be elaborated upon and have been set out here as the first stage in their exploration, to serve as an initial induction into the approach developed. Those individuals who are investigators especially need to develop new techniques, and I have outlined some aspects, although such explorations could merit a book to themselves. I do not want to give the impression that I suddenly decided about 4 years ago 'to examine this alien-abduction stuff' and have recently come up with the EM-pollution approach outlined. I have been investigating cases of various types since 1980 and, although the core of my cases could be said to number 50, I have in fact looked at many more cases than this, in various depths, over the years. It is only relatively recently, in 1994, that a synthesis between my developing viewpoint and that of the significant others listed in the acknowledgements came to a head.

Part of this development involved setting out some guidelines to enable investigators to find the same parameters that have been discovered. After all, it is the repeatability of experiments which lies at the heart of the scientific method, and the implementation of 'The 25 Questions' can now be regarded as an experiment to find out whether indicators of causative factors are present within a case. Of course, a series of mechanically presented questions may not produce the information contained within a situation and/or individual, and should not be regarded as final when exploring a case. Some people just do not have the information which is requested, or may not answer truthfully for various reasons, and 'The 25 Questions' are guidelines that should be backed up with on-site investigation, e.g. a field-survey. However, sensitively implemented, they are a good starting point that will give the investigator some idea of the severity or otherwise of a case, as they are intended to show evidence of prolonged and ongoing irradiation and the development of EH. In fact, many are compound questions which put a series of associated enquiries to the experiencer.

THE 25 QUESTIONS

1. Do you frequently get severe shocks from door handles, car bodywork, other surfaces?

2. Do you feel uncomfortable in synthetic materials (e.g. acrylic, nylon)?

3. Are you sensitive to perfumed products, aerosols, cigarette smoke, petrol, gas, make-up, aftershave, etc.?

4. Does electrical equipment go wrong or behave oddly in your presence?

5. Are there any foods/drinks that you either avoid or consume large amounts of? Do you have food allergies (e.g. chocolate, coffee, milk, food with artificial colouring or flavours, wheat products)?

6. Did you have a happy childhood? If no, give reason(s) briefly.

7. Do you ever have hairs on your body stand on end, feel suddenly cold or overheated, experience tingling or numbness?

8. Do you ever get a metallic taste in your mouth?

9. Do you get *déjà vu* strongly and often?

10. Do you ever get the overwhelming sensation that someone is in the room with you, watching, although you cannot see anyone?

11. Are you very sensitive to light? (Sunlight? Flickering light? Do you wear tinted glasses?)

12. Are you sensitive to medications (especially antibiotics)?

13. Do you have what could be called psychic experiences (e.g. ghostly encounters, OBEs, etc.)?

14. Do you find that objects in your home go missing or sometimes seem to behave oddly in any way?

15. Do light-bulbs seem to last for a very short period of time in your home?

16. Have you ever been close to a lightning strike or suffered major electro-cution? (Or defibrillation? Or electroconvulsive therapy/ECT?)

17. Do you ever see small lights darting about the room?

18. Does fluorescent light bother you at all?

19. Do you ever have periods where you lose all concentration, feel over-heated, see light flashes, lose muscle power in your legs and feel tingly and heavy?

20. Are there any of the following features near your home: a quarry, radio mast, power lines, reservoir, hill, military base, TV/radio station, radio ham?

21. Does time ever seem to slow down or pass in a flash?

22. Have you ever had periods of time for which you cannot account?

23. As an activity, do you write very much?

24. Have you ever had the experience of everything going very still, timeless and silent?

25. Do you ever get painful electrical rippling sensations under the skin?

The implications of these enquiries will be explored subsequently and will be applied to specific cases, including examples from the USA and Australia.

THE INTERDISCIPLINARY APPROACH

It will be noticed that the environmental health approach is a composite whereby a number of disciplines have been synthesized into a cohesive whole. Basically, I have discovered links between seemingly unrelated aspects where no relationships were thought to exist. This has been one of the major factors that has hindered general acceptance of the approach among specialists, and exposes a fundamental flaw in special-ization generally. This is an epistemological issue, i.e. the way that knowledge is contained and developed is through the academic nurture of individuals who become experts in their field. Such specialists, over the years of their development, become increasingly entrenched within their disciplines at the expense of a wider perspective. Electronic engi-neers are oblivious to the elements of holistic medicine; geologists are unconcerned about neurology; medical practitioners are unaware of electromagnetics and so on. Therefore, if there is a family of enigmatic phenomena which exists outside the boundaries of such disciplines, these events are destined to remain poorly understood, if not entirely unrecognized.

It requires an interdisciplinary traveller to visit these different trenches of specialization, recognize links and relationships, and synthesize them into a cohesive new approach. Such across-category visiting is a role that I have pursued in the formulation of the approach outlined above.

ELEMENTS OF THE ENVIRONMENTAL HEALTH APPROACH

The disciplines from which the environmental health approach evolved include the following:

- EM pollution
- Holistic medicine and clinical ecology
- Electromagnetics
- Bioelectromagnetics
- Neurology
- Psychology
- Physical geology
- Meteorology
- Atmospheric physics
- Electrical engineering.

This list is not exhaustive.

Electromagnetic pollution: a selective tour

WITH THE proliferation of electronic communication systems in the towns and cities of the world, we are all living in an invisible electromagnetic (EM) smog. Radio-frequency (RF) transmissions zip through our brains and bodies constantly in our schools and colleges, in our places of work and play, and in our homes. Television and radio antennae transmit constantly, as do mobile-phone systems, taxi-cab controls, police networks, airports, diplomatic wavebands, Citizens' Band (CB) radio enthusiasts, and radio hams. All of these sources, and more, contribute to an EM saturation of the atmosphere, the waves of which pass through all obstacles in their path, although some present more protection from these waves than others.

If we imagine these waves and beams as being like light, the whole country would be a blaze of illumination around the clock, everywhere we went. There would be great dazzling beams flooding our front-rooms and bedrooms, bathing us constantly in light from great lamps mounted on high points, such as tall buildings and hills, or specially constructed masts dotted strategically around the country. Laser-like transmissions would cut through this overall glare and constantly flicker and criss-cross over vast distances, alive with the buzz of electronic information.

However, these waves are not light, and although they are quite invisible to us, they contain electrical energy. Light is on one section of what is known as the *electromagnetic spectrum* and radio waves are on another. Nevertheless they can affect us and are responsible, on a long-term basis, for a catalogue of illnesses which some health specialists are only just beginning to appreciate. One of the reasons for this reluctance to accept the fact that such prolonged radiation is a real environmental health hazard, just as factory and car emissions are for example, is an economic one. Billions of dollars and pounds, etc. are invested in these in-place systems and changing such communication networks would be cripplingly expensive. In fact, it could require the development of an entirely new technology and, combined with whatever would be involved in dismantling the present one, would make such an epic project out of the question. Nobody could afford it.

Another and cheaper alternative may be *shielding*. Recently, some companies have made available radio-wave-absorbent materials which, applied to the roof and walls of a house as a highly specialized paint, could cut out a considerable section of the RF radiation. However, even this would have its restrictions, as in order to protect from the microwave section, e.g. radar emissions, such materials would have to be over 3cm (1in) thick. Also, magnetic fields just cannot be shielded out because of their extreme efficiency at penetrating all materials. However, the electrical-field component can be relatively easily shielded out using metallic meshes, and, for the domestic user, large folding screens, placed around such critical areas as the bed, would offer some protection. Such areas are critical as it is in the long period of immobility during the hours of sleep that people are especially subject to prolonged and uninterrupted irradiation. It is no coincidence that so many of these strange visitation events are experienced in the bedroom.

Thankfully, not all of us are affected, and it is people who live in what the World Health Organization (WHO) call 'hot spots' (WHO, 1993) electromagnetically speaking, who suffer from conditions not shared by others outside of such focal points. These hot spots can be relatively easily identified and plotted on maps, and the fields in question can be detected and measured by conventional field-meters, i.e. field-surveys, referred to as *dosimetric surveys*, can be carried out to determine the levels of exposure involved.

The issue of EM pollution has concerned many informed individuals and professional organizations for several decades now. There is extensive literature on the adverse health effects that prolonged exposure to power lines and microwave RF transmitters can cause, as well as a robust lobby in defence of the safety of these systems. The debate, however, is riddled with implicit concerns for vested interests, not the least of them being the maintenance of the electricity and telecommunications industries and, more recently, property prices. It is my opinion that fair and objective defensive assessments from specialists are impossible, as whole economies are potentially at risk (see also p. 9). Put bluntly, the companies who are involved in these industries are concerned that the floodgates of litigation will open and that they will be financially ruined. This is not the cool and calm climate needed to make objective assessments. It will therefore come as no surprise to the reader to learn that there is considerable political manoeuvring within the power and communication industries, where struggles for the hearts and minds of influential specialists, as well as the general public, take place through apparently unbiased studies and conferences. The newcomer to the issues of EM pollution will find before him or her a bewildering array of conflicting evidence from an equally daunting range of authorities. Without naming names, a conference solely on the subject of electromagnetic hypersensitivity (EH) was convened at a European city 2 years ago, which effectively exonerated both the power and telecommunication industries through the careful sponsorship of research individuals, who did this through the presentation of papers on their work. However, although I was at first appalled at the absurdity of some of the experimental conditions, the overall effect became understandable in the light of the fact that the conference was sponsored by a quango for radio communications. It is in just such a confusing climate that the unbiased investigator can settle issues for him or herself by going out and gathering information firsthand.

At this stage, we are probably in a similar position to when we were first confronted with the links between smoking and cancer: it is up to the individual to decide. Or, in some relatively recent cases, up to the courts to decide. However, as an investigator who has spent considerable time and energy on exploring the possible effects of EM pollution firsthand in the field I believe that I am in a position to give an informed opinion. And it is this:

> There is absolutely no doubt in my mind that prolonged exposure to electromagnetic fields in the environment induces real and tangible adverse health effects.

These include food allergies, chemical sensitivities, EH, epilepsy, myalgic encephalomyelitis (ME) and diabetic tendencies, as well as the wide range of unpleasant sensations and symptoms mentioned on p. 25. This list is not exhaustive as these are only the conditions and sensations that I personally have found. Such conditions as brain tumours and blood cancer appear to have been linked by population studies to EM exposures.

This chapter does not represent any attempt to compile an encyclopedic round-up of EM pollution, but instead it includes papers and information that have influenced me as an investigator. After all, the central aim of this book, and therefore this chapter, is to establish an understanding of EM phenomena and allow the reader to access this understanding.

The effects of EM pollution fall into three categories:

1. Environmental effects, i.e. effects on objects, materials and devices.

2. Health effects, i.e. the effects of fields on the human biological system.

3. Consciousness effects, i.e. the effects on the mind, with an emphasis on perception.

As may be expected, the latter two categories overlap and are intrinsically bound together.

SOURCES OF ELECTROMAGNETIC POLLUTION
RADIO-FREQUENCY FIELDS

In 1993 the WHO published a report on environmental health criteria consisting of a collection of studies and statements by a range of specialists on the increasing risks to the health of the populations of the world that RF fields represent (WHO, 1993). These fields include pulsed microwaves. Although there is a deliberately measured caution throughout, the report does make several unequivocal statements:

> *There is increasing concern about the possibility that RF exposure may play a role in the causation or promotion of cancer, specifically of the blood-forming organs or in the central nervous system. Similar uncertainties surround possible effects on reproduction, such as increased rates of spontaneous abortion and of congenital malformations. [WHO, 1993, p. 27.]*

And:

> *At frequencies below a few hundred kilohertz, the electrical stimulation of excitable membranes of nerves and muscle cells is a well established phenomenon. These effects exist at very high environmental field strengths, unlikely to occur in the general population. [WHO, 1993, p. 177.]*

The last sentence should of course be noted, and one of the first comments that many people make on hearing that RF fields are a health hazard is that the field strengths are far too weak to affect anyone. However, it should be remembered that the subjects of our study are those individuals who have developed EH, not the general population. Of course, common sense tells us that listening to a radio broadcast *per se* offers no hazard or EM stimulus whatsoever, but again, our concerns are focussed upon locations that the WHO terms 'hot spots'.

> *An RF hot spot may be defined as a point or small area in which the local values of electric and/or magnetic field strengths are significantly elevated above the typical ambient field levels ... [WHO, 1993, pp. 188–189.]*

So what are the frequency levels that can affect the human system? The report tells us:

> *For frequencies below several hundred kHz, the predominant effect is stimulation of excitable tissue resulting from currents directly induced in the body by the RF fields. [WHO, 1993, p. 176.]*

In this selective tour of EM pollution it is worth breaking off briefly to note this aspect of induced body currents, as it is a key concept in the understanding of the alien-abduction experience specifically. It introduces an identification of an unrecognized class of spontaneously occurring hallucinatory states.

Electrically driven visions

It was mentioned earlier that, typically, these internal visionary experiences are imbued with a 'super-real' quality, or at least a vividness that is indistinguishable from everyday reality. Neurological evidence shows that this is due to the fact that these strange super-visions, in historical as well as perceptual terms, are in an entirely different league from the many other types of hallucinatory experience. They are field-driven. That is to say, the subjective vividness of them is due to dynamic currents which course throughout the body and brain from these external sources. This important concept will be explored in detail in Chapter 3, but is mentioned here to plant a seed of recognition into the awareness of the reader.

NEAR FIELDS

One very common type of hot spot results from a component of RF transmissions: the reflected ground wave (Kravs, 1991, Chapter 6; Lynn, 1987, p. 41). This was covered in my previous book (Budden, 1995a), but since then additional information and insights have accumulated.

The diagram overleaf shows a location at the point of reflection in the path of a potent section of such RF transmissions. One component of a particular mode of radio signal, called the *space wave*, beams out from the antennae parallel to the ground. However, the other component actually bounces off the ground, and buildings located at the point of such reflections will have raised field levels, as a portion of the signal is deposited in this way. This loss of signal power is called *attenuation*, and radio engineers have tried, somewhat unsuccessfully, to design out this unwanted earthing effect. A significant portion of the RF field seeks a route to earth and irradiates buildings for the duration of the transmission, giving rise to what are referred to as *power surges* or *power spikes*. These will be explored subsequently as their ubiquitous occurrence is responsible for a range of commonplace electrical malfunctions, as well as some extremely unusual effects (see pp. 55-6).

The WHO report does in fact mention that, if in-phase beams of RF microwaves overlap, extremely high field strengths (*amplitudes*) can be reached. Such resulting power surges are due to clusters of RF-transmitting antennae positioned close together, and as an investigator I have found that it is at such potent focal points that a range of environmental illnesses mentioned earlier are often found. These are

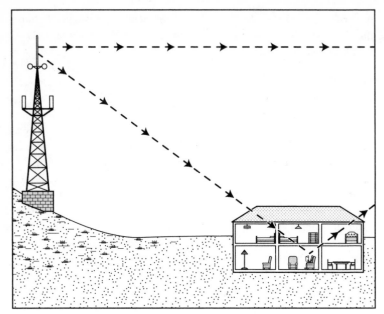

Diagram showing ground reflected radio waves from transmitting antenna in space-wave propagation.

equally intrinsically linked to a number of very strange experiences and events indeed.

Again, it is my experience as an investigator that, commonly, the point of reflection is between 450 and 750m (490 and 820yd) away from the transmitting antenna. This is only something that I have noticed as a working estimation, and is not any attempt to formulate an 'iron law' of any kind. Local conditions, such as uneven and hilly terrain, will influence this distance. The mathematical formula used by electronic engineers to calculate these near-field distances is quite complex (Kravs, 1991, Chapter 6; Lynn, 1987, p. 41), and factors such as the height of the mast in relation to the terrain, the type of antenna used and the way it is set up for specific transmission purposes all have to be taken into account. All of these aspects can be found in any technical manual on radio-wave propagation.

Metallic structures in and around these near-field locations, e.g. iron railings, cast-iron fireplaces, radiators, structural girders, car bodywork, iron conduits, bolts and nails, serve to increase the intensity of the fields at large in hot spots, as they are re-radiated and reflected from such bodies and surfaces. Especially potent in terms of intimately affecting the individual are: rings on fingers, as well as other jewellery, such as rings through ears and, recently, many other parts of the body; copper bangles; stainless-steel watches and their expanding straps; bedsprings; and even bra-cup stiffeners. Such metallic objects, which have prolonged contact with the skin or, at best, with only fabric in between, can produce electrical burns, especially in EH-status individuals. Such persisting marks, which can appear as bruises, have been taken, by investigators who favour the alien explanation for abduction experiences, as physical evidence for the intrusion of such beings into the lives of the experiencer. However, the WHO report tells us:

> *At frequencies below about 100MHz, currents can be induced in humans by physical contact with ungrounded metallic objects. From 300Hz to approximately 100kHz, such currents may result in the stimulation of electrically excitable tissues above the threshold of pain. At frequencies between approximately 100kHz and 100MHz, contact currents of sufficiently high density may cause burns. [WHO, 1993, p.176.]*

Doctors at the Breakspear Hospital in Hertfordshire, UK, where EH is treated, have often witnessed reacting subjects *actually during their visionary episodes* and relate that they frequently do so with their eyes open. Regarding the field-driven factor of the alien-abduction vision, it is clear that such physical sensations would provide more than enough cues for the imaging brain to incorporate into the internal drama and translate into all manner of mysterious and traumatic medical intrusions. In cases where seemingly enigmatic scarring is found, such epidermal traumas can be traced directly back to this type of electrical injury. It must also be remembered that the WHO report is commenting on the normal non-hypersensitive individual, and such physical effects (e.g. electrical burns and fasciculation) can be obtained at much lower field intensities in those suffering from what, in effect, is an EM allergy. These levels are, of course, not the most common form of RF irradiation and prolonged exposure at lower amplitudes, where the enhanced levels obtained with in-phase beams are not involved, are much more the norm. One of the most common sources of RF fields, and one which, typically, takes such irradiation into the heart of areas where one would perhaps least expect it (e.g. leafy suburban avenues) is the radio ham.

RADIO-HAM EXPOSURE

Over the past 3 years, during the development of the EM-pollution approach, I have repeatedly encountered cases involving hot spots induced by proximity to radio hams, and some cases to be presented (see Appendix) involve radio hams themselves. From these it is evident that such a pastime induces a range of adverse health effects in the operator and, if combined with another parameter – a major electrical event

(MEE) – will lead to the strange consciousness effects at the centre of our study: alien-encounter/formed-figure experiences. The young man who made a vivid internal expedition to the Falkland Islands with an imaginary British Army after suffering an electric shock was a radio ham, and so is 'Lori' of Ohio, USA (p. 224), who is also an experiencer.

Radio-ham enthusiasts often include a class of inspired amateurs who manufacture/modify their own equipment, which sometimes presses hard against regulation boundaries. Such modifications usually have the aim of utilizing greater transmitting potentials, which of course would extend their ability to propagate EM pollution. Users have to be licensed and it is illegal to 'propagate any plane wave', to use the right jargon, without one. However, once such official permission is obtained, anyone can send out powerful waves of EM energy into the environment. The effective radiated power relates to the strength of the transmission, 50W being typical.

There is little or no recognition of the adverse health effects on neighbours or those unlucky enough to be located in the near field, but as power surges and television interference (so common that it is referred to as TVI) are typically produced, hams do usually soon become aware if they are inducing any EM disruption to appliances because of complaints from neighbours. However, home-transmitters themselves are also subject to interference and, significantly, in addition to television sets and computers, fluorescent lighting can produce 'noise and mush'. (Poole, 1992.) This is because such illumination (except full-spectrum tubes) emits RFs and electric fields and is, therefore, also a common source of physiological disruption to EH-status individuals.

From an investigator's point of view, radio hams are easy to spot as they have characteristic transmitting antennae mounted on their roof or large masts erected in the garden. Sections of the EM spectrum are reserved for their use, known as *frequency designations*. However, although the subculture of the radio ham and the CB adds colour to the lives of many individuals, they are unaware that they are paying a price with their health for their communications, and, more unfortunately perhaps, so are their neighbours.

ELECTROMAGNETIC POLLUTION AND ITS EFFECTS ON HEALTH

EXPOSURE: A PREREQUISITE

It must be remembered that, with all field sources in the environment, unless the individuals whose homes are located in the hot spot are exposed for a sufficiently prolonged period, they will be subjected only marginally to its effects. This almost absurdly obvious truism seems an unnecessary statement to make but, during the presentation of the EM-pollution approach at lectures, on radio programmes, etc., it is clear that its parameters are often regarded blindly, with no attempt at understanding the principle behind them. For example, the husband of a well-known experiencer, who has herself appeared frequently on television, once challenged the approach developed by questioning why it was that he remained unaffected, while his wife continued to have ongoing experiences. The couple's home in Kent, UK, is between two rows of power lines about 100m (110yd) away from the house on either side, and, a kilometre or so away, three huge telecommunication towers beam their reflected ground waves down to the same restricted hot-spot area. However, the experiencer is at home most of the day with a child, while the husband spends his days away from the location at his place of work. This summarized example is presented here to illustrate the fact that individuals must have *exposure opportunity*, as it can usefully be termed, and the location of their home may be a necessary but not always a sufficient condition.

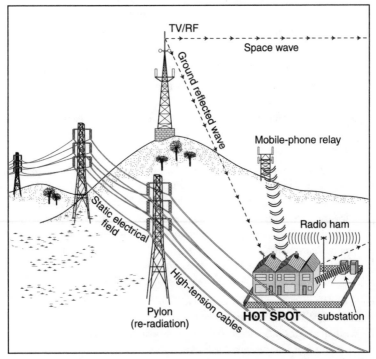

Electronic and electrical pollution – a scenario showing typical sources.

EFFECTS OF POWER LINES
AND ASSOCIATED INSTALLATIONS

When EM pollution is mentioned, many people tend to think of pylons and power lines, and are surprised to learn that transmitting RF antennae contribute to such environmental pollution. Also, the fundamental distinction between them is surprisingly blurred in the minds of many individuals. For example, television 'abductee' Maria Ward, during a radio programme for a station in Kent, UK, spoke of the 'near fields of a pylon'. Of course, power lines do not transmit electronic communication signals; they are simply conduits for the electricity of the national grid and are responsible for extremely low frequency (ELF) fields that can be synchronous with the natural frequencies of the human brain.

Australian researcher Bill Chalker wrote to me after reading of my approach, and related how 70 per cent of a sample of 40 experiencers in a survey carried out by Kelly 'Cahill' lived close to pylons, i.e. the power-line link was evident.

Also, Canadian investigator Lorne Goldfader, an extraterrestrial hypothesis (ETH) enthusiast of the UFO Research Institute of Canada (UFORIC), wrote an article in the veteran UFO periodical *Flying Saucer Review* which linked the homes of 'abductees' with power lines. He states:

> Over the last four years of intensive research into abduction reports, I have come across what seems to be an extraordinary and most interesting relationship. In almost every abduction case investigated by UFORIC and involving families with either small children or pregnant mothers, we have discovered the existence of power-grids ('Lego-like' hydroelectrical constructions) above or very near to the dwellings.

> When this situation became clear to us in the latter part of 1990, there followed the inevitable spate of speculation about such concepts as 'EM windows', using the grids to 'enter dimensionally', power charging of alien craft, etc. To be precise we should add that a possible relationship between reports of sightings of UFOs and the presence of the power grids had of course already been noted before 1990. What seems to be a completely new factor is the possibility that we have now established a link between the power grids and actual abductions by UFO.

> An Associated Press report dated November 14, 1992, cited a study made in Sweden which had found that 'children exposed to relatively weak magnetic fields from power lines near their homes develop leukemia at almost four times the expected rate'.

The study looked at 500,000 children and adults who lived near trans-mission lines.

It is my theory that the entities who control the abduction phenomenon may possibly be carrying out a survey of the genetic damage in the infants who live near these grids – and may even be correcting the harm done. [Goldfader, 1993.]

It is startling to see the elaborations that can arise from the discovery of a simple geographical link, if such data are interpreted through the extraterrestrial (ET) visitor mythology. However, putting aside such ideas, it is clear that Goldfader and UFORIC in Canada have found the same geographical correlations as Chalker in Australia noticed. Both act as independently arrived-at evidence, which supports my central premise that alien-abduction experiences are induced through prolonged exposure to EM fields in hot-spot locations.

However, Goldfader's evidence goes even further in its unwitting confirmation of the EM-pollution approach. It has already been mentioned that allergies are induced by prolonged EM exposure and are intrinsically linked to the alien-visitation experience. In fact, the title of a modest book I published (Budden, 1994), promoting 'UFOS – Psychic Close Encounters: The Electromagnetic Indictment', was actually entitled *Allergies and Aliens*. This correlation will be explored in depth in Chapter 3. However, after corresponding with Goldfader about his article in *Flying Saucer Review*, he wrote to say:

As far as the allergies go, I agree with you that many people (experiencers) do have them. How we discovered this 'correlation' [sic] is by asking every subject of a recent abduction or contact of any medical problems which began only after the encounters. A common response without our prompting was severe allergic symptoms accompanied by asthmatic attacks mostly with females and siblings, but not as often with adult males. [Chalker/Goldfader, private correspondence.]

Such allergic sensitivities may appear after experiences that constitute a major electrical event (MEE) if they are followed up by hot-spot exposure. Close proximity to an unclassified atmospheric phenomena (UAP) can offer high and sudden EM exposure comparable to that experienced from proximity to a lightning strike or ball lightning (BL), both of which will also act as an electrical initiation and trigger such sensitivities as allergies. As the reader will see in the Appendix, it is these two EM parameters, which occur with almost monotonous regularity across populations of 'abductees', that are the most significant and robust, i.e. the combination of MEE and subsequent hot-spot exposure.

Chalker is unclear about this aspect:

I have some concerns about cause and effect issues with the mechanism you are suggesting. In a number of cases sensitivity issues have only come up after the encounter not before. [Chalker, private correspondence.]

However, if such encounters involved proximity to light phenomena, then the above clarifies his concerns. Also, it is just as likely that such sensitivities are already there at subclinical levels and are only thrown into sharp relief when the percipient is field-exposed even further or, alternatively, that they seem to appear after the event due to the focus of the investigation enquiries. As an incidental aspect, Chalker does not appear to have made the distinction between objective light phenomena and subjective alien-abduction experiences, where the first triggers the second, and seems to assume that the reality status of the former is shared by the latter. Until investigators divide UFO encounters in this way, there will always be confusion between external phenomena and internal experiences. Such objective light phenomena have been consistently reported in close proximity to power lines, and are evidently an accidently produced form of BL. From the way that these electric fireballs have been produced in the laboratory, it is clear that unusual intermodulation effects are involved in their formation.

Returning to Goldfader's survey of experiencers, he mentions that, in addition to allergies, asthmatic attacks are triggered. Once again, he unwittingly provides evidence which supports the power-line link to abduction experiences.

ASTHMA AND ELECTROMAGNETIC POLLUTION

In the UK, John Holt, a Fellow of the Royal College of Radiologists, as one of a team of British and Australian scientists, has carried out studies which confirm a link between asthma and field exposure:

There is no question that factors such as air pollution and other antigens are involved. But I think our findings show that electromagnetic radiation has made it ten times worse. [Holt, 1996.]

These findings have come from tests led by Peter Finch, the Medical Director of the Centre for Immunology and Cancer Research at St Vincent's Hospital, Sydney, Australia. His team bathed cultures of human mast cells in EM fields for 10 minutes a day for a week. (Mast cells are a type of cell found throughout the body which produce histamine when exposed to *antigens*, a collective term for irritants.) Dr Holt stated that the production of histamine was double in the irradiated cells. [Holt, 1996.]

Asthma is part of an environmental-sensitivities syndrome, as treated at the Breakspear Hospital. So, as Goldfader has found that his experiencers, in addition to developing allergies and living under or near power lines, develop asthma, he provides yet another factor which supports the link between power-line exposure and alien-abduction experiences. In his accounts, Goldfader also provides yet another link by reporting another field effect on the body known as *fasciculation,* in which the experiencer feels an intense electrical rippling sensation in the muscles below the skin. It is Goldfader himself who has experienced this after a close encounter with an aerial light phenomenon.

THE THREAT TO HEALTH

It would appear that many health authorities are unaware of the threat to health that proximity to power lines presents. However, once again, there are huge economic concerns entangled in their policies towards the health threat that power lines induce. Repeated 'whitewashing' studies are made and published but, despite such 'evidence' of the harmless nature of power-line proximity, you can be sure that the people involved in producing these studies would not live near power lines themselves. The concept of 'prudent avoidance' is about as far as some will go towards an admission, and this basically says, 'We do not know if power lines are a health hazard or not, but, just in case, avoid them.' For me, as an investigator on-the-ground, these concerns are voiced far too conservatively, and there is no doubt in my mind that living near power lines and/or their associated electrical installations is an extreme risk to health.

My investigations have involved non-life-threatening conditions, although, in some cases, I have only looked through a window into these people's lives during a particular time period. Environmental sensitivities should be considered as a warning, and *it will be shown that the alien-abduction experience is a dramatized and symbolic form of this, warning that the health of the experiencer is under assault via EM intrusions.* That is to say, it has a definite biological survival role for the individual, and this key aspect will be covered extensively in Chapter 3. In terms of life-threatening conditions, the following local newspaper report is typical:

> *Paul O'Gorman died of leukaemia at the age of 14 on February 6th, 1987. His sister Jean, aged 29, died of breast cancer nine months later. Seven years on their father ... is still campaigning for the recognition of his belief that his son's death was caused by the electricity substation 30 metres from their Mill Hill home ... 'I believe that if we had not lived in that house my son would be alive,' said Mr O'Gorman. 'I know a lot of families who have lost children to leukaemia and the majority of*

> *them live near substations ... Six years ago I tried to sue the electricity company for the loss of Paul. There was not enough evidence' ... Roger Coghill, a leading British scientist in the electromagnetics field ... found eight out of ten studies point to a link between electromagnetic fields and childhood cancer. [Steiner, 1994.]*

Information in the same article confirms that the period of immobility during sleep is a critical aspect of irradiation, and it is no coincidence that so many visitation experiences take place then. However, in the following case, something more than environmental sensitivities and their accompanying consciousness effects was involved:

> *... a new case has come to light – that of the Studholmes, whose 13 year old son died of leukaemia ... [He] slept with his head against a wall with an electricity meter and burglar alarm on the other side. A normal reading of fields in a bedroom, measured in nanoTesla, is usually about 60.* **When the boy's pillow was measured it read 1,200. The wall reading was 3,400.** *[Steiner, 1994. My emphasis.]*

It is not known whether this child was an experiencer of any kind, but further probative evidence could certainly be obtained by exploring the background of such victims. However, so bizarre are such perceptions, which are usually completely repressed by both those who experience them and their families, that it would take a particularly empathetic and diligent investigator, who could assure them of the confidentiality of such revelations, to detect them. For a family trying to persuade the health authorities to take their complaints seriously, tales of alien visitation would not be considered the stuff of reliable testimony. For similar reasons, visitation experiences do not feature in published accounts or official reports on community power-line exposure; *they are just too weird.*

The fact that such visionary experiences arise as a result of the health hazard that EM pollution presents to the individual would also be too subtle and subjective to be cited as evidence of irradiation. Something far more tangible in adverse health-effect terms has to occur and, as if the death of the Studholme boy was not enough, another also occurred in close association:

Leukaemia death No. 2 in meter boy street

A neighbour of the boy who died of leukaemia after sleeping next to an electricity meter has also died of the disease. Jogger and half-marathon runner Norman Scholfield, 47, slept in a bungalow bedroom identical to that of Simon Studholme, 13. They lived only three doors apart in Little Lever, Manchester, and died within two years of each other. Simon's parents, Ray and Denise Studholme, have been given legal aid to sue electricity suppliers Norweb in a test case. [Anon., 1993a.]

The effects and sensations of field exposure are so marked, it is surprising that individuals do not become aware of their irradiation, but, as has been stressed, such sensations are evidently not linked to their cause by sufferers, hence the acute need for the visionary communications from the 'body consciousness' via the unconscious.

However, the array of sensations and conditions that are reported, such as tingling, black-outs, drop attacks, desynchronization, irregular heart-beat, food allergies, chemical sensitivities, EH, epilepsy, etc., are regularly found in alien-encounter percipients, as we shall see in the Appendix. Therefore, one of the primary aspects of such experiences, which seems to have escaped so many investigators and armchair theorists alike, is that *they are aberrant*. That is to say, they occur because the physiology of the experiencer is malfunctioning. Treatment centres such as the Breakspear Hospital do not seem to be particularly interested in 'the visions', as Dr Jean Monro, director of the hospital, called the hallucinatory experiences of those suffering from EH (although, according to Dr Monro, my book *Allergies and Aliens* was passed around the wards to selected patients). Also, environmental health groups, such as 'Powerwatch' (see Note 3), seem to see the correlation of their environmental concern with these consciousness effects as an unwelcome embarrassment, no doubt due to the 'flying saucer' connection. In fact, the alien-abduction experience, which has set the ufological world alight for so many decades, is really just one very small aspect of a much wider environmental health issue: EM pollution.

ELECTROMAGNETIC POLLUTION AND ITS EFFECTS ON THE ENVIRONMENT

POWER SURGES

The most instantly potent form of EM pollution in terms of inducing dramatic effects is the power surge. This represents a suddenly increased presence of EM energies in a location, usually caused by RF transmitters in the area. However, it should also be recognized that *geoelectromagnetic fields from fault lines* will also provide a sudden direct-current power spike in locations built over them and, usually, such places of power, having been irradiated in this way for sometimes hundreds of years, will have a haunted reputation.

ACTIVATION OF ELECTRICAL EQUIPMENT

One of the most dramatic effects of power surges on the interior environments of hot-spot locations is the spontaneous activation of electrical equipment and appliances. These are especially prone to do this if they are electronically sophisticated. As an example of this consider the following report on uncontrolled wheelchair movements from *Microwave News:*

> *Tests conducted by the FDA [Food and Drug Administration] have shown that certain wheelchairs are susceptible to EM interference. The agency found that some electronically controlled wheelchairs would unexpectedly stop, start or turn when exposed to RF/MW [microwave] radiation at strengths of 10 V/m or less, said Howard Bassen of FDA's Center for Devices and Radiological Health in Rockville, Maryland. Such field levels could occur in 'real world' situations, such as near a police car radio or hand-held walkie-talkie, he said. 'There are numerous reports of injuries due to unintended wheelchair movement,' Bassen explained ... Laboratory tests on the same wheelchair models did show that they were susceptible to low levels of radio-frequency/microwave radiation. [Anon., 1993b.]*

Such ghostly activations of electrical/electronic appliances in domestic environments have caused many of those involved in psychical research to regard such locations as 'haunted' and, on reading accounts of vigils at these places, one finds that virtually all of the phenomena reported can be identified as field effects of one kind or another. That is to say, the effects of power surges do not confine themselves only to electrical equipment, but have much wider ramifications. However, in this category I have found examples of radios which continue to play when unplugged, electric kettles which spontaneously activate and, probably most bizarre, a radio-controlled car which rocketed about the room erratically, even though the batteries had been removed. However, the time when I am most aware of the possibility of power surges is when I have my hand down the waste-disposal unit in the process of cleaning it ...

INTERMODULATION: a key concept

If there are multiples of fields irradiating a location, which include natural and artificial sources, effects on the environment and human system will be especially enhanced. This is due to what are known as *intermodulation effects*, in which the ever-changing fields mix and match, producing 'beats' and a variety of wave forms that are themselves in flux (e.g. step, square wave, saw-tooth, standing waves). Such mechanisms as re-radiation and reflection also modulate the strengths of the fields, and it is these *severely modulated energies* that have such a disruptive effect on the human system, which is unable to adapt to them effectively. This factor has been evident in the course of my own field investigations, and the WHO report tells us:

> When RF fields are amplitude modulated, effects in tissues have been noted that do not manifest themselves with unmodulated RF fields. Such effects are reported to have a complex dependence on intensity and ELF modulation frequency. [WHO, 1993, p.176.]

From this statement it can be seen that severely modulated fields are more potent in terms of their effect on the human system than constant uniform fields. In fact, it is this interaction of two or more fields which is responsible for a whole range of dramatic environmental effects, including the production of fireballs and the Hutchison effect (see p.62). Also, many laboratory test programmes in which the subjects are irradiated under controlled conditions *are confounded by the use of uniform sinusoidal fields* produced by signal generators, etc. because they do not replicate the severely modulated forms found in the environment.

Pulsed fields

Ever-changing pulsing regimes also disrupt human physiology more effectively than constant uniform fields, because the body is prevented from adapting due to the constant on/off effect; this presents more stimulation to the biological system, as it neither rests nor activates for any significant period of time. Again, this is also why many of the results of controlled studies are meaningless, i.e. they generally use constant non-pulsed fields on their laboratory subjects and not those ever-changing, in-flux fields found in the environment.

The ball-of-light phenomenon

Another fascinating property of intermodulation effects is the induction of what investigators in the UK refer to as the *ball-of-light phenomenon*. The interactions of high-voltage RF fields are of particular interest, as there is little doubt that they are responsible for a form of accidently produced BL which I have termed *electroforms*.

ELECTROFORMS

Evidence for this side-effect of EM pollution comes from the experiments of two brother researchers, Kenneth L. Corum and James F. Corum, in Morgantown, West Virginia, USA. They have successfully produced electric fireballs in the laboratory using dual Tesla coils. Following Tesla's original notes, they found that these artificial BLs *could be produced to order* by inducing an interaction of two radio frequencies:

a higher frequency wave imposed on lower frequency oscillations. Circumstantial evidence also supports this, as such aerial balls of light are often reported in association with radio/television masts in combination with geological faults, which can also emit RFs. This process of electric-fireball production is an important aspect of *intermodulation* (see also Chapter 5).

A further aspect is outlined in a Russian periodical which describes some of the devices and effects tried out in the covert and experimental 'techo-towns' set up in remote areas during the relative prosperity of the 1960s. Apparently, a novel form of street-lighting was produced by intersecting two beams of microwaves high in the air; this induced a bright blob-like form of BL that hovered in a stationary position. However, it never passed the prototype stage as it was found that the luminous phenomenon was attracted to overhead aircraft if they passed too low and, on many occasions, would shoot off at lightning speed towards them.

One may wonder if similar UAPs were accidently produced during the war years when the pulsed microwaves of radar were first used. This is an intriguing report of a deliberately induced intermodulation effect and perhaps provides an identification of the mysterious war-time 'foo fighters'. These were observed to be 'a dirty aluminium colour', which is, in fact, quite consistent with some of the variations in appearance of the electric fireballs recently produced by the Corum brothers. As mentioned, this breakthrough will be covered subsequently (see p. 175) although for years the artificial production of BL in the laboratory has been regarded as an impossibility.

PHYSICAL PHENOMENA AT 'HAUNTED' LOCATIONS

It is my experience that many psychical investigators tend to have strong protective feelings towards phenomena they regard as being permanently mysterious, and vigorously reject the idea that 'haunt-ings' take place due to hot-spot activity. I was shocked to find that the very organizations in the UK that are concerned with the study of psychical phenomena were the ones which actively preserved the enigmatic status of these phenomena and the ones which were not open to identifications that were alternatives to spirits of the dead, etc. or simply 'unknowns'. However, at the time of writing, 2 years after the launch of the environmental EM approach, many investigators and groups in the UK are equipping themselves with gaussmeters. The revolution has begun ...

SOUND PHENOMENA: the page effect

Consider the following from a report on a 'haunted' church:

> *At around 10.00 p.m., when it was still relatively light outside, the church's interior reached total darkness and clicking noises began to parade up and down the centre of the building. These noises continued on and off during the period of our stay, always travelling from the altar to the tower and occasionally back again. Once or twice we stood in the clicking noises' path, our torches searching for an explanation. But there wasn't one. The sounds seemed to ignore us and simply passed us by. [Veacock, 1994.]*

This 'click' phenomenon has also been reported as taking place during alien-contact/abduction experiences. Consider the following extract from a South African case:

> *At that time I was having these encounters about five times a week; the whole situation was so bizarre ... With my first encounters I heard a click-like sound, like the click of a key being turned in a keyhole ... the very next instant there was a hooded monk-like figure beside my bed. [Anon., 1993d]*

The click is an example of magnetostrictive acoustics, which result from rapid changes in magnetization. When a ferrous material is subjected to a magnetic field and the field suddenly drops, the sudden demagnetization produces an auditory sound wave, heard as a click (Burke, 1986). Similarly, banging and thumping sounds can be induced in ferrous conduits and fittings in buildings by magnetostrictive acoustics. The clicking phenomenon that occured in the church could be this effect on the nails in the floor.

THE MOVEMENT OF OBJECTS: intermodulation revisited

When considering these effects, it is a common reaction to doubt that fields with the required strengths or amplitudes are produced. However, as with so many situations, we do not really know what is possible until actual tests are implemented and, in this case, it is easy to be either unaware or underestimate the properties of intermodulation effects. It is these strange EM hybrids that provide many surprises in terms of what can happen at relatively low power levels. Also, it is not common knowledge that there are many dozen reproducible magnetic phenomena catalogued in textbooks on magnetism. The following is information taken from an encyclopedic tome – *The Handbook of Magnetic Phenomena* (Burke, 1986) – a text that is essential to those researching physical phenomena at 'haunted' locations.

Gyromagnetic effects: revolving objects

For example, it should be noted that a paramagnetic body tends to rotate when it is suddenly magnetized. Domestic objects subjected to a power surge will suddenly revolve and become subject to mechanical forcing fields, producing the Einstein-de-Hass effect (see Burke, 1986, p. 82). This is, of course, the stuff of poltergeist activity and such effects have been reported many times.

Psychical study organizations in the UK seemed somewhat outraged at any suggestion that relatively conventional explanations can be found for such physical phenomena and, in their attempt to counter them, claimed that only objects made of iron or steel would react in this way. As the reader will see, they are mistaken. Similarly, objections arose based on the assumption either that ultra-high field strengths would be needed (see p. 61), or that the non-ferrous environment, which is most of it, would not be affected by magnetic fields. Somewhat understandably, they were completely unaware of the Hutchison effect (see p. 62), which can produce the movement and levitation of objects *made of any material* through the interaction of fields at very low amplitudes and at a considerable distance from the source of those fields. In identifying phenomena at 'haunted' locations, it must be remembered that they all take place in the context of the EM hot spot and it is in these locations that the rules of reality are changed and the human system and the environment behave in a number of curious ways. The effects are intermittent, and some are due to cumulative processes.

The magnetite context

Particles of this naturally occurring magnetic oxide of iron are everywhere in our environment. It contaminates laboratories which require ultra-clean conditions. It is in the food we eat and the air that we breathe. It is in the cells of the brain and the bones of our bodies. Consider the following extracts from a report in *Nature:*

> For the past two decades, the study of the biologically precipitated ferromagnetic mineral magnetite (Fe_3O_4) has relied heavily on the use of ... [superconducting quantum interference device (SQUID)] magnetometers to quantify trace levels of magnetite in various biological and laboratory materials. It rapidly became clear that unique clean-laboratory techniques were required for this work because of the ubiquitous presence of ferromagnetic contamination. This contamination included ferromagnetic particulates present not only in the dust in the air, but also adsorbed onto the surfaces of laboratory equipment, present within glass and plastics, and even in reagent-grade laboratory chemicals and water. [Kobayashi et al., 1995]

And with reference to tissue cultures:

We have found that none of these materials is free of ferromagnetic particulate contamination ... A simple calculation shows that the mechanical energy present in a single 100nm magnetite crystal exposed to a 60Hz, 0.1 mT magnetic field is many times the thermal background noise. [Anon., 1995.]

The biological implications aside, there is evidence to suggest that hotspot locations, because of their enhanced magnetic-field levels, gradually attract and accumulate raised levels of magnetite particles. As poltergeist activity takes place in such locations, which can be irradiated naturally by fields from faults, this build-up of magnetic particles is probably instrumental in inducing magnetic properties in normally non-magnetic materials, such as cloth, paper, ceramics, etc., which gradually, over time, become impregnated with such particulates.

Before we leave the concept of magnetite impregnation, which the reader should note is yet another tangible and testable aspect that characterizes the EM-pollution approach, it should be mentioned here that researcher Anne Silk has carried out work on crop circles and correlated their locations with the near fields of RF transmitters. Crop-circle investigator Busty Taylor appeared on television in the UK in 1995, and showed viewers how wheat stalks and soil taken from crop circles could be picked up with a simple magnet. This, of course, implies magnetite impregnation at crop-circle sites, due to the cumulative effect described, implying that such sites (hoaxed examples aside) are indeed hot spots.

VANISHING AND APPEARING WATER:
microwave volatization and electrolysis

This effect is regarded as standard poltergeist activity, and it is significant to learn that it has also been reported as a close-encounter after-effect, i.e. it has been associated with electric fireballs. Once again, as with all of the phenomena under study, the two fields of psychical research and ufology are linked by a single commonality: electromagnetics. When water is subjected to 500MHz and above in the ultra-high-frequency (UHF) wavebands (commonly known as *microwaves*), the valency bonds of hydrogen and oxygen break down and the liquid changes state and volatizes, i.e. becomes gaseous (Ballone, 1993). This gas then disperses and the water vanishes. This can take place extremely quickly, depending on the volume of water involved and the field strengths.

The appearance of water is the other related phenomenon and is the above process in reverse. With any compound, of which water is an example, it takes energy to separate the constituents and, likewise, energy to cause them to recombine. Once again, it is no coincidence that electrical energies are involved in such a combination, and an electrical discharge of a volume of hydrogen and oxygen, present as a mixture will produce water. At 'haunted' locations, a small puddle of water is sometimes mysteriously found on the floor in the middle of the room. Also at such locations, I have found that electrical malfunctions due to power surges sometimes take the form of spontaneous electrical arcing in the wiring of the light-fitting which hangs from the ceiling in the middle of the room, or in the light-switches on the walls. Electrical arcing in the context of a UHF microwave field (which can blow flash-bulbs at a distance) could certainly volatize and recombine free atmospheric oxygen and hydrogen.

However, such mechanisms pale almost into obscurity because this phenomenon of the appearance of puddles of water and other liquids at poltergeist-active locations has been demonstrated during the operation of the Hutchison device; electrical engineer George Hathaway and John Hutchison himself have videoed the disturbance of water and other fluids during its operation. The levitation of quantities of fluids out of containers placed in EM-active areas is another intriguing phenomenon to watch, as the audiences of the Hutchison video will testify. Hutchison and Hathaway, during their experiments, videoed the behaviour of such substances as yogurt, a mixture of crushed ice and water and frozen orange juice, all in plastic pots. Probably most peculiar was the sight of pink yogurt slowly rising out of its container in a gooey peak before separating and taking off, quickly followed by the whole pot itself. Viewing such phenomena certainly convinces one that here is the duplication of many of the weird poltergeist effects recorded by psychical researchers for many decades.

One might object to this explanation on the grounds that poltergeists have been reported in pre-electrical eras, but a survey of the nature of earth energies, e.g. the emission of microwaves at fault lines, shows the incidence of robust natural hot spots. Also, until evidence arises which can demonstrate with a degree of reliability that the accounts of poltergeist activity in these eras are describing the same identifiable and discrete phenomenon, we should be cautious and take a healthily agnostic view, despite the mentioned constant of the presence of geoelectrical fields due to prolific faulting, mineralization, underground water, etc., which can produce powerful natural hot spots. However, when considering cases from past eras, we must not mistake folklore for data. This takes us into a region we cannot visit often enough, for it affects the very basis of the way we apprehend phenomena: what really happens and what does not?

ON EVIDENCE: THE QUESTION OF DATA

From a review of the literature that gives accounts of poltergeists in other historical periods, it is clear that many of the phenomena of yesteryear just do not occur today. Floating and self-animated gloves which beat in time to music, instantly constructed life-like dummies, poltergeist-constructed items of clothing (that were always conveniently burnt or otherwise destroyed so that they do not exist today), etc., are all examples of stories whose content has not been matched to any degree in carefully investigated cases today. As with so many classes of anomalies, we are looking at a mixture of mythology, hoaxes, delusions, wish fulfilment and lastly, but not least, genuine anomalies.

The debate about hauntings: anomalous physical phenomena

IT CAN be extremely disappointing for a great many of the people fascinated by physical effects at 'haunted' locations to learn that they are field effects of one kind or another. In fact, so shocking is this conclusion that many just refuse to accept it. This is not because the evidence is not convincing enough, but because 'hauntings', seen as the activity of incarnate entities, are close to the hearts and minds of many. However, I believe that truth really is stranger than fiction and I have found that, although the traditional realities of spirits may have been taken away, we have been given, for the first time, a way of predicting the conditions under which these events take place as part of a greater understanding. This may seem like cold comfort, but it is actually very empowering to be suddenly included in the magic circle, where amazing events are actually understood, and gives one the sense of being the conjurer rather than a passive member of a mystified audience. However, in order for this empowerment to be appreciated, it must be felt, and it is this that I offer the reader through the electromagnetic (EM) approach – the empowering position of genuine insight, which eventually brings with it a sense of awe that is in a different league from the simple fascination and woolly ignorance associated with ideas of playful spirits.

The real revolution in the area of physical paranormal phenomena is contained in the Hutchison effect. As we will see, although many events can be identified as 'conventional' EM effects, albeit obscure ones, there is the characteristic cluster which forms what is regarded as 'poltergeist activity'. The levitation of objects of any material, lights in the air, bending metal, spontaneous fires, the appearance of water, the movement of matter, electrical anomalies and the destruction of physical objects are all well known to psychical research. However, it is no coincidence that it is precisely this collection of events which is produced in the laboratory by the composite EM device put together by John Hutchison in British Columbia, Canada, in 1981. Therefore, let us trace the development of the EM-pollution approach from its early beginnings, when I was convinced that poltergeist activity took place in hot spots but had difficulty demonstrating it, to the sure-handedness of the spectacular Hutchison effect.

By May 1994, the EM-pollution approach had been developing for about 14 months and, by that stage, the identification of hot-spot activity was a routine matter for me. I had visited numerous locations with a TriField meter, having shown an investigator's interest in abduction experiences, 'hauntings', poltergeist activity, and mixtures of all manner of odd domestic occurrences (e.g. a kitchen cabinet that repeatedly threw itself off the wall, phone cards which 'wiped' themselves clean of credit, plastic lapel badges which 'melted', batteries which lost all power, cats which reacted to 'invisible intruders', flashbulbs which spontaneously popped and TV sets which turned themselves on and off in rapid succession). By this stage of the game, most of the hallmarks of hot-spot activity were clear to me.

It was in this climate that I began to see things which others did not. These were not hallucinations but connections between areas of study that had previously been regarded as unrelated. In just about every case file I read, examples of hot-spot activity jumped out at me from the page; it did not seem to matter whether I was reading about crop circles, haunted houses, alien abductions or covert psychotronic persecution. I began to think that I was suffering from 'investigator's bias', in which everything is interpreted in terms of 'the theory'. I now know that these across-category EM commonalities do in fact exist, and that electromagnetics is as important to the study of anomalies as genetics is to biology. The identifications of the sort of events listed above and earlier became almost casual and, the more I read and investigated, the surer I became that the EM-pollution approach was correct, although a little fine tuning was needed.

A HAUNTED PUBLIC HOUSE:
The White Hart Inn

One of the accounts of a 'haunting' I read was published in *Anomaly*, the in-house journal of the Association for the Scientific Study of Anomalous Phenomena (ASSAP). Written by UK investigator Tony Wells it was entitled 'The White Hart Inn' (Wells, 1994). It outlined the strange goings-on at a public house, which included the following:

1. A gas-tap on a carbon-dioxide container kept turning itself on and off.

2. The landlady felt something play with her hair and several women had felt themselves being touched on their back and shoulders.

3. Unspecified loud noises were heard, as well as 'thumps'.

4. A formed figure was seen to walk through a closed door.

5. More thumping and bumping noises occurred, which were described as sounding like someone running along an upstairs corridor.

6. The landlady felt as if someone was standing behind her and that she was being watched; simultaneously she felt a tingling sensation.

7. A door opened and closed spontaneously.

8. A strange musty smell appeared episodically.

9. Three women felt a pleasant tingling sensation in the spine accompanied by a distinctly sexual sensation.

Then, a series of phenomena were experienced by the ASSAP investigators themselves during an overnight visit:

10. Tony Wells heard a buzzing noise in his right ear during an investigation of the noise of someone mounting the stairs.

11. Tony Wells also felt so disorientated that he was unable to take notes or to concentrate and he generally 'felt extremely weird'.

12. A light went off on its own and, although the switch was in the off position, its click was not heard.

13. Tony Wells saw a blue flash.

14. Tony Wells and other investigators saw laser-like flashes come from the ceiling of the bar.

15. White flashing effects were seen by two or more investigators and, over a period of 5–10 minutes, light shining under a door was interrupted by shadows, although there was nobody on the other side to cause them.

The article also reports the incidence of epilepsy in the landlady, which had occurred since her teens.

COMMENT

In 1994 I wrote an article (Budden, 1994b) identifying these effects as being EM in origin and submitted it. The editor of *Anomaly*, Maurice Townsend, and the author of the article, Tony Wells, rejected the identification of EM hot-spot activity and co-authored an article in opposition, which was published *immediately following mine, in the same edition*. That was in May 1994, but 2 years later, ASSAP's General and External Affairs newsletters both contained reports of newly acquired equipment for their investigators. It included magnetometers and electric-field detectors. (Anon. 1996.)

ANALYSIS

Without the benefit of carrying out an on-site investigation, where a full field-survey could be implemented, an analysis can only be less than fully comprehensive. However, the following phenomena are readily identifiable:

Sensations of being touched

Psychologist Robert Ornstein relates:

> *Libet and his colleagues set out, following in Penfield's footsteps, to determine the nature of conscious experiences evoked by electrical stimulation of various parts of the brain. He discovered that by applying a series of electrical pulses to certain areas of the cortex in a particular pattern he could cause the patient to feel a nearly natural sensation of being touched on the arm. [Ornstein, 1991, p. 48.]*

The sensation of the hair being touched is due to the induction of rising hair follicles caused by static electrical fields and is termed *pilo-erection*.

Loud noises: thumps and bangs

The acoustical effects of magnetostrictive phenomena, such as the Page effect, have been covered on p.49, and it is evident that the sudden magnetization and demagnetization of such structural aspects as ferrous conduits (especially if electrical circuitry runs through them) and/or steel girders can produce thumps and bangs. This is especially likely if it occurs in conjunction with another magnetic effect which would amplify such sounds, a process termed *magneto-acoustic resonance*.

The *Handbook of Magnetic Phenomena* (Burke, 1986, p. 363) tells us that, when sound waves pass through any metal and a magnetic field is applied at right angles, a harmonic relationship is set up and sound levels suddenly rise. This is because the pressure waves created by sound replace the wave forms induced by an alternating electric current and interact with the magnetic field, producing an amplification effect. There would then be an accelerating cyclic effect in which the increased sound reacts even more with the magnetic field, producing even greater amplification, and so on. Once again, an on-site investigation would reveal if the loud noises emanated from areas where there were large expanses of metal, e.g. a cast-iron fireplace or radiators, in addition to structural girders.

Apparitions or formed figures

The report by Wells relates:

> Paul woke up to see a figure (apparently male) walk through the closed
> door of the main bedroom, and casually to the window. The figure turned
> to look at him, and then walked away out through the closed door ...
> This happened just after 4 a.m. He is short-sighted and had to scrabble
> for his watch and light his lighter to see the time. He believed his short-
> sightedness prevented him from making out the details of the apparition.
> [Wells, 1994, p. 5.]

Such apparitions are typical of those perceived by electromagnetically
hypersensitive (EH) individuals at hot-spot locations, and may be
entirely hallucinatory. Alternatively, there may be a place memory (see
p. 152) electromagnetically imbued in the fabric of the building. The
processes involved in the production of such a 'recording' offer an area
of uncharted research possibilities. My feeling on the nature of this
'recording effect' is that imagery of people is imprinted into a field in
the building and this acts as the medium which both stores and triggers
the perceptual effects known as 'place memories' in suitably sensitive
individuals, i.e. those who are EH.

Sounds of footsteps

Again, this effect can be produced by magnetostrictive acoustics, whereby
a series of abrupt changes in magnetization along, for instance, metal pipes
running the length of a hall, produces a succession of thumps that sound
exactly like someone walking along the hall in heavy boots to anyone in
the rooms below. However, it is the magnetic field that is moving, giving
the effect of the progression associated with the sound of footsteps.

The feeling of an invisible entity watching

This is probably the most common perceptual effect associated with
fields in EH individuals. It is an epileptiform phenomenon known as
'the sense of presence', and has been induced in a clinical setting. It is
caused by the stimulation of the temporal lobes of the brain and, in this
case, it is certainly no coincidence that it was experienced by the landlady of the inn, who was already suffering from epilepsy. It has been
shown on p. 114 how exposure to a magnetic field is able to introduce
electricity into the brain, thereby inducing a seizure, probably through
the mechanism of eddy currents.

The spontaneous opening and closing of a door

This would seem to have been induced by a direct magnetic effect on
the ferrous fittings of the door, such as the hinges (if they were of the
long type which stretches across the width) or the iron latch mentioned
in the report. However, there is another strong possibility, which would

have been detected had the investigators used a seismograph or other vibration detector. The Mercalli table, which shows the effects on the environment of tremors, does in fact list 'doors may swing' as an indicator of light tectonic activity, i.e. earth movement. This, of course, is entirely consistent with the identification of this location as a hot spot and, in fact, a major surface fault is located only 300m (330yd) to the north of the town in which the inn is situated. Also, the ironstone mineralization of the strata in which the fault lies has supported an iron industry since Roman times; it would add to the general ambient magnetic climate, as non-magnetic ironstone could re-radiate geoelectromagnetic fields.

However, in addition, a look at the directory of radio hams compiled by the Radio Society of Great Britain, shows, at the last count, seven radio-frequency (RF) transmitters at distances from the inn which would irradiate it by intense fields, should they all be transmitting simultaneously, because of overlapping signal zones.

Tingling and sexual sensations

A tingling sensation can be induced by direct electrostatic stimulation of the nerve endings in the skin and is known as 'somesthesia'. Alternatively, stimulation of areas of the brain (left supra-medial surface of the gyrus) can also induce feelings of tingling (Simpson & Fitch, 1988). Sexual sensations can be induced by the stimulation of the septal area.

Strange light effects, e.g. 'a laser-like flash from the ceiling'

The *Handbook of Magnetic Phenomena* contains dozens of uncommon effects produced by the interaction of light and magnetic fields. It is not at all surprising, therefore, that such effects in their various forms should be observed at this location, and it is further evidence of its hot-spot status. Examples of unusual light phenomena abound. *Magnetorefraction* is the term used to describe how the refractive index of a material is changed upon exposure to a magnetic field (Burke, 1986, p. 138). In the Cotton-Moulton effect, some dielectric (i.e. non-magnetic) materials become double-refractive. In the Kerr magneto-optic effect, light reflected from the surface of a magnetized material is elliptically polarized. *Heiligenschein* produces a metallic-looking surface when light shines through water droplets in a magnetic field. As a general guide, the properties of different materials, in terms of how light behaves, are modified by the presence of magnetic fields.

Perhaps more immediately recognizable in the case of the 'haunted' inn is the magnetophosphene effect. If the human head is subjected to a magnetic field that is varying at a rate between 10 and 100Hz and whose strength is between 200 and 1000Gs, the subject will see flashes of light

(Ruttan *et al.*, 1990). These register in the upper left quadrant of the visual field, which is circumstantially correct, as they were reported as coming from the ceiling area.

However, it should be noted that this visual phenomenon embodies an important implication − that of shared hallucination. Such neurological constants mean that, if two or more people are irradiated in the same way, at the same time and in the same place, they can all be induced to perceive the same hallucinatory flash of light. There is evidence to indicate that this mechanism is involved in the shared perception of more complex imagery. But, whatever the effects involved, the important factor is really just to demonstrate the magnetic context, which has been achieved by the numerous cross-referring systemic and environmental effects identified.

Relocation of objects

In the ASSAP article (Wells, 1994) also mentions the mysterious reloca-tion of domestic objects, although no movement was actually observed and things were just found in unexpected places. Again, it is my expe-rience that such apparent relocations are a result of epileptiform seizures. *Automatism* is the term used to describe the behaviour of a seized indi-vidual who carries out some activity but has absolutely no memory of having done so. It is during these periods that objects are used and replaced in different places. This is also the so-called 'missing time' of abduction experiences, and can last from a few minutes to several days. There are consistent accounts of objects vanishing near electrical gener-ators, and there may be another range of mechanisms at work − known as the Hutchison effect.

Buzzing noises, unwellness

To conclude this analysis of the White Hart Inn account, there is some-thing else that I have noticed: author Tony Wells relates that, on entering the building, he began to feel extremely unwell. He reports:

> *I felt extremely weird throughout the majority of the time at the inn and was unable to concentrate enough to take notes.*

And:

> *I did not hear any footsteps on the stairs, but did hear a buzzing noise in my right ear.*

And, commenting on subsequent visits:

> *As per the other visits, I had felt weird throughout the evening, and was interested to note that one of the medium's assistants was feeling similar sensations.*

The buzzing noise is extremely reminiscent of a phenomenon called *microwave hearing*, which is caused by prolonged exposure and induced sensitivity to RF fields. Alternatively, a characteristic buzzing effect can be produced by electrical stimulation of the primary receptive areas of the brain, and an EH-status subject would be especially prone to this. Also, I have frequently found that it is the RF frequencies from geological sources, to which the brain is especially sensitive, resulting in visual, auditory and olfactory focal seizures. Interestingly, the generalized disorientation, which also involves the loss of ability to concentrate and write, as described by Wells, are clear signs and symptoms of subclinical levels of EH straight out of the information pamphlets on EH issued by the Breakspear Hospital, which treats the disorder.

I have found that EH symptoms are frequently an occupational hazard, so to speak, of investigators, especially if they spend long hours in 'haunted' hot-spot locations during overnight vigils. It is doubly ironic that this was the investigator who argued strongly against the identification of hot-spot activity and EH, publishing his objections. However, as outlined on p. 62, it is the Hutchison effect which shows how intermodulating fields produce vigorous poltergeist activity, and which is the stimulus behind a vast array of physical environmental anomalies, otherwise known as 'destructive hauntings'.

THE POLTERGEIST MACHINE

Anyone who has read anything about poltergeist phenomena will be aware of the more spectacular aspects. Again, the arena of the debate which took place in *Anomaly* provides a springboard from which to launch the issues involved. The Enfield poltergeist case in the UK (Playfair, 1981) is surely one of the most spectacular and well-documented cases in relatively recent times, and one of the investigators, Maurice Grosse, after following the *Anomaly* debate, commented:

> *Albert's enthusiasm for his suppositions does him credit, but the [article]
> 'The White Hart Inn: A Reply' in* Anomaly *16, displays a distinct lack
> of practical experience of psychic phenomena ... I look forward with great
> interest to the day when flying boxes, stones, toys, heavy items of furniture,
> plus spontaneous fires and water phenomena, together with the passage of
> matter through matter, levitation, metal-bending, to name just a few exam-
> ples of poltergeist high jinks I have personally experienced, can be explained
> by electromagnetic and bioelectromagnetic activity. [Grosse, 1995.]*

The tone of this piece will give the reader some idea as to what I have been up against when presenting the EM approach to well-known psychical researchers in the UK, and although I have already made substantial inroads into such entrenched positions with the mechanisms presented earlier, I can now, with a certain pleasure, take this opportunity to direct Grosse's attention to the Hutchison effect.

THE HUTCHISON EFFECT:
a lift and disruption system

Canadian EM researcher John Hutchison has unintentionally produced a range of effects which previously were regarded as the exclusive characteristics of poltergeist phenomena. Very basically, what he has done is to combine EM apparatus from different technologies within the confines of a single location. A company called Hathaway Consulting Services in Canada has taken over the research and development of the device. George Hathaway, in a report, relates:

> The system is a single entity, made up of many discrete components. It has many interrelated parts, unfortunately continually being added to by the inventor. It was discovered fortuitously by Hutchison, who was experimenting with early Tesla systems and static machines such as Van de Graaf generators. The main thing about this technology, apart from its unusual phenomenology, is that it is highly transitory. The phenomena come and go virtually as they please. One has to sit with this apparatus for from between six hours and six days before one actually sees something occurring. [Hathaway & Hutchison, 1992]

It is no coincidence that poltergeist phenomena also share this unpredictability. The report continues:

> The Hutchison Effect is divided primarily into two categories of phenomena: propulsive and energetic. The system is capable of inducing lift and translation in bodies of any material. That means it will propel bodies upwards, and it will also move them sideways. There are actually four kinds of trajectories which are capable of being produced. It also has very strange energetic properties including severely disrupting inter-molecular bonds in any material resulting in catastrophic and disruptive fracturing. It is also capable of causing controlled plastic deformation in metals, creating unusual aurora-like lighting effects in mid-air, causing changes in the chemical composition of metals, and other long-range effects at distances up to and around 80 feet (24 metres) away from the central core of the apparatus—all at low power and at a distance.

The implications for domestic poltergeist effects and aerial-light phenomena in the environment, known as UFOs, are far-reaching. The reader will note that, once again, unusual intermodulation effects between the clashing fields and wave forms are at the centre of these phenomena, and it is no surprise to find that such mechanisms are at work during poltergeist activity, through different sources of EM pollution, e.g. geological faults, microwave repeaters, power lines, etc., at hot-spot locations. In fact, the comprehensive description of the Enfield events in *This House Is Haunted* (Playfair, 1981) provides us with extreme examples of EM hot-spot activity involving both the environment and EH individuals.

One of the objections to electromagnetism being the cause of poltergeist phenomena, which was argued by the editor of *Anomaly*, Maurice Townsend, was that non-ferrous materials would not be affected. I have already shown how the ubiquitous presence of magnetite could begin to address this objection (p. 50) but the Hutchison effect goes much further and actually demonstrates that intermodulations transcend such apparent dielectric restrictions, and all manner of materials are levitated, including planks of wood and cartons of yogurt! Hathaway's report describes the trajectories of affected objects and, once again, they are especially reminiscent of the way in which objects in poltergeist activity behave:

> There are four main modes of trajectory that these objects can follow if they so choose to take off. There is a slow looping arc where the objects will basically take off very slowly in a matter of a couple of seconds and loop back and fall somewhere else. It is almost as if the earth moves underneath them whilst they are in flight, and they fall back in different locations. The second type of trajectory is a ballistic take-off. In other words, there is an impulse of energy at the beginning of the trajectory with no further power applied to the lifting thereafter, and the object hits the ceiling and comes back down. A third type of trajectory is a powered one where there appears to be a continuous application of lifting force. The fourth trajectory is hovering – where objects just rise up and sit there. The objects can be of any material whatsoever: sheet metal, wood, styrofoam, lead, copper, zinc or amalgams; they all either take off or they burst apart, or they do nothing, that's 99% of the time.

The report then relates an aspect which seems to explain why some objects and not others are affected by poltergeist energies. Part of the selectivity relates not to their iron content, but to their geometry:

> The objects that are lifted in the first part of this section are of the order of a few pounds. All of them lift off with a twist, i.e. they spiral as they lift off. There has to be a particular geometry with respect to the downward direction, i.e. gravity, for them to take off. Some objects, if you lay them on their sides, won't take off. If you turn them on their ends, they will take off. The geometrical form of the objects, their composition and their

relationship to their environment, the field structure around them that is being created by the device, all play a part in how these things take off.

One of the objections raised concerns the amount of energy that is required to induce these effects, in order to dismiss the feasibility of their occurrence under environmental conditions. I have emphasized the exceptional properties of intermodulation effects and it therefore comes as no real surprise that the report refers to them occurring 'all at low power and at a distance'. But what power levels are involved to begin with exactly? The report tells us:

All components are powered from a single 15 amp, 110 volt power supply.

This is the ordinary standard mains electricity that is used in Canada, and a field-survey carried out by Hathaway showed that, for much of the time, the fields present in and around the device could be measured in microvolts (7000–100 000)! The report goes on to describe other effects produced, which are extremely reminiscent of the weird thermal phenomena associated with poltergeist activity:

Sometimes, instead of lifting objects, John Hutchison will purposely try to destroy them. In one case, a quarter inch rat-tail file rested on a plywood base and was prevented from taking off by two plywood struts. Also, some coins were placed beside the file. The file began to glow white hot although there was no scorching of the wooden plywood struts holding it down, and the coins were not affected. This is explainable in terms of radio-frequency heating theory as eddy current heating on the surface can occur, and the metal can be almost cool to the touch very soon afterwards. However, it is still unusual that there is no conductive heat transferred to the wood.

And:

*From time to time there are scorch marks on the wooden boards from other experiments, and the apparatus **can induce fires spontaneously in parts of the laboratory if you are not careful**. [My emphasis.]*

Such 'destructive hauntings' should, of course, carry a hazard warning, and the closing section of the report does exactly that:

I must caution anyone who is pursuing this line of experimentation, that it is an extremely dangerous apparatus. It has never knocked any of my dental fillings out, but certainly has the potential for doing so. It has smashed mirrors eighty feet [25 metres] away. Also its effects cannot be pinpointed easily, as it has overturned large metal objects of about sixty pounds [27 Kilograms] about 100 feet [30 metres] away. The active area where things happen can only be guessed at, but often something occurs unexpectedly at a fairly remote location, e.g. the apparatus is capable of starting fires in concrete which manifest as small bursts of flame here and there, and it will cause your main circuits to have problems. Fuses, circuit-breakers and large bulbs have been tripped or blown.

Hathaway Consulting Services have also met with some problematic aspects with respect to obtaining funds to develop the Hutchison project. The report relates:

The device tends to destroy itself, a classic example being when we had some important potential investors visit the laboratory. On the morning of a demonstration for them it blew one of its own transformers apart.

Highly relevant to the unusual luminous effects associated with poltergeist outbreaks and UFOs, or, more accurately, with unclassified atmospheric phenomena (UAP) sightings, are the light phenomena that the device can induce:

John was filming in 1981 and all of a sudden a sheet of iridescence descended between the camera and the apparatus, seen as a sheet of light. It had a strange pinkish centre to it and it hovered there for a while, and then disappeared. John thought he was hallucinating, but when he watched the recording it turned out that something was definitely there.

In my last book, *UFOs – Psychic Close Encounters* (Budden, 1995a) I introduced the concept of 'domestic UAPs', i.e. light phenomena in the homes of experiencers. I pointed out that, if the same effects were observed in an outdoor setting, they would be called UFOs, the point, of course, being that setting dictates not only the identification of such phenomena, but who collects such data. If they occur during poltergeist activity, psychical researchers will be involved; if in the landscape, ufologists. However, they are both phenomena basically the same, with the same basic cause.

However, for most readers, the poltergeist-related phenomena which probably come to mind are those involving the spontaneous movement of objects, and some of them, as Maurice Grosse pointed out in the list he gave, are massive and heavy. Hathaway's report on the Hutchison effect mentions, almost as an incidental fact during comments on a video recording, that:

In this same video, we observed heavier objects taking off, including a 19 pound (8.6 kg) bronze cylinder, and also water in a cup vibrating.

With regard to this levitating bronze cylinder, Hathaway analysed the film of its rising frame by frame and found that, in its short trajectory to the ceiling, it was travelling at 70km/h (45mph)! However, such public evidence as a film has not been forthcoming on the Enfield events, although Grosse did make many intriguing tape-recordings. In terms of evidence, I would have thought that continuous filming would have been an important investigative tool. However, such limitations do not apply to the Hutchison device, and the Hathaway report tells us:

> *Early in 1987 when several unusual phenomena occurred, they were filmed by a television crew and shown on the national news.*

In fact, a video-recording sent to me by Hutchison shows his device featured on Canadian, American and Japanese national television news during the 1980s. It must also be remembered that 'The Hutchison Story' as it may be dubbed, broke in the media in the early 1980s and, over the past 17 years, has been investigated by numerous electrical engineers and several scientific institutions, as well as official technical departments. These include the Max Planck Institute in Berlin, McDonnell Douglas (August 1985) and Los Alamos in the USA, whose report on the visit to Hutchison's laboratory in June 1983 is officially classified, even to John himself! However, it is available under the Freedom of Information Act in the USA.

THE BRITISH SCENE

For certain reasons, little information on the Hutchison effect has reached the UK, and its presentation here is its first public disclosure, apart from a limited-edition report that I wrote in late 1996, whose distribution was largely confined to the UFO/paranormal/Fortean subculture [Budden, 1996/7b]. However, despite the thorough exploration of the Hutchison effect by the established scientific and governmental institutions mentioned above, English non-scientist John Rimmer self-published an article (Rimmer, 1997) ridiculing Hutchison and his device. He writes that 'John Rimmer thought Heath Robinson was the king of the strange devices, until he found out about Mr Hutchinson's [sic] Amazing Machine', and goes on to imply that the Hutchison effect is an elaborate hoax. I suspect that this article will haunt him for years to come, as responses via correspondence from scientists from America, Canada and Europe already indicate.

It must be noted, however, that, in the 1980s, such subject matter had not been recognized by the media to the extent which it is today. Such areas of interest were still 'in the closet' as it were, and existed as a relatively isolated subculture, as opposed to the recent boom in UFO- and paranormal-orientated programmes on TV, newspapers and media in general.

On viewing the Hutchison video, it is clear that no connections with the paranormal are being claimed and, in the various national TV news features, it was depicted as an electrical engineering curiosity. Of course, the EM approach did not exist in the 1980s, and I had not brought the significance of such an approach to the attention of the specialized study groups and societies, or published the material available today. Therefore, the present popular context for the Hutchison effect was not there in the media and, like much of Tesla's work, the significance of the effect was not generally realized at the time of its discovery. Although this position remains to a lesser extent today, it is my hope that a new generation of psychical researchers will grow up fully aware of the fundamental significance of the Hutchison effect in the understanding of poltergeist phenomena and other physical anomalies.

THE ENFIELD POLTERGEIST AND THE HUTCHISON EFFECT

About a year ago I did in fact track down the semi-detached house in Enfield, north London, UK, where the events took place, partly by matching it with the photograph on the front of *This House is Haunted* (Playfair, 1981), and spoke briefly with 'Mrs Harper', who was the mother of the two adolescents at the centre of the activity. This was about 15 years after Playfair's book was written and I did not expect to find any further background information. However, I was intrigued by the proximity of the railway system, power lines, reservoir and equidistant positions of Luton and Stanstead airports, not to mention an electrical substation in the front garden of a neighbour, especially as Playfair did test the location with a magnetometer and found that power surges occurred at the same time as objects were thrown about:

> *From the landing, we could keep an eye on the dial of the machine, and in the following forty minutes Janet's pillow was twice thrown across the room, just as it had been the previous evening in my presence ... And each time the needle on the magnetometer did indeed deflect ... we called off the experiment once we were satisfied that it seemed possible that there was a link between poltergeist activity and anomalous behaviour of the surrounding magnetic field. [Playfair, 1981].*

It is especially frustrating that scientists were not in charge of collecting data, as one gets the general impression that, despite their use of a field-meter, the investigators considered 'the poltergeist' to be some type of interdimensional entity from the 'other side', according to Playfair's book. Until all notions of alien intelligences or spirits from the other side, the astral plane, or wherever, are swept out of the thinking of ufology and psychical research, no progress towards an understanding of such phenomena can be made.

Returning to the detection of magnetic fields at the Enfield location, a link can be made with Canadian researcher Mel Winfield's comments. He suggested that the effects associated with Hutchison's device were 'due to a method of making the electromagnetic fields involved spin and swirl in some unknown way'.

Once again we are considering a field-interaction approach involving ever-changing and severe modulations, and, as such combinations are quite evidently able to produce dramatic effects that are not possible with single-field conditions, we should regard the robust Enfield activity as the environmental product of two or more field sources. Phenomena at Enfield included the spontaneous movement of a 23kg (50lb) iron radiator, which appeared to wrench itself out of the brickwork holding it and is a good example of the severe disruptions to materials that Hutchison recorded on film and video. Unfortunately, because of the time that has elapsed since activity died down, it is not possible to carry out a reliable field-survey of the property today. This is because transmitters have been switched off, power cables moved, airport homing beacons relocated, radar redirected, etc. Nevertheless, it is clear that the curious forms of destruction associated with the mayhem of 'destructive hauntings' are more than matched by those produced by Hutchison's device which, it should be remembered, operates at low power. During its operation solid metal bars were fractured and actually frayed, fires started in remote parts of the building and also *inside* blocks of concrete, liquids levitated, mirrors smashed 24m (80ft) away from the centre of the device, water mains burst, pieces of wood were discovered inside a shattered aluminium block, etc.

Such effects will surely be a comfort to those who think that the EM-pollution approach strips enigmas of their mystery and it will become clear that truth really is stranger than fiction. In effect, I am merely redirecting the mysteries into more scientifically orientated areas of enquiry. Through electromagnetics we are now entering the next weird world and glimpsing aspects of uncharted territory. As Hutchison comments on the operation of the device:

> *The idea is to excite the surface skin of the masses and their atoms to create an unstable space-time situation. This might allow the fields from the Tesla coils and RF generation equipment to lock up in a local space-time situation. My thought is that now a small amount of energy is released from the vast reservoir of space-time at the sub-atomic level to create a disruptive or movement effect. [In Budden 1996/97a.]*

Suddenly we find that we have moved away from the spiritualistic ideas of disembodied intelligences to considering the physics involved in poltergeist activity. However, Hutchison found that not everyone appreciated the breakthrough he had made and, in a long-distance phone conversation in 1996, he told me of an incident when a Super 8 film of the device in action was shown to officials associated with the Defense Technical Information Center in Canada. When a series of sequences showing heavy objects levitating and hovering appeared, one of the generals present was so outraged that he immediately got up, approached the projector and wrenched the spool of film from its mounting, throwing it across the room before storming out of the building. Apparently he was involved in anti-gravity research and had spent vast quantities of his budget on complex prototype development, only to achieve a much weaker version of the levitation effects that Hutchison had produced using standard and self-constructed equipment at a fraction of the cost.

THE VANCOUVER EXPERIMENT: observations

In August 1985, Jack Houck of McDonnell Douglas investigated the Hutchison effect. He writes:

The equipment belongs to Hutchison and is in his residence. The area in which the majority of the effects occur is determined empirically. Often major events occur outside of the intended 'target area' where test objects were placed. In the early days of their experimentation, many hovering and apparently antigravity-type events occurred ... Lately, most of the observed effects have been metal exploding or bending, and objects moving horizontally or expanding or contracting. A group of scientists from Los Alamos had witnessed an experiment last year ... On 13 and 14 August, 1985, this author had the opportunity to witness two evenings of experiments ... There were some very interesting events captured on video tape ... Aluminium foil pieces and some plastic samples were observed to slide as if hit by an impulse ... I was satisfied that no fraudulence was occurring, and was impressed by the fact that most of the events were covered by the video camera. However, some of the biggest events occurred outside of the intended target area. The first evening, a gun barrel and a very heavy (60lb [27kg]) brass cylinder were hurled from a shelf in the back corner of the room onto the floor. Simultaneously, on the opposite side of the room toward the back, three other objects were hurled to the ground. One was a heavy aluminium bar. It was bent 30 degrees ... another object was a [7kg] brass bushing. These objects can be seen falling in the video recording. [See Note 4.]

At the end of an experiment on 14 August, a water-main burst in the street outside of Hutchison's residence ...

Interestingly, Houck was familiar with the characteristics of phenomena that had been identified as psychokinetic (PK) and was struck by the many similarities to the Hutchison effect. He asks if Hutchison was stimulating the same type of energy or fields, or if his device acted as a PK amplifier? However, a co-worker, Alex Pezarro, believes that the device creates a type of field that causes energy to be dumped into the objects.

However, it seems that the term 'psychokinetic' is entirely misleading and that, for many decades, investigators and psychical researchers have ascribed aspects of the mind to phenomena that have only marginal links with the psyche. That is to say, such phenomena are not psychical in any sense, but are electromagnetic and/or bioelectromagnetic in nature, and not the product of some kind of vague mind-energy called 'psychokinesis'. In fact, there is little evidence to show that the mind has anything whatsoever to do with these spontaneous effects. This is in contrast to experimental data such as that obtained by Rhine (in Taylor, 1975) who found that some subjects could influence the outcome of dice throws. The two areas appear to be different and it seems that the laboratory results showing physical objects seemingly influenced by the will were convincing enough to be erroneously generalized to apply to other areas where objects mysteriously moved, i.e. poltergeist activity. However, this is a fundamental error of conceptualization, as it is evident that the well-documented cluster of phenomena attributed to poltergeists is electromagnetic and bioelectromagnetic in nature and this outlook in psychical research needs to be radically revised.

STOP PRESS: the latest

Nicholas Reiter, originator of 'Reiter's response' (a specific response induced in experiencers by intracranial magnetic stimulation), has recently entered the experimental arena to generate the Hutchison effect using apparatus which he himself has designed. Basically, Reiter's aim is to build a 'probability generator', a device which will generate chaotic wave forms within a confined area using spark gaps, magnetic coils and other field-generating apparatus. The rationale behind this rests on a working assumption that although, under normal conditions, any disturbance of the molecular or atomic structure of matter and its relationship to the environment (e.g. the effect of gravity upon it) is highly improbable, it is possible (this being the key word) that fields may interfere with such usually stable parameters. The clue that such interference effects exist comes from a school of thought in psychokinetic research that suggests, for example, that although it is highly *unlikely* that you will be able to pass your hand through a solid wooden table, it is *possible* if, by sheer chance, all the intermolecular spaces in your hand and the table line up and coincide, offering no resistance. It is a concept similar to the suggestion that, if an infinite number of monkeys sat down and banged on an infinite number of typewriters for an infinite length of time, eventually one of them would, by chance, write the complete works of Shakespeare.

By producing a constantly changing flux of fields within a small area, many permutations would present themselves in terms of their potential for disturbing the atomic or molecular structure of objects. Eventually, the right combination of frequency, wave form, or amplitude would occur at the right place and an effect would take place. Without the discovery of the Hutchison effect, this would seem like interesting theoretical speculation, but it is a model that does fit the observations, in that Hutchison has set up a system that produces this super-EM chaos and does get some very dramatic results with low power inputs. Thick metal bars *do* twist and explode, heavy bronze cylinders *do* levitate at speeds of 70km/hr (45 mph) and hover, etc., but one has to wait for up to a week sometimes, or a day on other occasions, until the right permutation occurs. The more chaos, the more chances will present themselves.

Once again, the power of intermodulation effects should be fully realized, as should the fact that this EM chaos is sometimes produced accidently at hot-spot locations, where poltergeist activity occurs. However, the most intriguing aspect is that, if the human organism can emit fields, people can become part of the EM chaos, and the introduction of a biological system injects a range of permutations which is in a completely different league from even the most complex electronic instruments. And this, I suspect, is what happens when EH subjects enter a hot-spot location, because, as a symptom of their condition, they do in fact emit fields as a whole-body effect.

Irradiation: biological effects and the holistic medicine connection

THE CLINICAL conditions responsible for the visionary consciousness effects described are electromagnetic hypersensitivity (EH) and multiple allergy. One of the aspects that have prevented professionals and scientists from appreciating the authenticity of these perceptions is the fact that they associate them with psychosis, and do not realize that the people who experience them on an episodic basis are not suffering from any form of mental illness but have, instead, developed environmental sensitivities. It is through these sensitivities that perfectly sane individuals experience perceptions of visitors that seem to be from another galaxy or another dimension.

This absence of understanding on the part of the medical world is partly due to the fact that there is an ideological cold war between medical orthodoxy and holistic medicine (clinical ecology). One cannot help but wonder if there is again an economic strand to this conflict, because holistic medicine involves the use of non-drug-related treatments and the pharmacological industry may feel under threat.

However, it is essential to grasp one important aspect relating to how and why these experiences are triggered. That is to say, the nature and dynamics of the environmental sensitivities acquired by experiencers are embodied within the ethos of holistic medicine and, by becoming familiar with the principles of this environmental approach to the health and well-being of individuals, one can also gain valuable insights into such perceptual phenomena as visitations, 'hauntings' and alien-contact/abduction experiences. It is a pity that such causative processes do not lie within more *status quo* medicine, as there is often the whiff of unorthodoxy associated with unregulated holistic approaches. Nevertheless, in order to understand these strange perceptions, at least mainstream holistic medicine needs to be understood.

However, there is also the additional range of bioelectromagnetic effects which are induced in the human body but unrelated to environmental sensitivities, and which are superimposed on those triggered by hypersensitivity to fields and other impinging aspects of the environment, including foods and chemicals. That is to say, we also need to be aware that there is an established field of study which is primarily concerned with the ways that the human biological system behaves when subjected to electromagnetic (EM) fields.

But how are EM fields and foods/chemicals related, and how do they interact and contribute to the triggering of visitations and alien-abduction experiences, etc.? The short answer to this is that they all contribute to the physiological load that the brain/body has to cope with at any one time, and these weird experiences are, in fact, symptoms of a failure of the body to adapt to them; basically, such experiences are symptomatic of a breakdown of the body's regulatory systems. This brings us to an extremely important aspect of holistic medicine, because it provides insights as to why experiences are triggered on some occasions and not on others, i.e. it depends on whether the experiencer has exceeded a personal threshold in terms of the physiological load his or her body is coping with, and this aspect is embodied in a concept called the *load phenomenon*.

THE LOAD PHENOMENON EXAMINED

This concept was introduced in the blueprint of the EM-pollution approach (p.22), and refers to a physiological overload. Information from the Breakspear Hospital, Hertfordshire, UK, relates:

> *To understand the load phenomenon and the effects of overload one has to regard the body as having to reach a threshold above which symptoms will occur. The threshold is not fixed – it can be lowered by stress, infection and general factors such as lack of sleep, but to reach the threshold, the effects are cumulative as the body interacts when it encounters environmental agents. Once the threshold is reached, symptoms will be produced. [Breakspear Hospital, 1994.]*

As the hallucinatory realities perceived are, in actuality, symptoms, this load-phenomenon concept must also apply to them and, as mentioned, provides us with some insight as to why experiences are triggered on one occasion but not on another. An extremely important aspect of load is how EM-field exposure relates to food allergies and chemical sensitivities. During the period leading up to an alien-abduction experience/visitation, etc. the body accumulates stressors, as the extract above relates. These are also foods and chemicals taken in by the body to which it has become sensitized. But how do potential experiencers acquire these food allergies and chemical sensitivities in the first place, when the primary factor affecting them is the EM fields from local RF transmitters and/or power lines, etc.? That is to say, although they are living in a hot spot, they also become allergic to a range of foods (allergies to wheat, sugar, milk and additives are common) and sensitive to an array of chemicals (gas, cigarette smoke, perfume, aerosols and other volatile products); exposure to these will then contribute to the load-phenomenon threshold and, ultimately, visitation experiences. As all of us are exposed to these on a regular basis, how does irradiation by fields induce a hypersensitivity to them?

THE ALLERGY-RELAY ASPECT OF ELECTROMAGNETIC FIELDS

Dr C.W. Smith and Dr Jean Monro, of the Breakspear Hospital, have both worked extensively with patients suffering from multiple allergies/chemical sensitivities and EH. They have developed a protocol whereby the symptoms of these patients can be neutralized by exposing them to an EM frequency. Basically, they have discovered that there is an interchangeability between chemicals, foods and EM fields in terms of the symptoms which they can induce in patients, and they have developed a conceptual system to account for this practical treatment method of removing symptoms. They have explored the processes involved in the acquisition of food allergies/chemical sensitivities, and have found that an EM field can act as a 'carrier' for allergies which then 'infects' the patients' reactions to foods and substances that are usually tolerated. Consider an extract from the epic *Electromagnetic Man*:

> It seems that a new allergic response can be acquired, or transferred, by being exposed for a sufficiently long time to some hitherto innocuous substance while reacting strongly to an existing allergen. In such circumstances it seems that exposure to an electromagnetic frequency can sensitise the patient, so that their specific pattern of allergic responses is triggered on subsequently encountering that particular frequency. In general the pattern of allergic responses is the same whether the trigger is chemical, environmental, nutritional, or electrical. In principle, such an accurate 'memory' for frequency is no different to the 'absolute pitch' facility that many musicians possess. [Smith & Best, 1989, p. 87.]

As I understand this, if an individual who is already allergic to wheat products eats something containing gluten (the 'active ingredient', to which people react allergically) and is simultaneously irradiated by radio-frequency (RF) microwaves from a nearby TV-station transmitter, his/her system will associate that frequency with an allergic reaction, and react to that field alone on another occasion – a position analagous to classical conditioning. However, if during such an irradiation and subsequent allergic reaction the individual smokes a cigarette, or at least inhales smoke passively, his/her body then associates the allergic reaction 'carried' by the field with tobacco smoke, and becomes sensitized to it. This is a type of 'relay' mechanism whereby an allergic reaction is transferred from gluten in a wheat product to an RF frequency and then passed on to cigarette smoke. Among my case files of experiencers, I have some who have reported that they are hypersensitive to tobacco smoke, literally giving up smoking overnight, no doubt due to this effect. They may sometimes attribute this near-miracle of effortless abstention to part of a health-promoting process endowed upon them by alien intelligences who are preparing them for life after an atomic war, but the effect is real enough.

However, this 'relay effect' is not without its critics and, in fact, the holistic approach, which I regard as a valuable addition to medicine, has come under considerable attack from *status quo* medical circles, including questions being raised as to whether allergies themselves really exist. I do not take a partisan approach myself, though as we will see, I cannot escape the tenets of the holistic approach as they have predicted so many aspects that I have found in the field. But, in the *Bulletin of Anomalous Experience*, Dr David Gotlib, after reading my book *Allergies and Aliens*, comments:

> *Mr Budden draws heavily on the theories and methods of clinical ecology, a field which, at least in North America, has yet to achieve credibility within mainstream medicine. Many of the symptoms Budden cites as attributable to environmental sensitivity are also anxiety symptoms, and some psychiatrists and allergy specialists think that 'environmental sensitivity' syndromes are not immunologic illnesses, as clinical ecology claims, but anxiety disorders akin to agoraphobia. Mr Budden's explanation of the involvement of electromagnetism in developing environmental allergies is also controversial. I wondered why, since we are all swimming in a sea of chemicals and electromagnetic pollution, we are not all suffering massive generalized allergic reactions, not to mention encounter experiences. [Gotlib, 1994.]*

Dr Gotlib's objections are easily answered. To focus on the last aspect, as to why the general population is not affected, it is immediately obvious that it is only those individuals who live in EM hot spots and have developed EH that have reactions and experiences, and then only on an episodic basis.

To regard allergic reactions as phobias is equally easily answered, because phobic reactions to stimuli involve an engagement of attention and direct observation of that stimulus. If a spider was placed in an opaque sealed container and placed close to a patient suffering from arachnophobia, he/she would not react because he/she would be unaware of the spider's presence. However, on two occasions, I have been present when friends have been rushed to hospital after eating an ingredient to which they were allergic and which, unbeknown to them, was added to a dish in a restaurant (a nut allergy actually). It was their bodies which did the reacting, as they were unaware of the presence of the allergen. How could a phobia of an ingredient manifest itself if the sufferer was unaware of its presence? Evidently, food allergies cannot be phobias.

Regarding the 'relay' mechanism of fields acting as a 'carrier' of allergic reactions, I am unable to carry out direct experimentation myself to determine its validity. However, I know that Drs Smith and Monro and their colleagues have done so. As an investigator in the field, I can only support their conclusions because such a relay mechanism accounts for why experiencers who are irradiated by fields on a regular basis have consistently acquired sensitivities to a range of foods and chemicals. That is to say, their conclusions on this fit precisely with what I have also found in the field. For example, during one interview we had to move into another room because I had turned the gas fire on while waiting for the subject to arrive and a minute amount of gas had escaped into the room before I lit it. To my astonishment, it was not only detected but also triggered a reaction in the subject. Usually, the development of such sensitivities would require massive and frequent exposures to the chemical to which the subjects were sensitive and, as none of them report such exceptional exposures, their sensitivities must be due to another cause, i.e. the 'allergy relay' mechanism of the fields which irradiate their homes.

However, I also have another, more personal reason for my certainty. My wife suffers from multiple allergies and chemical sensitivities, the result of spending her childhood close to the powerful radar and communication systems of a military base in Essex, UK. Over the past 7 years of coping with exposures, observing reactions, visiting allergy specialists and generally absorbing practical and empirically acquired information, I have developed an insider's perspective of what is involved in the triggering and development of such sensitivities. I have also been intrigued by the fresh descriptions of her visitation experiences minutes after they have occurred ...

Returning to the load phenomenon, we can now appreciate how the triggering threshold may be breached and symptoms, including visitations, precipitated. It is important to realize that EH sufferers are subject to fields which carry an *allergic payload*, as opposed to, and in addition to, 'uncontaminated' fields. In a way, the fields and frequencies that they are regularly subjected to in hot spots have become personalized with their own specific *allergenic tags;* this additional specific potency would add to the levels of the load-phenomenon threshold, so that they may be triggered to undergo an experience whenever they are exposed to these frequencies, wherever they are.

It must be stated, however, that typically it is not food allergies or chemical sensitivities alone which act as triggers, and there seems to be an EM-sensitivities component to the total stimuli of the load phenomenon. This is probably because it is the electrical energy that fields provide which is active in the electrically destabilized brain and produces hallucinatory epileptiform visual seizures. It may now be appreciated that EH is but one strand to the environmental sensitivities which experiencers develop, and which induce their exceptional and bizarre perceptions, and also to how the different elements combine and interact. Having stated this, however, hypersensitivity to fields is the primary condition which triggers these perceptions, supplemented and intrinsically linked with food allergies and chemical sensitivities. It would seem that the brain can be the reactive organ during an allergic reaction to foods and/or chemicals:

> *The cause and effect of food allergies affecting the brain have been well documented in medical journals since the 1920s. In fact, the subject was documented as far back as the seventeenth century by Robert Burton who regarded certain foods as 'engendering melancholy humours in the body' and wrote 'all that comes from milk increases melancholy' in his* Anatomy of Melancholy. *[Rothea, 1991.]*

THE ROLE OF THE PINEAL IN THE ABDUCTION VISION

When considering the mechanisms and processes that would sustain hallucinatory/visionary experiences, as well as a range of spontaneously occurring anomalous sensations, it would certainly seem that parts of the brain are kicked into activity by the intrusions of fluctuating EM fields from the environment. For example, although foods are traditionally considered to trigger migraine attacks, there is also a school of thought that regards anomalous electrical activity to be a major contributory factor. When normally quiescent brain areas are activated in this way, altered states can be precipitated, although it must be emphasized that, before altered states of mind can occur, there must be an altered state of body.

In addition to the electrically destabilized brain, the work of Dr Serena Roney-Dougal, a pioneer in her field, has shown that field-stimulated hallucinatory chemicals can also be at work. She maintains that a group of hallucinogenic neurohormones are produced primarily in the pineal gland in response to irradiation by naturally occurring magnetic fields. She states:

> I have suggested that the pineal gland makes a hallucinogen which could well take us into an altered state that is psi-conducive and which affects us at physical, emotional and psychic levels. Shifts in the intensity of the earth's magnetic field (EMF) appears to be one of the environmental conditions which affect pineal activity and psychic sensitivity. [Roney-Dougal, 1991.]

The implications for the EM-pollution approach are tremendous. Obviously, if the pineal can be triggered into activity to produce these psychohormones by natural energies from the earth, then the influence of the more potent intermodulation effects from RF transmitters and power lines could be formidable. What hallucinogenic compounds are produced? Of the pineal, Roney-Dougal relates:

> The pineal is found right in the centre of our brain ... No other part of the brain contains so much serotonin, a neurotransmitter, 5-hydroxy-trytamine (5HT), that works at the synapses, or is capable of making the neurohormone melatonin, which is almost certainly a precursor of the possibly psi-conducive pinoline ...

However, Roney-Dougal extends this by introducing another class of psycho-active compounds:

> ... together with serotonin and melatonin in the pineal gland and the retina, there is another class of compounds called beta-carbolines, which are produced by the pineal gland and which are chemically very similar to the alkaloids of Banisteriopsis ... a vine whose active ingredients are harmaline and other harmala alkaloids ... used by a large number of South American tribes in order to induce visions ... in combination with other plants as Prestonia amazonica and Psychotria viridis (Cawa) which have hallucinogenic properties ... the active ingredient being dimethoxy-tryptamine (DMT)"

Therefore, we are implicating not only direct EM effects on the brain and body in the visionary drama of the alien-abduction experience, but also the increased presence of hallucinatory compounds, albeit EM-induced through the irradiation of the pineal gland. However, there is additional circumstantial evidence which is indicative of the involvement of these psycho-active compounds.

From the many descriptions of the alien-abduction/contact experience, it is evident that, in many cases, we are considering a complex and convoluted drama where the 'abductees' feel that they are floated bodily out of the normal surroundings of bedroom, car, countryside, etc. into alien realms, and given a guided tour of alien environments, including interiors of 'the craft' or expansive chambers where all manner of strange exhibits and procedures take place, albeit with symbolic overtones. In the following example, from *The Andreasson Affair*, the percipient is describing a sequence where she is being given just such a guided tour and she and her alien hosts have been floating through various scenarios guided by a track on the floor, reminiscent of the colour-coded lines painted on the floors in hospitals to guide visitors to their destination, which may have been the origin of such imagery:

The track curved upward. This new area was vast.

It's beautiful here … we are still going along and it seems like mist or sea or something off to the side … And we're like on a narrow passage of land and we're gliding across it … And I see – I don't know if they are fish or what. It looks like a combination of bird and fish. And it seems like it's haze all over, and fog, and yet it's light so I can see. And we are going someplace, I don't know where it is, up ahead … Betty peered down upon strange plants, mist-enshrouded water, and a distant complex of buildings. The sheer vastness of this alien realm overwhelmed her senses … It reminded her of some legendary underground kingdom. *[Fowler, 1980.]*

From this and other experiences, it is clear that these extended visions can be comparable to the mescalin-induced realities described by Aldous Huxley in *Doors of Perception* and *Heaven and Hell*, and also to the spiritual worlds of the astral traveller. It is entirely consistent, therefore, to learn that the harmala alkaloids, which Roney-Dougal compares chemically to those magnetically induced in the pineal, have been used traditionally by South American tribes, via their consumption of plants which contain it, to enter other non-corporeal worlds:

The anthropomorphic evidence, however, points to the harmala alkaloids being more than merely hallucinogenic, the people reporting out-of-body experiences which they consider to be spirit travelling. This use of a psychotropic plant … matches that of the witches' 'flying ointment'. Other reported experiences can best be compared to clairvoyance and remote viewing. [Roney-Dougal, 1991.]

For those who have harboured doubts that the simple focal seizures of the irradiated brain could produce such complex visions, and that there must be some other factor involved if the EM-pollution approach is to account for the evidence, this electrochemical addition should certainly satisfy them. The discovery of Roney-Dougal's work from my own point of view was a startling revelation. For over 12 years I had been investigating a particularly 'high strangeness' case in which the witness had come extremely close to three earth lights as luminous spheres. She had reported that pencil-thin beams of light came from them and focussed upon a spot on her forehead, just above the bridge of her nose. It had not escaped my attention that a continuation of the line that these beams made was directly on-target for the pineal gland. The woman's experience was atypically complex and lengthy, and involved prolonged hallucinatory realities. It now seems that the hallucinogenic compounds in the pineal gland which Roney-Dougal describes were being stimulated to facilitate the experience.

MAGNETITE AND THE PINEAL

Probably the most convincing indictment of the pineal's role in visitation and other psychical experiences comes about as a number of independent but cross-referring factors. Let us consider these:

1. Roney-Dougal maintains that magnetic fields stimulate the pineal gland to produce hallucinogenic neurohormones, albeit from natural geomagnetic and atmospheric sources.

2. Dr Jean Monro, who treats EH at the Breakspear Hospital, has found that this clinical condition is acutely enhanced in patients who have undergone a major electrical event (MEE), e.g. proximity to a lightning strike.

3. I have found that, typically, 'abductees' have developed EH and have undergone one or more MEEs in their lives.

4. As detailed on p. 84, Manchester zoologists Baker, Mather and Kennaugh found significant deposits of the iron-based mineral, magnetite, in the pineal. Therefore, a strong circumstantial picture arises whereby those individuals who have acquired enhanced levels of endogenous magnetism in the pineal by exposure to an MEE (which induces increased magnetism in the residual magnetite deposits there, making for a more active pineal in terms of its secretions of hallucinogenic neurohormones) are the people who would be expected to have abduction and other 'high strangeness' visitation experiences on an episodic basis. In fact, this is the case. That is to say, some types of experiencer carry around their own internally irradiated pineal, as the magnetite particles there have been made more magnetic by a close exposure to a lightning strike or some other MEE. But this is not all.

The same Manchester zoologists found even more significant levels of magnetite in the walls of the sphenoid and ethmoid bones of human sinuses. These, anatomically, are close to the underside of the temporal lobes of the brain, as evidenced by the use of nasopharyngeal electrodes in electroencephalograms (EEGs) to detect temporal-lobe epilepsy (TLE); these are placed high up in the nostrils. It would appear therefore, that an MEE would also magnetize these deposits in the sinuses, which would be another endogenous magnetic site, irradiating the temporal lobes. It would certainly appear that there are two internal magnetic sites that stimulate the parts of the brain which are key active areas of 'abductions', visitation experiences or other psychical events.

TYPES OF ELECTROMAGNETIC HYPERSENSITIVITY

For a sufferer of EH, the onset of exposure to a field which he/she is especially sensitive to usually begins with a distinct sense of unease and a loss of concentration and muscle strength, especially in the legs, which refuse to work. Head pains, weakness and the inability to read or write without extreme difficulty occur, and these soon develop into a 'zombie-like' state in which the subject may become completely mute. A peculiar sensation of becoming increasingly overheated and a detachment from the immediate surroundings is typical. The subject may see a bright radiating light, along with a pulsing feeling in the temples, or a tight-band sensation around the head, and may eventually lapse into unconsciousness and fall to the ground in a drop attack. The subject, if sitting or prone, will just pass out. Alternatively, a blank/mute state may set in, sometimes referred to as a 'blank-out', in which consciousness is retained but time seems to pass unnoticed, and a heavy tingling sensation is felt throughout the body, especially in the extremities. These symptoms wear off gradually once the subject is away from the field source.

Also during this allergic reaction to fields, EH can mimic epileptiform conditions; the subject may go about a routine task, such as driving between familiar destinations, going out for a walk and coming back, getting undressed and putting him/herself to bed, and have absolutely no memory of having done so. This effect, along with black-outs and blank-outs produces the 'time lapse' or 'missing-time' effect of alien-abduction experiences, and such automatic behaviour, as it is called, has often been observed at the Breakspear Hospital, where EH is treated and videoed for medical training purposes.

However, such extreme altered reactivity is an acute reaction, and mild reactions may occur in which EH subjects are able to adapt and re-radiate fields as a whole-body effect, causing electrical equipment in their presence to malfunction. Dr Jean Monro described this with an analogy to sound: it is as if patients are being subjected to a general ambient noise, while they emit a pure musical note, i.e. the field emitted is surprisingly coherent and their body acts as an oscillator. Fields of 2MHz have been recorded from subjects and can be picked up as static when a tape-recorder is placed on their lap. I have recorded some unusual sounds from experiencers while recording interviews, e.g. a periodic 'boing' effect which I have called the *electronic gulp*.

In another less severe reaction, described to me by Dr Jean Monro, the subjects do not lose consciousness but become immobilized while they are preoccupied with their inner visions, sometimes with their eyes open; they may be able to describe what they are experiencing as it occurs. A good example of this is the Maureen Puddy case in Australia (p. 262), in which investigators were actually present during just such a visionary period. Also, it is precisely this type of reactivity that is recalled during the regressive hypnosis sessions of 'abductees' and it is clear that these experiences are entirely subjective. Such regressions fuel the belief that real physical aliens are at work, as it is difficult not to be persuaded by the testimony that these regressed subjects report. But we should be, because they are describing vivid inner experiences which are prefaced by descriptions of their objective environment and the onset of EH symptoms. There are many examples of the 'alien-activity' part of the experience but a good example of the EH-onset symptoms seems to be the case of Mrs Elsie Oakensen, of Church Stowe, Northamptonshire, UK, whose full account was presented in my first book. To reproduce the relevant section:

> *The witness did report a short amnesiac period or 'time lapse'. This was investigated by regressive hypnosis and, instead of an alien abduction story emerging, she recalled: 'I got hotter and hotter ... the pressure hurt my head.' Then 'a brilliant pure white light, very bright' hit her full on from the front. It throbbed with circles radiating out from the centre: 'The pain in my head was intense ... I felt no reaction in my legs ... I was very frightened.' [Budden, 1995a.]*

TYPES A AND B

After collecting many cases of EH over the past 3 years, it would seem that there are two types (at least) of this condition, which could be referred to as 'chronic' and 'acute', the fundamental difference being whether or not an MEE occurred with the experiencer. Basically, type A involves prolonged irradiation at a hot spot, often where the fields involved emanate from a natural geological source, i.e. tectonic activity at faults. Individuals with type A tend to hallucinate formed figures that do not include aliens or alien-abduction experiences, e.g. guardian angels, child-figures, apparitions. Type B, however, involves an MEE and hot-spot irradiation from artificial sources, especially power lines and RF transmitters. An MEE is when the individual undergoes a sudden and massive influx of electrical energy into the body as a result of proximity to, for example, a lightning strike or suffering major electrocution. MEEs include:

1. Being struck by lightning or being close to a lightning strike.

2. Proximity to ball lightning (BL), St Elmo's fire, corona discharges, etc.

3. Proximity to unclassified light phenomena (UAPs) e.g. earth lights (Devereux & McCartney 1982) or 'electroforms', as accidently produced electric fireballs from the interaction of powerful RF transmitters, power lines, electrical installations, etc. Exotic forms have been observed and regarded as UFOs.

4. Proximity to a tornado; these produce powerful fields and electrical discharges of lightning may accompany them.

5. Major electrocution; shocks of higher voltages for longer periods than simple domestic contacts.

6. Electroconvulsive therapy (ECT); such charges through the brain will amount to an exceptional electrical event.

7. Defibrillation [see Note 5]; resuscitation by this method also induces exceptional encounters with electrical currents.

8. Controlled electrical demonstrations; e.g. the Science Museum in London, UK, used to discharge a spectacular million-volt spark daily to inspire young scientists.

This list is not exhaustive.

Permanent changes to the body are precipitated after such MEEs, although obviously some are more potent than others. Such massive exposures set the body up for an acute form of EH in later life, although some experiencers have reported abduction experiences and other visitations within weeks of the event. This is where the other major parameter of the cause of these experiences is also met, i.e. hot-spot exposure. Physical bodily changes precipitated by MEEs are due to the fact that, when an electrical current enters the body, it will flow along the blood vessels, nerves and the pathway of the cerebrospinal fluid. The brain stem is the hardest hit due to the fact that the central nervous system (CNS) is confined to one narrow pathway in that area of the body. Lightning will widen the space between blood and brain cells, i.e. they are forced apart and the integrity of the normally impervious blood/brain barrier is breached. The neurological textbooks express their own specialized aspects which are reproduced here for readers with the advantage of medical knowledge:

> *Respiratory insufficiency may result in anoxic encephalopathy and gener-*
> *alised seizures. Damage to the cerebrum may result in hemiplegia or*
> *homonymous hemianopia. The passage of an electric current through the*
> *brain stem can produce Parkinsonism, cranial nerve deficits, or corti-*
> *cospinal tract involvement with spasticity ... Passage of an electrical*
> *current through a limb may be followed by peripheral nerve involvement*
> *producing painful neuralgias, muscle weakness, fasciculations and atrophy*
> *... [Gilroy, 1990, p. 340.]*

I have found fasciculation (see p. 23) in numerous experiencers whose event involved close proximity to anomalous atmospheric phenomena/ UAPs, sometimes linked to power lines. This is mentioned here to underscore the fact that lightning and UAPs 'identified' as UFOs amount to comparable electrical phenomena.

ROLE OF ORGANIC MAGNETITE

Basically, it could be said that some MEEs widen and dilate selective vessels of the body so that blood flow is altered. However, there is another significant effect that an MEE will precipitate, which relates to the deposits of particles of magnetite in the body. Magnetite, or 'lode-stone', is a naturally occurring mineral, which, as we have seen (p. 50), is ubiquitous in its particulate presence in the environment. However, it is somewhat surprising to learn that it is also present at relatively concentrated levels within the human body.

Three biologists working in the Department of Zoology at the University of Manchester, UK, discovered and investigated deposits of magnetite in the walls of the sphenoid/ethmoid bones in the sinus complex of man. Baker, Mather and Kennaugh isolated and photographed these areas of magnetism. We will be turning our attention to these specific sites on p. 86, as they have important implications for certain physical effects reported after alien-abduction experiences. It is these microscopic particles of this mineral compound in the cells of the brain, which could introduce an endogenous magnetic field into the brain when subjected to an MEE, that are especially significant. Author Dr G. L. Little relates:

> *For many years it was not known how or why electromagnetic fields altered*
> *brain chemistry − and human experience. Now, with the 1992 discovery*
> *of the substance magnetite found in quantities in human brain cells, the*
> *answer is probably before us ... Quite simply, magnetite aligns itself to the*

field of whatever electromagnetic – or geomagnetic – force that the person is in. This alignment of magnetite subtly alters the ionic flow in the brain's cells and thus can increase the flow of neurotransmitters in some brain areas while decreasing the flow in others [through inhibition] ... [Little, 1994.]

Neurologists working on epilepsy at the University Hospital, Zurich, Switzerland, have also been concerned with what they term *iron biomineralization* in the human brain. A report on their activities relates:

In 1993 and 1994 the project partners reported that weak DC magnetic fields induced a response in the brain wave activities of patients with drug-resistant Mesial Temporal Lobe Epilepsy ... the goal is to examine human brain tissue using magnetic methods in order to verify the existence of biomineralized ferromagnetic iron oxide magnetite in human hippocampal tissue. Recent magnetic analysis of samples of tissue which has been dissected from brain tissue ... indicates that the magnetite is not the result of post-mortem changes in the brain's iron chemistry ... the project could lead ... to understanding the role of magnetite in the functioning of the central nervous system ... [Kuster et al., 1993–4]

Whatever processes can be gauged to be in effect, the enhanced magnetism of these cellular particles would again represent an additional endogenous magnetism within the brain of the EH-status individual. Its presence would increase the individual's sensitivity to magnetic fields because of constant exposure to internal fields, which although small compared with external fields, are located in an extremely sensitive and strategic area – the brain tissue itself.

It would follow that their every exposure to a magnetic field would involve a micro-intermodulation effect due to the acquired polarity of these internal particles (via the MEEs), and the potency of intermodulations generally (see on p. 46). In Chapter 4, p. 114, an extract from a *New Scientist* report shows how an electrical induction effect in the brain can be produced by intracranial irradiation with simple magnets to alleviate depression. From this, it is not difficult to see how micro-seizures in the brain could be induced when the acquired field of the particle meets the in-coming field, thus inducing an intermodulation effect. It is the mechanism of eddy currents produced by these micro-intermodulations which could kindle seizures at focal points in the brain. These simple seizures produce hallucinations and perceptual disorders which can be recognized, either inset into the more complex matrix of alien-abduction and other visitation experiences, or occurring in isolation in percipients at 'haunted' locations, which are, of course, hot spots. To conclude this section on the effects of MEEs, consider this list of seizure-induced psychosensory phenomena taken from the textbook

Basic Neurology by Dr John Gilroy. These have been consistently regarded as 'haunting phenomena' by psychical investigators and as alien activity by ufologists when considered in conjunction with the direct effects of fields on the environment that have been explored:

> *Visual hallucinations are usually elementary and consist of flashes or balls of light. Occasionally ... complex stereotyped visual phenomena such as a landscape or a human figure. Auditory hallucinations usually take the form of hissing or ringing ... buzzing or bell-like sounds ... but the hallucinatory experience may present as the voice of persons known or unknown and the patient is often able to remember the details of the conversation after the attack ... Hallucinations of smell are often intense and unpleasant ... An intense feeling of fear or dread is not unusual ... attacks may vary in one individual from a relatively brief period with few symptoms to an extremely complex constellation ...' [Gilroy, 1990, pp. 72–73]*

This short catalogue is not exhaustive, but has been interpreted by researchers from both areas as examples of mysterious phenomena, demonstrating a duality of error in psychical and 'abductological' circles, e.g. the fear reaction during abductions and the same effect during hauntings; strange anomalous smells occurring in both types of experience; lights in the air also occurring in both, as do human figures and landscapes. However, they can be properly identified as epileptiform perceptions induced by field exposure.

'ALIEN NASAL IMPLANTS' IDENTIFIED

In Baker, Mather and Kennaugh's paper in *Nature*, on magnetic bones in human sinuses, they state:

> *Histological examination was carried out on tissue from all of the regions tested magnetometrically ... Although a scattering of iron-staining material was found throughout the soft tissues (including the brain) and in the bone marrow, extensive concentrations of ferric iron were found only within the bone of the sphenoid/ethmoid sinus complex. These concentrations were in the form of a continuous layer of iron-staining material, apparently particulate, approximately 2 micromillimetres thick and about 5 micromillimetres beneath the surface of the bone. The bone itself is about 200 micromillimetres thick ... our impression is that the iron layer is most conspicuous beneath the surface of the bone that forms the inner wall of the sinus. Occasionally, however, there is an iron layer about 5 micromillimetres beneath both inner and outer surfaces. [Baker et al., 1983.]*

A microphotograph of this layer is reproduced in the picture section of this book, and the researchers also offer hypotheses about its function:

One possibility is that the sinus bones are part of a storage or dumping site for iron. The apparent absence of deposits in an anaemic subject suggests that the material is withdrawn as the subject becomes iron-deficient. A second possibility is that the magnetic deposits are concerned with magnetic-field detection. Experiments suggest that humans can detect direction by reference to the ambient magnetic field ... The sphenoid/ethmoid sinuses coincide with the region deduced from orientation experiments to be the site of a magnetoreceptor. A third possibility is that the magnetic material is involved in some way with growth and repair of bones ... such interpretations need not be mutually exclusive. [Baker et al., 1983.]

It is surely no coincidence that EEG testing for TLE involves electrodes which pass high up into the sinuses through the nostrils. It is suggested that the close proximity of these deposits to the temporal-lobe region of the brain re-radiates magnetic fields to these areas, enhancing the endogenous magnetism they would already provide. The experiential effects of irradiating the temporal lobes have been investigated by Persinger and his colleagues, and these also correspond with the hallucinatory sensations reported by experiencers, e.g. sense of presence, desynchronization, magnetophosphenes.

Furthermore, it is suggested here that, when these deposits are subjected to magnetic fields, they are also traumatically disturbed by them, so that sudden gyromagnetic movement induces a rupturing of the tiny blood vessels, resulting in minor nose-bleeds. This is the centre piece of the 'alien implant' mythology, which says that, during the aliens' invasive tampering with humans, they insert minute monitoring devices into the sinuses; 'abductees' have consistently reported minor nose-bleeds as a post-abduction phenomenon.

THE WORK OF NICHOLAS REITER

The EM researcher/investigator Nicholas Reiter, from Gibsonburg, Ohio, USA, has carried out some unique experiments on experiencers, including 'abductees'. There are two central areas of his investigations involving magnetic fields.

MAGNETIC-FIELD DETECTORS AT 'ABDUCTION' SITES

Magnetic-field detectors were placed in the homes of experiencers across the USA and a pattern emerged in which these devices were triggered on the occasions when an experience was reported but not at other times. Also, this pattern was not established when the detectors were placed in the homes of non-experiencers, as controls. This of course supports the EM-pollution approach, which maintains that environmental fields trigger alien-abduction and related experiences in EH subjects.

THE MAGNETIC RESPONSE TEST: Reiter's response

Numerous individual experiencers and non-experiencers were tested by placing strong magnets (1000–2000Gs) on different areas of the skull (see diagram) A pattern emerged whereby experiencers displayed a 'magnetic response' as a range of distinct sensations and non-experiencers did not. These included one where the experiencer described the feeling as like a 'bubble' rising under pressure within the sinuses. Readers may deduce for themselves that this is an effect on the enhanced magnetism of the particulate layer of magnetite, discovered by the Manchester zoologists described on pp. 84 and 86.

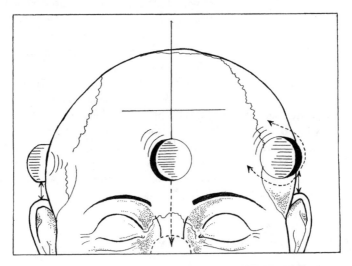

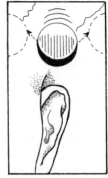

Reiter's response: the magnetic response test. Diagrams showing three primary positions for placing magnets on the head of test subjects. Dotted lines indicate movement of magnets during testing in order to enhance response. EH subjects experience a range of sensations such as ears 'popping', flashes of light, pressure and vibration inside the head. Non-EH subjects feel nothing.
(Poppy Palin)

It is significant also, that author/experiencer Whitley Strieber suffered nose-bleeds after experiences, as well as an uncomfortable sensation of 'knots' in the sinuses; interestingly, so did his family, who lived at the same location and so would have also been subject to the effects of irradiation. However, Strieber underwent multiple MEEs earlier in life. (See Budden, 1995b.)

The words of Reiter himself transmit not only the substance and complexity of his investigations, but also his evident confidence and enthusiasm:

> *During the winter of 1990/91 a short series of unique experiments relating to the UFO abduction phenomenon were conducted in the Dallas, Texas area by a close friend and research associate, Ms Barbara Boyle. Fundamentally, it was observed that several individuals who were UFO abduction experiencers were subject to a very peculiar, vivid sensation when a strong permanent magnet was held near their heads. What was tentatively called the Magnetic Implant Response (MIR) consisted of a mixture of physical feelings, such as nausea and pressure, mixed with a variety of disturbing mental associations. In at least one of these cases, the area of the volunteer's head where the sensation occurred corresponded to a location where the volunteer had recalled, under hypnosis, 'aliens doing something to him ...' [See Note 6.]*

Reiter then extended this small sample of experiencers to 50 subjects chosen at random, still using the magnetic implant response (MIR) as a label. Building on the work of Budd Hopkins *et al.*, who had published the conclusion that aliens inserted a monitoring device into the 'abductee', Reiter, at this early stage of his investigations, was wondering:

> *Was the field of the powerful magnet affecting or interfering with a brain implant?*

However, after completing 'The Random Series' of 50 subjects, to Reiter's credit, he renamed the effects he obtained with a more neutral term – the magnetic response (MR). What effects did he discover? Consider a selection:

1. Subject felt slight feeling of 'pressure' behind right ear. Subject felt very strong sensation at a region above the nose. Felt as though a 'bubble of pressure' was trying to move down and out of the nose, from somewhere up behind the eyes.

2. Subject felt a strong, uncomfortable sensation of 'pressure' at the left temple, slightly above ear level (close to where the magnet is applied for the magnetic response test).

3. Felt a strong sensation toward back of head, on left side, behind and below left ear. 'Felt like something surprising me ... Hair on back of neck going up ... Felt like panic.'

4. Felt strong sensation of uneasiness and confusion when magnet was passed over left ear/temple region. Was clearly upset.

5. Felt a weird sensation behind right ear. Also felt something unusual behind left eye whenever right ear zone was accessed ... verbal elaboration difficult ... visual impression of white and blue flashing lights in left eye ... very unnerved by the experience.

6. Sensation between and behind eyes ... could feel hair rising up on the head ... became uneasy.

7. Response behind left ear ... felt very intense sensation of pressure ... subject became animated and nervous to the point of trembling ... said that the response location seemed to be near where she had a tumour removed about two years previously.

8. Sensation behind left ear ... like poles of magnets pushing each other ... felt chills and shivers ... odd sensation behind eyes.

9. Sensation behind and below left ear ... felt uncomfortable like a migraine headache.

10. Felt throbbing pain behind and below left ear ... became nervous and 'distant' after test.

From these investigations, Reiter came to the following conclusions:

1. The MR is an objective phenomenon, with both physical and mental symptoms.

2. The MR, first discovered by Barbara Boyle with the help of UFO 'abductee' volunteers, has proven itself a replicable phenomenon. Symptoms of the effect have remained constant.

3. The MR appears to affect 1 in 3.6 individuals, or 14 out of 50 (randomly chosen).

4. It seems to be a 'quantum' sort of effect! Not one individual tested was indeterminant about whether or not they could feel the MR. *The effect either was a definite sensation, or was entirely non-existent.*

5. The locations of the MR are consistent and form a distinctive pattern of occurrence.

6. The MR seems to manifest itself with fairly even distribution across genders, occupations, social status and age groups, with one noticeable and

possibly significant exception. Of the 50 volunteers tested, 10 individuals fell into the age group of 61 years or older. Of these 10, not one tested positive for the MR!

Reiter then goes on to identify the distinguishing factor between positive and negative responders, but before we discuss this, how can the results he obtained with this random 50 be interpreted?

Immediately, the fact that both physical and mental effects were induced attracts me to the conclusion that epileptiform sensations were involved. If there were no mental effects, we could perhaps conclude that only the deposits of magnetite were being affected by the magnets, but the feelings of fear and apprehension are typical of the mental phenomena evoked by the stimulation of the temporal lobes of the brain, as are the light flashes, typical of magnetophosphenes (Halgren *et al.*, 1978). Once again, the consistency of the MR is indicative of the consistency of the effects of fields across populations of experiencers, i.e. those who have developed EH and multiple allergies.

The trend for older subjects to be free of the MR mirrors the marked scarcity of alien-abduction experiences before the 1960s. In *Allergies and Aliens* I proposed that this reflects the absence of high EM-pollution levels in the environment and the accelerated proliferation of electronic communication systems in the last 30 years or so. This, of course, implies that the difference between the two groups that Reiter found – MR positive and MR negative – is the tendency for the MR-positive subjects to be experiencers of some type and the MR-negative subjects to be non-experiencers; this was, in fact, the case. Reiter relates:

> The most obvious difference between the two groups concerned the experiencing of the anomalous! The life-histories of the MR positive volunteers had a tendency to be filled with encounters with ghostly activity, poltergeists and UFOs. The MR negative tended to have very few occurrences of this sort.

I have illustrated this with the following chart:

	MR+	MR-
1. UFO sightings	5	2
2. Ghostly encounters	7	1
3. Poltergeist activity	4	0
4. Strange entities	3	0
5. ESP or psychic phenomena	2	3

It became clear to me that, in some way, the Magnetic Response was linked to the Anomalous. The following is a list of 'symptoms' or *classical characteristics of the UFO abduction experience which I specifically enquired about:*

1. Periods of missing time during waking hours.

2. Scars, welts or bruises appearing overnight, or to which no remembered origin can be attributed.

3. Nocturnal bleeding from nose, ears or mouth.

4. 'Visitors' in bedroom; either in dream or waking state.

5. Close encounter with a UFO.

6. Chronic 'ear-ringing' or noises in the head.

Results have been charted as follows:

ABOVE ITEM	MR+ (nine)	MR- (eight)
1.	3	0
2.	7	0
3.	6	0
4.	3	2
5.	5	1
6.	3	1

In conjunction with the above chart I shall state:

From the MR+ group, there are four individuals who have experienced four or more out of six characteristics congruently. [Reiter, 1994.]

Of course, an immediate criticism of this section of Reiter's investigations is that his sample is too small to indicate anything significant. My answer to this would be to ask why, if nothing could be shown from this sample, does it confirm my EM-pollution approach so precisely? That is to say, if EH is centrally instrumental in the induction of the visitation experience, whether such experiences feature 'aliens' or 'ghosts', then the individuals who showed a positive response to the magnetic fields from the 2000Gs magnet should be experiencers of some type. This in fact was the case.

Reiter goes on to ask:

How are we to interpret this? ... it seems that our two choices, as to the origin of the MR, are the following:

1. It is the result of a naturally occurring sensitivity to strong magnetic fields.

2. It the result of some special condition imposed by an external force, either selectively, or by chance on some humans.

Occam's Razor (the simplest explanation is the most likely) would dictate that the far more likely explanation would be the first ...

However, there seems to be certain inconsistencies with conditions that the first would probably contain. Consider the following questions:

1. Why the 'go/no go' appearance of the MR? It was either a distinct sensation or was not felt at all.

2. If natural, would it not be observed more often?

3. Why did none of the volunteers in the Random Series who were in the 61 or over age bracket experience the MR?

4. While geo-magnetically induced hallucinations would explain such things as ghosts and UFOs, in the light of the natural explanation, how does one relate such a natural susceptibility to mysterious night bleeding, or nocturnally appearing scars, welts or bruises?

5. A strong MR, in several cases, seemed to elicit very disturbing and ill defined memories from somewhere in the volunteer's past. If a natural effect, why the unnatural manner of manifestation? [Reiter, 1994]

The Occam's Razor rule has always seemed absurd to me. Surely we are looking for *the* answer, no matter how complex, not simply *an* answer. These are the posers that Reiter presents and the reader will, by now, have some idea as to how these questions may be answered in the light of the EM-pollution approach:

Question 1

The 'go/no go' aspect, as Reiter puts it, relates of course to the development or non-development of EH and hot-spot exposure. At the time of writing Reiter has implemented my '25 Questions' to some of the experiencers in his files and the few results that have come in have indeed indicated EH/multiple allergies and hot-spot exposure, including the incidence of MEEs. These will be covered in the Appendix.

Questions 2 and 3

As EH/multiple-allergy syndrome is the very opposite of anything 'natural', the incidence of the MR as Reiter has detected it is consistent with the selective randomness of the development of environmental sensitivities.

The question of why older volunteers did not show a tendency to display the MR has already been partially answered in terms of the development of EM pollution, especially the absence of the proliferation of RF telecommunication systems. This aspect also indicates that deposits of magnetite were not present in the sinuses; the Manchester zoologists found that it was absent in people with anaemia, which is likely to be more common in older volunteers. Also, without hot-spot exposure during the volunteers' formative years, or MEEs, any magnetite deposit present would not display the enhanced magnetism to induce the intermodulation required. This is not to say that this age bracket (60-plus) could never be experiencers and display the MR, only that Reiter's sample did not. Also, significantly, Dr Jacqueline Parkin, Senior Registrar at St Mary's Hospital, London, UK, has found that allergic responses do not occur readily in the elderly. Dr Parkin relates:

> With advancing years, the immune system demonstrates diminished reactivity, as judged by a reduction in lymphocyte responses, type 1 skin test reactivity and IgE levels. Allergic disorders would therefore be expected to be less common in the elderly. [Parkin, 1990, p. 42.]

This underlines the fact that EH is involved in the MR, as this condition is, in effect, an 'electrical allergy', especially as we have seen its close relationship with food allergies and chemical sensitivities.

Question 4

The mention of 'geo-magnetically induced hallucinations' refers to Persinger's well-known work [Ruttan et al., 1990]; Reiter asks about physical trauma as post-encounter effects and, of course, this is due to the gyromagnetic movements of the magnetite layer. The 'scars, welts and bruising' are due, I have found, to the re-radiation and concentration of electrical as well as magnetic fields from jewellery and other non-earthed metallic objects in contact or near-contact with the skin of the hypersensitive experiencer, as mentioned on p. 36. This effect can also induce electrical burns, especially if microwaves from a powerful RF transmitter at point-blank range are involved, and the heating effect of RF fields, known as *diathermy*, is well known. In relation to such metallic objects close to the body, comments from the 1993 WHO report, on the role of ungrounded metallic objects, have already been given on p.37. Comments from the same report, on the use of safety measures, provide another indicator of the possible hazards involved:

> Safety glasses have also been proposed for RF protection, but there is no convincing evidence that any of them are effective. On the contrary, they may act as receiving antennas and locally enhance the field. [WHO, 1993, p. 191.]

It is suggested that metallic objects close to the body will act as antennae in the same way. Basically then, the experiencer reacts allergically to irradiation and, as well as the induction of consciousness effects, traumas to the skin are produced. Specifically, recent experiments by Dr John Holt at the Royal College of Radiologists, London, UK, in which the body's mast cells have been irradiated by EM fields, have shown that histamine is produced (Holt, 1996). This well-known allergen can induce severe welts and burn-like marks on the skin as a result of allergic reactions, as well as many other dramatic effects. In fact, Holt linked his findings with asthmatic attacks, and I have personally seen the red skin patterning of allergic urticaria in experiencers living in hot-spot locations.

Question 5

The induction of mental effects, including past memories, is entirely consistent with epileptiform phenomena and Reiter, just as Persinger has done in controlled conditions, has induced seizure-like effects through MR testing, probably also in the temporal lobes.

Reiter's concluding comments in effect point the way towards the EM-pollution approach, for his unique experiments certainly support it:

> *The MR is a real entity, of this I no longer have any doubt. More impor-*
> *tantly, it is one of few solid handles I have ever encountered for grasping*
> *the shifting illusion-filled crucible of the anomalous. [Reiter, 1994.]*

If we regard the MR as a breakthrough, in that it represents a tangible/repeatable/consistent factor, the parameters of the EM-pollution approach will appear even more so, because, as the reader will see from the case files in the Appendix, we are dealing with multiples of consistent factors which can be repeatedly predicted. However, Reiter's investigations do not end here and, in fact, this presentation so far has simplified them in order to communicate their essence. Reiter also found that the MR could be 'quenched' by a discharge from a Tesla coil, an effect that seems to swamp it by triggering different brain areas. In fact Dr C. W. Smith and Dr Jean Monro, from their work with EH patients, emphasize that reactions in patients are extremely frequency-specific. It is relevant that one experiencer described the MR effect as like a migraine, because studies have shown that certain frequencies alleviate symptoms of this condition (Pickering, 1993, p. 25). Reiter also tried to detect the MR in animals, but this seems to be straying outside of our area of study.

REITER'S MAGNETIC EVENT MARKERS: an experiment with field detectors in the homes of experiencers

As mentioned at the beginning of this section on his work, Reiter also extended his and Barbara Boyle's pioneering MR work to a unique and ground-breaking project entirely of his own design and conception. He states:

> *By late 1992, I was convinced that magnetic fields or modulation were*

very deeply connected with the abduction experience. Prior research and literature in this area is limited, but is quite available and very interesting. Michael Persinger et al. have theorized that geo-magnetic interactions with the human brain and neurological processes are responsible for some hallucinatory experiences, such as death-bed visitations or religious visions. He presents evidence that electromagnetic fields from earth faults played a role in a Canadian case involving ghostly entities and poltergeist activity. [Reiter, 1994.]

Reiter then makes a statement that focusses more precisely on the experiences of 'abductees', and shows even further that field exposure and the abduction event are closely linked:

*An extraordinary significant clue to the magnetic connection presented itself to me in the form of testimony from four independent experiencers/abductees. **These individuals, each without knowledge of the other, reported that the sensations of the magnetic response were quite similar to those experienced either before or during an abduction event!** [My emphasis.]*

I do agree with Reiter here; such amazing admissions link magnetic fields and abduction experiences phenomenologically. That is to say, it is the experiences of the 'abductees' themselves that have made this direct link, as opposed to any indirect deductions.

Also, quite independently from Reiter, I have been given a revealing testimony from an experiencer, although not directly. However, it is its very old, independent and unrelated nature which provides it with its power. In the autumn of 1994, a few months after *Allergies and Aliens* was published, well-known author, investigator and scientist Jacques Vallée wrote to me from San Francisco, USA, and congratulated me on the then new EM-pollution approach. Shortly after this he sent me copies of some pages from a book published in 1957 on old Adamski-style contactees: *Flying Saucer Pilgrimage* by Bryant and Helen Reeve. They were about Orfeo Angelucci, a man living in Los Angeles in 1955, who claimed that he was in regular contact with 'space visitors'. Vallée had ringed certain passages on Angelucci's health problems:

His big problem has always been his precarious health and his extremely nervous sensibilities, which have caused him endless suffering and pain both preceding and during any thunderstorm or electric storm. Whenever an electric storm approaches he goes through a regular series of distressing 'symptoms' starting with a prickling sensation in his hands, arms, back and feet. It was this physical problem that led the family to move to California where storms are less frequent. We mention this because these physical symptoms were later to become, for Angelucci, an almost infallible warning of the approach of a space-craft or a prelude to a space-contact. [Reeve & Reeve, 1957, pp. 222–223.]

And:

He had moved to California and was working in the Lockheed Aircraft Corporation plant at Burbank ... On May 23, 1952, late at night he felt the strange physical symptoms which usually preceded an electrical storm. He went outside to find an unusually clear and beautiful night. It puzzled him that there was no storm to account for the distressing symptoms ... he caught sight of an oval-shaped object travelling ahead of him in the air... two fireballs descended and hovered in the air ... They were fluorescent green in colour and about three feet in diameter. [Reeve & Reeve, 1957.]

Vallée's written comments said:

This seems to confirm the pattern you have discovered. [Private correspondence.]

Probably the most interesting aspect of this correlation is that it innocently confirms the authenticity of Angelucci's testimony, and it is quite evident that this man did in fact have such experiences, albeit interpreted through the extraterrestial hypothesis (ETH) mythology.

Field studies

Returning to Reiter's investigations, he relates:

The choice seemed completely natural to begin the search for physical abduction event evidence with a device which would register or record the presence of a magnetic field. To my knowledge, no other abduction researcher has ever attempted the distribution of magnetic field detectors to experiencers for in-home use. [Reiter, 1994.]

Here was an investigator devising a simple but definitive method for gaining evidence that magnetic fields trigger visitation experiences, which, unbeknown to him, was one of the major premises of the EM-pollution approach I would develop 2 years hence, many thousand kilometres away from Gibsonburg, Ohio, USA, in Brentford, Middlesex, UK. As if this were not enough, Reiter also made the same connection with phenomena studied by psychical investigators at 'haunted' locations:

There also exists a very limited body of literature from psychic investigators and 'ghost hunters' which reports that magnetic and electromagnetic disturbances have been looked for and confirmed in haunted houses or buildings. [Reiter, 1994.]

Reiter's intent was to find the answers to three basic questions:

1. Are abduction experiences, and other anomalous activities accompanied by measurable magnetic disturbances?

2. Is it possible to show statistically that experiencers of anomalous activities are prone to magnetic disturbances to some extent beyond that observed by non-experiencers?

3. Would the presence of even a small mechanical detection device alter the 'routine' of abduction-type intrusions into some people's lives?

This last question does reveal some differences in our outlook at this stage, however, as the EM-pollution approach implies that no external alien-abduction event takes place, although the presence of UAPs/electric fireballs does involve an external EM phenomenon.

Considering Reiter's unique strategies, he relates:

> *Objectives defined, I next settled on an operating strategy. A quantity of no less than ten discrete magnetic field indicators would be built by myself and distributed to volunteers ... these I dubbed Magnetic Event Markers or MEMs and they would be set up by the experiencers themselves, and also non-experiencers as controls. In almost all cases, even those of non-experiencers, this location was the bedroom of the volunteer. [Reiter, 1994.]*

A MEM is given in the picture section and, to summarize Reiter's description, it is a purely mechanical indicator in which a magnetic pointer is suspended between two fixed bars that have been coated with adhesive rubber on their inner surfaces. If the pointer is deflected from magnetic north by a field it will stick to this inner surface. It can easily be reset by the user, and it should be sensitive to magnetic disturbances at or slightly below the ambient geomagnetic field strength, typically 0.5 gauss in most of North America. However, at the same time, the MEM should be insensitive to microgauss and low milligauss variations so that overhead planes or passing trucks will not trigger it. Quantitively speaking, the MEM only provides an indication of a magnetic event. Magnitude and direction of the activating field will not be discernible, except to confirm that the said field is stronger than the minimum needed to cause a deflection.

Reiter then sent MEMs to many non-experiencers and experiencers across the USA and key extracts from them will provide us with an intriguing finale, remembering that Reiter colour-coded his experiencers for confidentiality and convenience, and activation of the MEM is referred to as a 'stick', because the magnetic pointer deflects and actually sticks to the adhesive on the inner surface of the bar magnets:

...I received a telephone call from Mr Green. He informed me that during the night something unusual had occurred in his house, and in the morning he had discovered a 'stick' on the MEM. That evening I paid Mr Green a visit. Green told me that he had vague memories of being up and moving about the house in the small hours of the morning. Furthermore, he described a disturbing recollection of 'something' having sex with him. Starting the day after, Mr Green's penis became red and inflamed and remained in that state for several days. When we spoke by phone, Green had mentioned that he had been unable to reset his MEM after the nocturnal 'stick' ...

Soreness, swelling and irritation of the male genitals is a condition that I have encountered in a significant minority of my own cases. It is due to diathermy, a heating effect of RF-field exposure, and J. F. Corum *et al.*, in their work 'ANSI standards for microwave radiation' relate:

*... the microwave hazard to humans is either the excess rise in total body temperature or the selective heating of sensitive parts of the body. (An increase in body temperature of 1 degree centigrade is considered excessive.) The central issue is 'reversible' versus 'irreversible' effects resulting from the electromagnetic interaction. Localized heating of the body is most dangerous where there is little opportunity for heat exchange with surrounding tissue, such as the brain, **the genitals**, the lens of the eye, the liver, the gall bladder and the gastronomical tract. [Corum, Green & Pinzone, 1996. My emphasis]*

Corum *et al.* include specific calculations for diathermic heating effects on the human body, and readers interested in the more technical aspects are advised to obtain a copy of this work. It should be noticed here how the induced body (ie. genitalia) currents and heating of the penis were translated into 'something having sex' with Mr Green. One can only consider the feasibility of such an event taking place without his consent to realize its internal and hallucinatory nature, the stimulation of the septal area of the brain being instrumental in this. The sense of 'being up and moving about the house' is an equally typical description of automatic behaviour. Reiter continues with his description of the events surrounding Mr Green:

I personally verified that the MEM could not be reset. To me it appeared that the dresser, or even the plastic of the MEM base was charged electrostatically, however no measurements were available to confirm this. [Reiter, 1994.]

He continues:

Miss Pink kept a log of MEM sticks and unusual events ... A total of ten sticks were recorded, all of them apparently nocturnal ... In her words ...

> *visual flashbacks of taller beings ... awoke to find a stick; slight nose-bleed ... stick; strong emotional event; definitely not a dream ... stick; lost 25 minutes on watch ... Mrs Brown's experiences seem to fall into several categories: Abduction events; Out-of-body experiences; Noted presence of invisible entities; Unusual electrical activity around the house e.g. lights blowing out, garage door-opener activating spontaneously ... etc. [Reiter, 1994.]*

Mrs Brown's rich catalogue of phenomena to accompany sticks on the MEM are recorded in tabular form in Reiter's records. I could continue describing his results, but the details given so far are enough to give the reader an idea of the positive correlations obtained, and the success of his investigations using MEMs. To conclude this section on Reiter's pioneering work, however, consider the definitive statement made by him after these results:

> *The MEM project has served its purpose. We have acquired evidence which suggests that abduction events and related anomalies possess a physical reality in the form of detectable, measurable magnetic field disturbances ... I remain personally available as a consultant and source of assistance to the serious investigator, who seeks to do work along these lines. Moving with a quiet, determined pace, using simple instruments and cleverness, we will uncover the secrets of this greatest of enigmas. [Reiter, 1994].*

Until I discovered Reiter and his work via the editor of the *Bulletin of Anomalous Experience*, Dr David Gotlib, I had assumed that expensive field-monitoring equipment would be needed to show others the reality of what I already knew, i.e. that EM fields trigger the experiences. Reiter has enlightened me in this respect. However, at the time of writing, Nicholas Reiter has applied to the Fund for UFO Research in order to repeat his investigative experiment with sophisticated field-logging electronics. To date, after some considerable time, no funding has been forthcoming and my own communications with the fund organizers make me wonder if the ETH is the primary motivational force behind serious investigation in the USA.

Human consciousness effects: electroclinical syndromes

WHY ALIENS AND WHY ABDUCTION?

Food allergies are less strongly associated with electromagnetic hypersensitivity (EH) than chemical sensitivities. That is to say, sensitivities to such substances as domestic gas, cigarette smoke, perfume, aftershave lotion, aerosols, petrol and other volatile chemical compounds are typically in close association with EH. In fact, oddly enough, it would seem that, to some extent, EH can be induced by massive or prolonged exposures to chemicals; indeed, one of the first diagnostic enquiries at the Breakspear Hospital is to ask whether the patient has ever been sprayed by pesticide (closely followed by protective enclosure in a Faraday cage which screens out all external fields).

One reason for this trend relates to the control that we have over what enters our bodily system. If a certain food or drink makes us feel unpleasant, we avoid it. Also, many people are aware of what constitutes an unhealthy diet and are moderate in their intake. However, avoiding exposure to cigarette smoke, car fumes or even perfume is less within our control as such substances are ubiquitously abroad in the environments of urban life. However, we can be aware of such chemicals and modify our exposure time. The same cannot be said for electromagnetic (EM) fields. Even in hot spots we are unable consciously to detect prolonged exposures, which, nevertheless, as we will see further, have a detrimental effect on our system. Even when early symptoms occur, such as tingling, headaches and fatigue, we are unaware of their cause, and places of work, for example, just gain the reputation for suffering from 'sick building syndrome' or subsequently, at a later stage of exposure, homes become 'haunted'.

However, although the conscious mind may be unaware of exposure to EM fields, the body is not, and the effects of the fields register within it. For example, one of the dangers to cells and tissues is the formation of free radicals due to EM-field exposure. Basically, free radicals can be regarded as half a chemical searching for the other half in order to become stable. On molecular levels, this can involve them taking *electrochemical bites* out of living tissue in order to access its oxygen content and this, over time, can induce a measure of degeneration. The bonds between an electron pair are broken by irradiation and, when a single electron is released, damaging free radicals are produced. Also, allergies induce the formation of immunoglobin or histamine, which cause all manner of physiological disruptions to the body's systems. If such reactions were induced by food or chemicals, we would be more aware of the connection between the allergen and the reaction and take steps to avoid or exclude the offending substance.

All manner of cumulative disturbances can be induced by fields but, as we are unaware of them or their cause, we do nothing about them and, in fact, are unable to prevent their intrusions into our body. But such fields do register with the body, and our immune system especially is alerted as prolonged field exposure alters immunocompetence. Therefore, the body will eventually be aware of unwanted and uncontrollable intrusions. This absence of control is due to our conscious minds, i.e. our selves, being unaware of these intrusions, but the body will register 'intruders without consent'.

The body can tell the difference between self and non-self fields. The subtle organic fields which flow around our body from the brain to the organs, and the impulses which flow from our sense organs to the brain for example, are very different from the fierce electrifications of pulsed microwaves from a TV-station transmitter. The body will alert its immune system to bacterial intruders, which register as 'foreign', or 'alien'; similarly, organs transplanted from one body into another must have a high degree of compatibility to be accepted. Such compatibility/incompatibility assessments take place at molecular levels in the cells, which use EM frequencies as intercellular communications. Surely then, when external fields whose frequencies have been 'contaminated' via the 'relay mechanism', so that they are identified as allergic, irradiate the body, they will also register as harmful and 'not of this body'.

THE BODY'S FIELDS: ELECTROCHEMISTRY

There is an obvious and well-established reason why the body should apprehend in-coming fields from the environment as entirely alien and at odds with its own fields. This is to do with the fact that the nerves do not act as 'wires' conducting electricity, but are living membranes in and around which chemical reactions take place; the 'current' is really a 'chemical message' which is passed along the 'circuitry' of the nervous system. Dr W. S. Eidelman describes the differences between simple electrical conduction and the electrochemistry in the body, using a historical perspective:

... in the 1840s, Emil Dubois-Reymond demonstrated a measurable electrical impulse traveling down a nerve. He, like Galvani, believed he had found the life-current. So it was Dubois-Reymond's turn to make the claim that electricity ran through the nervous system, like currents running through wires ... It was soon shown that the impulse he had found could not possibly be a true electric current, for two reasons. First, the impulse traveled much too slowly for electricity, and second, nerves did not have the proper insulation or resistance to conduct a current. They just did not measure up as wires!

But if ... this ... was not an electric current, what was it? Julius Bernstein ... solved the mystery in 1868. This is what he found:

All cell membranes have an electrical polarization. Sodium ions, with a positive charge (atoms missing one electron), sit on the outside of the membrane. Chloride ions, with a negative charge (atoms having an extra electron) sit on the inside of the membrane. When the nerve is stimulated, at the top of the nerve, the ions switch places across the membrane, changing the electrical polarization for a moment. Then they return to their normal places. This change of electrical potential moves down the nerve as if it was a true current, and Bernstein called it 'action potential'. The conclusions of the scientists were that this action potential was not true electricity. It was accepted as 'electro-chemistry', with the accent on chemistry, water chemistry ... [Eidelman, 1995]

These historical highlights show us how totally alien the intrusions of electronically produced fields and fields from power lines are to the nervous system, with its organic electrochemical mechanisms. Galvani found that he could stimulate the muscles of a frog's leg by applying a current to the correct nerve, but, in effect, he was triggering the required chemical reactions along the nerves. Normally, the body acts as a natural semi-conductor; however, when we are considering EH-status individuals, whose bodies have been physically changed by a major electrical event (MEE) so that they exhibit a greatly enhanced body conductivity, such invasive environmental fields have more of a 'free run'. They register in the body acutely and, eventually, after adverse health effects have become established as sensitivities, they will be expressed in terms of imagery. However, the situation is worse than this, because certain field frequencies may duplicate allergic reactions. There is no doubt in my mind, despite Dr Gotlib's objections, that 'allergenic tags' do rub off on to specific frequencies which the body then identifies as allergens. Therefore, not only are the fields entering the body as 'intruders without consent', and being identified as 'not of this body', they also carry an allergenic tag that the body would, if it were able, reject as a harmful 'alien' energy. As the conscious mind is unaware of these harmful intrusions, although individuals do, of course, know that they are feeling unwell, the body will recruit the unconscious mind to communicate them to the conscious. One form of these communications is the alien-abduction experience.

That is to say, the unconscious selects, from its image-bank, imagery that the conscious mind, i.e. the individual, would regard as depictions of aliens. The image banks of everyone are stuffed with all manner of imagery from science-fiction films and TV programmes, which it collects subliminally. However, as with the raw material that makes up our dreams, such images are highly personalized and are not just plucked out of *Star Wars* or *Star Trek* unaltered but are mixed and matched with personal attitudes and feelings. For example, there may be creatures that we feel are 'alien' on a subliminal level because of past associations that have been forgotten. I have two cases in my files where the experiencer saw spacemen with animal heads. One involved three astronauts, standing in front of a landed flying saucer in the grounds of Reading University; these were quite human apart from their scaly lizard heads, complete with glistening reptilian eyes. The other, a bedroom visitation, also involved three entities, who wore robes and had wolves heads from whose eyes shone laser-like beams of light. Unaltered Daleks or Klingons straight from science-fiction productions do not usually appear.

The point I am making is that, although the body apprehends these external and artificial fields as alien to its system, the unconscious, in its symbolic communications to the conscious mind, will select imagery of aliens from its image banks, and will present it to the conscious mind as personalized alien forms. Just as there are recurring types of dream, e.g. flying dreams, wish-fulfilment dreams, nudity in public, pursuit but paralysed, etc., we get consistent types of aliens across populations of experiencers. (This aspect of consistency of 'aliens' is covered at length in *UFOs – Psychic Close Encounters* [Budden, 1995a].)

In a very real sense, the fields *are* the alien intruders, and the language reflects this, i.e. foreign objects in the body are unwanted intrusions, and foreigners are also known as aliens. This reflection in the language is not trivial, as the language and communications of the unconscious, as they are expressed in dreams, have an oddly literal quality about them. I am reminded of how a computer was programmed to translate English into Russian. British proverbs were tested and the saying 'Out of sight, out of mind' came out as 'Blind and insane'. With a similarly literal translation, in the language of the unconscious, the fields are apprehended as alien intruders in the body and, further, alien imagery also represents field frequencies that have acquired an 'allergenic tag'.

THE EXTRATERRESTRIAL THEME EQUATION

There is also another factor that would contribute to the body's identification of electronically produced fields as alien or, to be more precise, extraterrestrial (ET). Our body and consciousness have developed within a powerful field that originates from, and is closely identified with, the Earth. This field is called *gravity*. This is a force that is essential for our biological functioning, as tests of astronauts in zero-gravity conditions have shown.

However, if the body is irradiated for an extremely prolonged period with an artificially produced field, e.g. from a microwave transmitter, it will be registered by the body as being 'not of the Earth', and the literal translation of this would surely be 'extraterrestrial', and appropriate imagery from the mind's stock will be recruited to express this. I believe that it is this sort of super-literal interpretation, which is entirely consistent with the selection of dream imagery, that contributes to the depiction of ETs in the abduction vision.

The alien form

It is suggested that the electronically produced fields from transmitters in the environment can carry allergic reactions to the body, which responds by producing hallucinatory experiences involving imagery of aliens. However, it will be noticed that the mechanism involved is epileptiform in nature, i.e. electrical activity is set up in the brain, although at times pinoline or other beta-carbolines from the pineal, which is magnetosensitive, may be involved.

In my previous book (Budden, 1995a), I suggested that, because parts of the brain are repeatedly stimulated, the *gray* as a consistent type of entity is hallucinated, and that this is another reason why a consistent type of entity is reported. That is to say, as the body image is encoded in the physical structure of the brain, e.g. the somatotropic organization of the cortex (see diagram overleaf), it follows that repeated EM stimulation of the same areas simultaneously will induce a humanoid figure as hallucination. It seems that, if the right combination of brain areas and type of stimulation (i.e. voltage, magnetic or electrical field, etc.) could be found experimentally, such formed figures as the gray, which reflect the structure of the central nervous system (CNS) when it is abnormally stimulated by irradiation, could be induced. Are there any other indications that support this idea that grays as a specific formed-figure hallucination are such an 'epileptiform constant'?

Whitley Strieber is a well-known experiencer, whose encounters with grays have been extensively documented in his books. In his efforts to understand what was happening to him, he underwent a number of very thorough neurological tests. These are equally well documented in a book on temporal-lobe epilepsy (TLE) called *Seized* by Eve LaPlante (LaPlante, 1993). Consider a selected extract which tells of these tests after an abduction experience:

> *Several months later he had an EEG [electroencephalogram] with 'nasopharyngeal' electrodes, placed at the back of the nose, which are 'not very effective at detecting EEG abnormalities' according to Howard Blume, a neurosurgeon. This single test showed no abnormalities. During the recording, Strieber experienced no symptoms, which further reduced the possibility of finding signs of a disorder. An EEG with ordinary electrodes that Strieber had a year later was also normal, as was a CAT scan. However, an MRI (magnetic resonance imaging) brain scan*

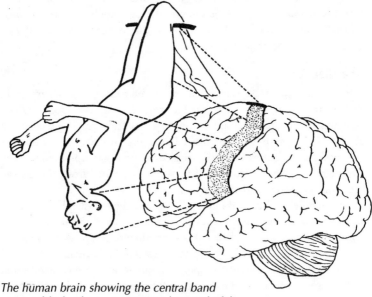

The human brain showing the central band responsible for the movement and control of the various body areas, which are physically encoded, or 'hard-wired', at the various sites of the brain indicated.

In this diagram, these sites are shown projected on to the whole body, indicating which brain areas correspond to which body areas. Rapid and successive ripples of electromagnetic stimulation across the somatotropic band would certainly suggest why images of humanoids occur so frequently in samples of formed-figure hallucinations. The humanoid is too much like us, and really is not alien enough to be extraterrestrial. Close encounters with such 'ETs' say more about the witness than about the nature of life on other planets.

(Courtesy of McGraw-Hill, *Basic Neurology* by John Gilroy: Pergamon Press, 1990)

> *showed 'occasional punctate foci of high signal intensity' in his left temporoparietal region, suggesting scarring that could lead to temporal lobe epilepsy ... his alien creatures would be true in the medical sense if indeed they resulted in seizures:* **they would be the psychic representations of abnormal electrical activity in his brain**. *[LaPlante, 1993, pp. 107–108. My emphasis.]*

It was startling to find such independent support for the gray as an epileptiform constant and, although Strieber still insists that his aliens are tangible, he has conceded that the effects I have identified are also real. In response to an article I wrote for the *MUFON Journal*, (Budden, 1995b) he stated:

> *I think that all the phenomena that Budden describes are real, and that some kind of electrosensitivity must facilitate an encounter or even generate it, but I also think that the visitors are real, and can certainly act independently of those of us who face them. [Strieber, 1995.]*

However, it must be remembered that this was in a periodical for UFO buffs and, in *Seized*, he is quoted as saying something different:

> *It's a terribly important and fundamentally human experience – perceptions that come from the level of the mind that isn't interrupted by the rational structures that animate most of our thought. It's a kind of memory, a form of perception, or mechanism of consciousness, something inexplicable that the mind attaches an explanation to, probably the same thing that caused people to believe in the old gods and myths ... It probably starts in the human mind. [LaPlante, 1993, p. 109.]*

The reader can decide how close Strieber comes to the approach explored in these pages. However, psychologists researching human hallucinations have, in fact, found that consistent images occur as constants, including those that they describe as the human form in caricature. This is covered in more detail in the Appendix.

WHY ABDUCTION?

When posing this question, we are asking why does this visionary dramatization occur so consistently across populations of experiencers? Why does this specific theme occur, as opposed to any other? Clearly, it is a variation on visitation where, instead of visitors coming into our environment, we are taken to theirs (remembering, of course, that we are dealing with the themes of a visionary reality). Something must be triggered physiologically or, more probably, neurologically in the whole body that is quite distinct and radically different from straight visual hallucination but nevertheless is superimposed on it. After all, it is the body that is depicted as being removed. It would seem inescapable, therefore, to conclude that abduction relates to the destabilization of body image, whereby the body is depicted as being taken away to another realm, as a type of dramatized out-of-body experience (OBE), and it is no coincidence that this perceptual phenomenon is reported as occurring at the onset of abductions. Consider the following examples:

> *She awoke and sat up one night to feel that there was someone else in the room [sense of presence due to temporal-lobe stimulation]. The next moment, a luminous formed figure emerged from the middle of the bed and remained as if half embedded up to the waist. It extended an unusually long arm and she felt its touch on her wrist as it jerked her whole body out of the bed and both floated towards the window. Outside, feeling that she was floating in the air she got an impression of the gardens below her. Her next memory was being immobile on a table with two 'grays' looming over her. [Budden, 1994.]*

And:

> *I unaccountably awoke in the middle of the night, walked out alone and watched calmly as a UFO approached and drew me aboard on a light beam. The creatures stripped me and subjected me to various unpleasant, invasive procedures, including opening my head and tampering with various things there. [Ring, 1992.]*

From these and many other examples, it is evident that the overriding sensation is one of being floated upwards at the onset of the experience. Investigator Budd Hopkins once related to me an account of an abduction experience in which the woman involved was kneeling on a sofa during a party and felt her body image being drawn up through a closed window. Hopkins commented and wondered why it was that sometimes the 'visitors' took the real body and at other times 'the inner body'. In the second example above, there could hardly be a better layman's translation of epileptiform activity (i.e. erratic electrical activity in the brain) than 'opening my head and tampering with various things there', unless we consider the identification of cranial electricity in one of Hopkins's cases. The following extract describes an experiencer's hypnotically obtained recollections:

> *Dan suddenly jumps and begins to shiver. Tears come to his eyes and he is obviously very frightened. I ask what happened, what he felt. He answers very softly, and I have to ask him twice before I can make out the single word of his answer: 'Electricity … electricity.' I ask if he feels it through his whole body – 'Just the head …' [Hopkins, 1987.]*

Significantly, a study by the National Radiological Protection Board in the UK tells us:

> *When a biological system is exposed to radiofrequency or microwave radiation, electric and magnetic fields are induced within it. These internally induced fields give rise to ionic currents and molecular excitations within the tissue which result in heating ... A heterogenous object such as the head can also undergo layer resonance – a focusing effect which causes an enhanced power transmission through surface layers (i.e. the skull).* **Hence, there is a concern with power deposition in the head,** *particularly in the eyes and the brain at radiofrequencies and microwave frequencies. [Dimbylow, 1990. My emphasis.]*

This is an example of where official concerns for radio-frequency (RF) field exposure match the sensations reported by an experiencer. Some abduction experiences begin with a bright light and sudden changes of scene reminiscent of dreams. In fact, experiencers seem to have difficulty in telling the difference between a dream and an abduction experience, and there is evidently a graduation from the former to the latter, a continuum of reality simulation, where some experiences are easily identified as dreams, but others less so. This is, of course, consistent with the nature of these experiences which are produced in the brain, and it would also be consistent to regard the intensity of the subjective reality of them as dependent on the intensity of the fields induced in it at any one time. That is to say, these visions are more vivid, 'real' and undream-like if they are driven by the intrusion of external fields, such as pulsed microwaves, through the cranium, as opposed to the natural organic electricity of the brain. It is evident, however, that dreams of abductions lead on to experiences where the abduction event is felt to be very real and undream-like. This is because the condition in which the electrical activity of the brain is destabilized is a progressive one, i.e. it increases over time. Continued exposure to fields from the environment entrains areas of brain cells to activate, or 'fire'. This firing produces hallucinations and is called *kindling*; the experimental work by well-known neurologist G. V. Goddard confirms this.

Goddard's experiments have shown that epileptiform or erratic electrical activity in the brain does occur as a permanent condition when the brain is subjected to very low current intensities, at levels which are certainly exceeded by those found during field surveys of experiencers' homes. He and other neurologists found that daily low-level electrical stimulation produces a permanent destabilization of the brain's normal electrical activity, and this has been borne out by both the findings of investigators into the paranormal and the sufferers of such induced epilepsy who have initiated litigation against power companies in the

British courts in the early 1990s. The conclusions of such neurologists tell us unequivocally that:

> *Kindling is the phenomenon whereby repeated low-level electrical stimulation of discrete brain regions (e.g. amygdala or hippocampus) results in progressive behavioural and electrographic seizures **and a permanent epileptiform state**. [Goddard, 1967. My emphasis. See also Goddard et al., 1969.]*

These findings by Goddard are extremely significant for the EM-pollution approach, as they have shown experimentally what has been predicted as being an outcome of hot-spot exposure. Therefore, extending these experimental results, the work of Professor Michael Persinger? shows that a form of OBE or disembodiment can occur during the magnetic stimulation of the temporal lobes of the brain and, according to Goddard *et al.*, once this tendency has been established by daily irradiation, *it remains*. In fact, Persinger speaks of 'temporal lobe lability' as a varying tendency in the population, and such sensitivity does seem to play a significant part in the induction of OBEs. As 'abductions' (otherwise known as CE4s or Close Encounters of the Fourth Kind) are a form of OBE, then the stimulation of the temporal lobes is also involved in the induction of this destabilization of the body image. However, it would also seem that such a profound sensation of bodily removal involves other more radical disturbances to the body by fields.

Electromagnetic disturbance of proprioceptors

One option is that the proprioceptors distributed throughout the body, which are responsible for monitoring posture and orientation, become paralysed as a result of overstimulation of the neurones by induced body currents. Information reaches the brain from these receptors which are present in all the muscles and usually send volleys of impulses to the brain whenever there is movement to update the total body image. If these impulses are disturbed by EM fields, body-image information falls below a certain threshold. If this absence of neural information about the orientation of the body in space is replaced with EM-induced vestibular sensations from the temporal lobes, i.e. floating feelings, an OBE is produced. Such vestibular sensations have been induced under controlled conditions by subjecting the temporal lobes to extremely low frequency (ELF) magnetic fields (see p. 113).

> *Stimulation of the temporal lobe, and specifically of two structures within the limbic system, the hippocampus and amygdala, is known to generate intense hallucinatory activity that may nevertheless seem distinctly real to the individual in the manner of the waking dream. Among the*

impressions that can be produced in this way are the sense of presence, apparitions, floating and spinning sensations, out-of-body experiences, hearing inner voices, powerful convictions of deep meaningfulness, and afterward, amnesia or a sense of time loss. [Ring, 1992.]

Parietal-lobe seizures

Overstimulation of other brain areas can also induce comparable OBE effects, which is even more relevant to the induction of these perceptions as it relates to the effects of EM trauma to the brain. If focal seizures (points in the brain where heightened electrical discharge takes place) are induced by electrification, repeated disturbances to the body image can occur. For example, neurological studies tell us that the parietal lobe stores information responsible for body image and, when damaged through lesion, disordered corporeal awareness and disorganized visual spatial conceptions are induced. Such defects are said to be *gnosic* (Simpson & Fitch, 1988). This is another reason for the consistency of experiences, i.e. stimulation of the same brain areas induces the same effects across populations of experiencers, because they all possess the same brain structures/functions.

Perhaps now we can begin to appreciate the elements which combine to induce the alien-abduction experience as a consistent set of perceptual events. The EH body apprehends the incoming fields as intrusive and alien to its system, especially if they are 'tagged' with an allergic response relayed from allergenic foods and/or chemicals; the resulting visions are driven by these fields producing sensations both by direct stimulation of the body via induced body currents and through triggering focal seizures in the brain itself. This mixing and matching induces visual hallucination and persisting allergic responses in the skin, etc. as post-encounter effects, e.g. electrical burns through microwave exposures.

Out-of-body experiences during surgery

It should not escape us that OBEs frequently occur during surgical operations on the body, and abduction experiences also involve exactly that, i.e. apparent operations on the body. That is to say, there is a *thematic matching*, in which two parallel elements are involved. One is a real physical operation on the body and the other is a hallucinatory match in which the percipient is also laid out on an operating table and altered, albeit by aliens. Both involve a disturbance to the body image: the real operation through a physiological reaction to the anesthetic (to which the patient is allergic) and the 'abduction operation' through the anesthetizing effects of EM fields. It should not be surprising, therefore, that the OBE and a hallucination of bodily interference after the body is 'taken over' occur side by side, as it were, in the same experience – an alien abduction, where one develops out of the other. Incidently, it should also not escape us that, in both epileptiform activity and an alien-abduction experience, the body is 'seized', which is not just a quirk of language.

Out-of-body experiences and anesthetics

If we consider the very consistent accounts of patients who, during a surgical operation, experience the phenomenon of seeming to hover above the operating table near the ceiling, looking down and being able to describe the conversation and actions of the surgeons and medical staff, we are again considering a disturbance to the body image. After the event patients come to the conclusion that their consciousness has left the physical body. However, what is really happening here is that the patient has become partially conscious during the operation and is paralysed but still able to hear and sometimes feel what is happening and going on around him/her in the theatre (e.g. the surgeons' conversations, the general hurried activity, the comments made by the nursing staff, the new oxygen cylinder being brought forward). Meanwhile, the patient is having a vivid hallucination that incorporates the paralysed body image, which is seemingly floating above. In fact, such a visualization of the room, i.e. a plan-view from above, is the simplest mode of picturing it which the brain can cope with.

This hallucination provides the patient with an image of what their body and general layout of the operating table, etc. looks like, but it is not a direct observation; it is really a reconstruction based on what they *think* it looks like, i.e. it is based on memory. The actual activity by the surgeons and staff, etc. is genuinely heard and felt but incorporated and constantly fed into this vivid visual reconstruction, as the patient hears/feels it happening. That is to say, the auditory and tactile cues are translated into visual imagery within the OBE, which is a visualization of the operating theatre layout. It is in this way that the patient gains some genuine knowledge of what goes on during the operation, just like someone who was eavesdropping with their eyes shut, and only *appears* to have seen it directly.

One patient heard a doctor ask for the plastic hat to be removed from her head, and felt a paramedic take it; this real event appeared to the patient in her OBE visualization. The paramedic in question was astounded when, after the operation, the patient was able to tell him about his actions. However, her knowledge came about because she heard the surgeon ask the paramedic to remove the surgical hat during the operation, which he did, and which she also felt.

This selective-consciousness explanation is provided to demonstrate the extent to which conditions and stimuli external to the body can be incorporated into the body-centred hallucination, otherwise known as an OBE or alien-abduction experience. Fields do not, of course, enter the consciousness via the sense organs, as ordinary stimuli do, but directly via the brain and body, which makes for an even more effective way of cueing the hallucinatory experience in progress at the time of the irradiation.

Professor Michael Persinger, head of neuroscience at Laurentian University, Ontario, Canada, is well known for his work on the controlled induction of hallucinatory experiences by irradiating the temporal lobes with ELF milligauss magnetic fields. This process is carried out in a chamber where the subject wears a modified crash-helmet, fitted with solenoids to stimulate the pulsed firing of the temporal lobes. In case readers doubt the vividness of the sensation of being grabbed by aliens, which is induced by magnetic fields, consider the following description by a subject undergoing the irradiation:

> I was wide awake through. Nothing seemed to happen for the first ten minutes or so ... Then suddenly my doubts vanished. 'I'm swaying. It's like being on a hammock.' Then it felt for all the world as though two hands had grabbed my shoulders and were bodily yanking me upright. I knew I was still lying in the reclining chair, but someone or something was pulling me up. Something seemed to get hold of my leg and pull it, distort it, and drag it up the wall. I felt as though I had been stretched half way up to the ceiling. Then came the emotions. Totally out of the blue, but intensely and vividly, I suddenly felt angry – not just mildly cross but that clear-minded anger out of which you act – but there was no-one and nothing to act on. After about ten seconds, it was gone. Later it was replaced by an equally sudden attack of fear. I was terrified of nothing in particular ... I felt weak and disorientated for a couple of hours after coming out of the chamber. [Blackmore, 1994.]

This was a set of controlled and directed magnetic-field pulses, which were aimed at specific brain sites. It is not difficult to imagine how experiences that feel identical to 'reality' could be induced by irradiating other brain areas, such as the visual cortex or the language areas (Broca's and Werninke's areas).

In fact, the subject's description of irradiation in Persinger's chamber given above was by Dr Susan Blackmore at Bristol University, UK. She states:

> Persinger applied a silent and invisible force to my brain and created a specific experience for me. He claimed that he was imitating the basic sequences of the processes of memory and perception and that he could control my experience. Could he have done it from a distance? Could it be done on a wider scale? [Blackmore, 1994.]

However, what if the irradiation took place without our knowledge? Without knowing that such irradiation is occurring, what baseline of reference could we use to remind ourselves that such lifelike visual and auditory experiences were in fact hallucinations? Also, what if, also unbeknown to us, our brain and body had been specifically altered to be especially sensitive to the stimulus inducing these experiences by an encounter with a lightning strike when we were young? The point I am making is that experiencers are at the mercy of their condition when, after moving house into a hot-spot location, they mysteriously find that they become ill and are suddenly invaded by aliens. They certainly have the overwhelming feeling that 'It is happening to me' as opposed to 'I am doing it'.

ELECTROMAGNETICALLY INDUCED CONSCIOUSNESS EFFECTS

Minute electrical currents from the sense organs enter the brain and are processed into something which we recognize as reality. Light from the eyes is translated into electrical impulses. Sound in the hearing mechanism is also turned into a change in potential difference along nerve fibres. And so on for the other three senses. If the bundles of nerve fibres from these sense organs are stimulated artificially to replace the usual neural traffic of impulses, anomalous sensations will register in the brain. Alternatively, the skull is entirely transparent to magnetic fields, and such fields do in fact induce electric currents directly into the brain.

Another study was reported in *New Scientist* and describes the work of Mark George and his colleagues at the National Institute of Mental Health near Washington, DC. George and his colleagues found that patients suffering from depression would over time, again respond to strong magnets placed at strategic points on the skull. The article relates:

> ... the researchers believe the magnetic pulses work by mimicking the effects of electroconvulsive therapy ... But there is one big difference. Unlike ECT, transcranial magnetic stimulation isn't designed to cause seizures and convulsions. The rapid pulses of magnetism it 'fires' into the head stimulate brain tissue in a more precise manner than ECT, producing electrical effects that revive activity in the outer folds of the brain, in an area of the cortex needed for the expression of a normal range of emotions.

And on the precise mechanism(s) involved:

> Think of magnetic pulses as a clean and efficient way of 'injecting' small amounts of electricity into the brain, says Rothwell. The laws of

electromagnetism dictate that whenever a conducting coil moves within a magnetic field, electricity must flow in the coil. In transcranial magnetic stimulation, it is the magnetic field that moves, or oscillates, and the coil, in the form of the brain cells, which stays put. But the result is the same: the production of electricity. [George et al., 1995.]

One may wonder with this reasoning, how brain cells could be regarded as conductive coils, but one could come to the rescue of this objection by quoting from studies which show that brain cells contain microscopic particles of magnetite (naturally occurring magnetic iron oxide). One objection to the identification of alien-contact/abduction experiences as electrically driven visions could be that they involve normal mundane reality, albeit intertwined with more exotic scenarios. Experiencers frequently relate, somewhat absurdly in some cases, how the aliens fit in with their domestic environment. For example:

I looked out of the window and saw an alien walking up the front garden path to the door. [June of Coventry, see p. 254]

Evidently, the electrical stimulation of the brain can in fact induce a perceptual reality that is quite 'normal' and mundane. Neurologists since the pioneering work of Wilder Penfield have experimented with direct stimulation of the brain with electrodes in fully conscious patients. Consider the following from *The Nervous System*, a textbook that has been reprinted on numerous occasions:

It is rather surprising that such crude investigation as the application of an electric current through an electrode should produce normal phenomena, normal movements, visual hallucinations, and the recall of scenes from the past. One might have expected that it would produce some sort of chaos or caricature of normal phenomena. But in fact it imitates normal functioning of the brain to a surprising degree. One notes too that all the phenomena caused by electrical stimulation in these patients also occur spontaneously as part of their epilepsy. [Nathan, 1988, pp. 223–224.]

I would also urge the reader to note that, with EH subjects, no contact with the brain is required to produce hallucinatory experimental effects, and a powerful EM field rippling through the rooms of their home is more than sufficient to trigger their experiences, especially during the long periods of immobility during sleep, because it is then that the body is irradiated for prolonged periods.

It will also be noted that the WHO report (WHO, 1993) mentions the production of induced body currents, not only currents in the brain, and this traffic of anomalously induced electrical impulses is evidently a two-way process. That is to say, we have considered nervous impulses from the brain to the body, but we must also examine the implications of direct EM stimulation and activity in the body. In terms of experiential effects during the alien-abduction experience, we must surely identify a recurring feature that typifies these events: the quasi-medical examination.

To appreciate the nature and experience of this *field-driven* vision, we must picture the experiencer prone in bed during the night at the onset of a period of irradiation which has caused them to exceed their load-phenomenon threshold. Remember that they would be in a hot-spot location. A typical RF hot spot is described in the WHO report:

> *RF hot spots may be produced by an intersection of narrow beams of RF energy ... by the reflection of fields from conducting surfaces (standing waves), or by induced currents flowing in conductive objects exposed to ambient RF fields (re-radiation). [WHO, 1993, p. 109.]*

These are microwaves (MW) and a further extract from the WHO report tells us that the whole body is never irradiated, but is erratically exposed:

> *RF hot spots are characterised by very rapid spatial variation of the fields and, typically, result in partial body exposures of individuals near the hot spots. Uniform exposure of the body is essentially impossible because of the high spatial gradient of the fields associated with RF hot spots. [WHO, 1993, p. 189.]*

The picture this conjures up in terms of bodily exposures or in the language of the report-specific absorption rates (SARs) is of a flickering field in which various parts of the body (and brain) are irradiated in rapid succession. However, it must be remembered that the body and brain are not fitted with convenient on/off switches and some areas, once triggered into activity, continue when the field drops. As an example of this, Persinger found that the temporal lobes of his test subjects could activate after his sessions of controlled irradiation had ended, and subjects would report spontaneous seizures days afterwards. However, the field-stimulated body can provide cues which produce imagery. Just as external stimuli, such as sounds, can intrude into dreams and are incorporated into the dream content, field-stimulated tingling, numbness, changes in temperature, paralysis, floating and other bodily sensations are the raw experiential material for the abduction narrative. As fields intrude into the body in this dynamic way, it is entirely appropriate that a similar experiential scenario occurs: the medical examination. After all, it is the body which is being interfered with by such energies.

ANOMALOUS RESONANCE

However, it must be stated that the precise trigger for alien-abduction experiences *per se*, as opposed to any other depiction of formed figures, is unclear. A variant on the OBE is involved, but some abduction experiences have such deeply meaningful outcomes for the experiencer, that it is clear that a more radical shift occurs in the brain and body which transcends simple field exposure. After much thought and searching of the literature on bioelectromagnetics, I suspect that the trigger for these supremely significant and deeply spiritual abductions is bodily resonance. A prime example of an experience which had such fundamental psycho-spiritual effects for the percipient is contained in *The Andreasson Affair* (Fowler, 1980).

'Resonance' is a term that has become a misused buzz-word among those who seem to appreciate the involvement of electromagnetics in anomalies generally, but in a somewhat vague and unfocussed way. However, there are genuine clinical aspects which do support the idea that, in certain circumstances of irradiation, the body can become 'tuned' to a fixed combination of field frequencies in its immediate environment. That is to say, a sort of harmonic resonance is set up throughout the irradiated body, which has profound consequences for the experiencer, who would most certainly be in an altered state during such periods of resonance. It has been stated that the hypersensitive body apprehends artificial fields as alien intrusions into its natural organic electrical activity and eventually depicts this unnatural invasion as alien imagery. Extending this, if the body is totally integrated into the fields irradiating it, by becoming 'tuned' and resonating to the frequencies around it, the body, in effect, acts as another electrical unit, emits coherent fields, and is involved or 'taken over' by fields on a more fundamental level. It is thought that it is precisely this physical resonance of the body that acts as a trigger for alien-abduction experiences.

Clinical practitioners Choy, Monro and Smith, in a paper for *Clinical Ecology*, discuss an experiment to determine which frequency range is involved when allergens begin to interact with the physiological system of a patient. They state:

> ... 100 GHz was suspected of being responsible for the patient-allergen interaction. This is exactly the part of the frequency spectrum in which Frölich predicted coherent electrical vibrations in the cell membranes of biological systems. It would appear that the allergen acts as a resonator, while the reacting allergic subject acts as the active device in electronic terms: coupling the two together would trigger the allergic reaction. This might be considered to be analagous to a control system becoming unstable

or oscillatory, remembering that allergy is also defined as – the failure of a regulatory system. [Choy et al., 1986, p. 96.]

From this, it can be discerned that microwave frequencies abroad in the environment are, in fact, in the same range as those implicated in certain allergic reactions, and that such reactivity is due to 'electrical vibrations in the cell membranes, setting up a critical resonance' so that the body of the allergic subject acts as if it were an electronic device. It may be that the alien–abduction experience sometimes involves a radically *altered state of body* in which its physical structure is integrated into the field frequencies that regularly irradiate it through resonance. This state would surely register with the individual biological system as the ultimate invasion by energies totally alien to its functioning. Could this be thought of as the bioelectromagnetic version of *The Invasion of the Body Snatchers?*

As outlined earlier, one of the effects that result from temporal-lobe stimulation is a hallucinatory epileptiform sensation called the 'sense of presence' in which the subject has the overwhelming feeling that someone or something is in the room with them *and that they are being watched intently.* A bodily examination is merely *a cued extension* of this overwhelming feeling of being examined by some alien other. Once this mindset is triggered, stimulated body areas become specific focal points on which imagery is based, otherwise known as the 'medical-examination' stage of the abduction experience.

THE VISIONARY AND LIGHTNING

People who have been struck by lightning have frequently been reported as developing psychic sensitivities, and there is no doubt that these are due to their EH status. However, it should be mentioned, as it is not generally realized, that encounters with high levels of electricity actually shape the lives of individuals. While they may recover completely from the shock itself, and forget about it, such surges of energy alter the electrical ambience of the body and brain, and, in later life, can determine such artistic activities as writing and painting, and sensitivity generally.

It can also permanently alter temperament, and individuals who have had an MEE may later experience intense feelings of meaningfulness and a visionary reverence for nature, especially the heavens at night, waking up with an intense urge to 'commune with nature', frequently with generalized sexual undertones. This is due to an increased lability of the temporal lobes, which are the most electrically unstable part of the brain and govern such 'mystical' sensations.

Also, I am sure that, in some cases, the echoes of an MEE in formative years are felt so strongly that affected children may feel they are 'changelings', so different are they from the parents and other family members, who may show a complete absence of artistic sensitivity and visionary awareness. They are, in fact, 'electrical changelings'. Indeed, one's whole personal history may be entirely re-interpreted in the light of a close encounter with high levels of electricity in early years.

When I was 13 years old, two other boys and myself climbed over a security fence into a train-shunting yard. We meandered about for a while and stopped when we came across a rusty rail. We argued about whether it still carried electricity or not and, to settle the matter, in my teenage wisdom, I stepped on it. My father had just mended my shoes by banging metal 'Blakeys' into the soles, and there was a blue flash and a bang and I was hurled a metre or so into the air, landing in a heap some distance away. The argument was settled, the rail was indeed live and, although I was shaken, I went home and said nothing to my parents. It was the sort of nightmarish scenario that all worrying parents imagine in their darkest hours; except it really happened to their son.

A few weeks after the incident, I began to take an extraordinarily sudden and intense interest in Japanese art and, to the bemusement of my parents, began painting ancient Oriental scenes throughout the night, or frequently awoke with intense feelings of meaningfulness about nature and the universe; these, I would have thought, were not typical preoccupations of a 13-year-old boy! This was soon followed by the writing of long passages of stream-of-consciousness prose poetry, with strongly surreal imagery. Today, I am a writer ...

HYPERGRAPHIA

Another parameter of the alien-contact/abduction experience is the incidence of a profuse writing activity. Of course, this may occur 'naturally', and this factor is not a primary parameter, unlike food allergies, chemical sensitivities or a history of psychic experiences. However, there is something strangely distinctive about the writing activities artificially induced in experiencers by MEEs and/or hot-spot exposure. Writing activity suddenly acquired through this odd epileptiform condition usually shows a preoccupation with a characteristic set of topics. The individual is said to have become *religiose* (Nathan, 1988), as opposed to religious, because their 'writing mania' typically covers such areas as the destiny of mankind, what religion really is, how crystals allow the chosen ones to tune into the creative force of the universe, and other themes of apparent cosmological significance.

This personalized creative theosophy may strongly preoccupy the experiencer; many hours a day may be spent actually writing it all down, or it may come in episodic bursts of feverish activity. The content of the alien-contact/abduction experience itself is usually the path to writing long treatises on the significance of the cosmos, as well as on the apparently rich world of activity in the astral plane. Frequently, experiencers feel that they are not in control but that they are just the 'aerial' and information is being channelled through them. They may be surprised, as are their friends and family, at their apparent knowledge of technical matters (intricate designs of the engine of a flying saucer, usually based on some kind of anti-gravity device involving free energy, are popular subjects.)

As an investigator who asks experiencers whether they write very much, I have frequently been shown several volumes of closely written ledgers, which I am usually forbidden to read, as it is secret knowledge which would be too powerful for my mental processes. It is easy to mock the writing of hypergraphic experiencers, who include 'astral travellers', or those who have OBEs on a regular basis, but quite often there are strangely accurate nuggets of insight that do deserve attention.

After traumatic or spectacular alien-contact/abduction experiences in particular, themes relating to health, nutrition and the environment are common, appearing to be written ideologies for the complete overhaul of life-style, including dietary changes, such as vegetarianism, and sometimes cessation of smoking and drinking. However, it must be remembered that these are not merely changes of heart, but *physiological changes* that reflect the newly enhanced sensitivities to chemicals, foods and the environment.

The content of these treatises acts as the 'written word' for beliefs about the purity of foods and the environment, but the subjects' apparent abstinence is not due to self-discipline, but is to avoid allergic reactions. That is to say, during the abduction vision, which can be triggered by proximity to power lines or an electric fireball, their body cannot cope with the suddenly and dramatically increased load threshold, and the sensitivities which have been at subclinical levels become overt. The writing often embodies this physiological revolution, and a code of practice about pure food and a pure environment is sometimes wrapped up in these philosophical/cosmological outpourings. After all, this is the biological survival function of these experiences. Hypergraphic examples of the writings of an 'astral traveller' are shown in the picture section.

By now, it can be seen that a picture of a special type of individual is being built. These individuals are hypersensitive to EM fields, especially of a specific frequency, and have other environmental sensitivities as well. They have increased internal magnetism, and are prone to epileptiform sensations, due to the destabilized electrical activity of the brain. Also, allergies to food contribute to an overall load that their body is coping with on a full-time basis and, if that physiological threshold is exceeded, they are likely to undergo hallucinatory experiences. However, they are usually totally unaware of their state of altered reactivity, and think that they live in a haunted house, are prone to spectacular psychic experiences or, for some reason, their life has been invaded by aliens with their own agendas.

AUTOMATIC BEHAVIOUR

I have been asked if experiencers/'abductees' could be regarded as epileptics, and the answer to this is in the negative. However, they are prone to seizures, or syncopes, if they have lived in a hot spot for some time and have had exposure opportunity, e.g. are at home most of the day and subject to fields from whatever source is inducing the hot spot. This is because such daily irradiation can induce kindling, i.e. a state where the electrical activity of the brain is erratic and unstable. The study by neurologist G. V. Goddard confirms this precisely (see p. 109).

I have found repeated examples of different types of seizure in experiencers. A well-known 'abductee', RR, who has appeared on television frequently in the UK, told me how she had gone shopping with her mother, who told RR to stay in the car, while she went to a local store. Reluctantly, RR agreed and, according to her, complied, but was surprised when, after she had been waiting for a while, idly watching the people who went by, her irate mother suddenly came up to the window and asked where she had been. Her mother insisted that, when she had returned to the car, RR was not there and so, somewhat annoyed, she had gone off to look for her. However, RR's quite sincere version was that she had simply not moved. This is a case of automatic behaviour, where RR had evidently left the vehicle and returned, and had absolutely no memory of having done so. Very often, people who exhibit this behaviour do rebellious things that they would really like to do, but are normally inhibited from doing. RR related that she had felt a twinge of resentment at being made to stay in the car, as she had been made to do when she was a child.

Another experiencer, also exhibiting an automatism, burst into his employer's office and told him that, if he did not get higher wages, he would leave. He was puzzled to find extra money in his pay-packet at the end of the week. An experiencer who lives in Coventry, UK, awoke one morning to find potatoes around the edge of the bath. Earlier, she had told me about her obsessively tidy mother, who used to say 'A place for everything, and everything in its place'. Another woman, who insisted that her house was haunted, was reluctantly persuaded to knit a jumper by her husband. After a few days of struggling with a tortuous knitting pattern, she came down one morning to find that it had vanished, forcing her to abandon the knitting. The 'ghost' was blamed for this mysterious event. She found the pattern a year later, folded up into a tiny square and tucked under a jar at the back of a kitchen cupboard. In many cases, it would certainly appear that automatisms allow the individual to do what they really want but usually do not dare to do.

THE RELIGIOSE OUTLOOK

A number of experiencers (or, in some cases, investigators) display a newly acquired religious fervour, if not fanaticism at times. Such extremes of feelings and behaviour, which seem out of character to those who know the experiencers well, can be the result of the development of an epileptiform symptom, in which they are said to have become *religiose*, as opposed to religious. Such anomalous religious preoccupations occur in people in hot-spot locations and I have several tapes full of non-stop incoherent religious ramblings from individuals who had no prior disposition towards religion; this seems to be the verbal equivalent of hypergraphia (see p.119). Another form seems to be quasi-scientific in theme, and such preoccupations are displayed as a strange non-stop, almost involuntary rambling, usually concerned with how science has taken a fundamentally wrong turning in its history, and how they can correct this with their convoluted theories and outlandish concepts. Basically, it seems to be a form of rampant fundamentalism that re-writes just about any major area of thought, including that of ET visitation.

BODY CONSCIOUSNESS

From the identification of types of seizure, with an emphasis on aberrant electrical activity in the brain, it would be only too easy to see the human organism as a compartmentalized machine. However, this is a fundamental mistake and does not conform to the holistic ethos which allows us an understanding of the visitation experience in all its forms. The hallucinatory experiences that arise are so often the result of the cumulative effects of stressors, which allow the regulatory systems to function as they should only intermittently, and the body then begins to put out urgent messages to that effect. Returning to the key concept of the load phenomenon, Dr Jean Monro tells us:

> Foods eaten daily are required as a source of nutrients for survival but **they are also a major environmental stress on the body**. [Breakspear Hospital, 1994. My emphasis.]

One of the earliest messages of physiological malfunction that the body expresses is in the form of food allergies and, as we have seen, these can develop through being irradiated by fields via the 'relay effect' (see p. 74). Following closely on this, other environmental sensitivities arise, e.g. an intolerance to chemicals. EH apparently develops when these are well established, and is an indicator of a maladapted end-state.

This new stage, in terms of the maladapted body system, brings with it a number of typical signs and symptoms which reflect a heightened sensitivity to the environment, known as *altered reactivity*. This occurs because the body can detect small field concentrations that were previously beyond its scope. One experiencer, a retired miner living in Yorkshire, UK, told me how he could sense the fields of a transformer which had been embedded in a wall as a space-saving strategy. He was also useful to amateur electricians, because he could tell them where the wiring ran through the walls without instrumentation. Another experiencer related how people began to give off 'vibes', much to her surprise, and, when they sat next to her on the train, she knew by how they 'felt' whether or not they were in good health. This is, of course, not easily verified, but is related here as it illustrates a subjective aspect of what it is like to develop such sensitivities; many EH-status individuals become involved in healing because of this acquired sensitivity.

HYPERAESTHESIA

Further on in the continuum of developing sensitivities, a cross-over occurs, where non-EM aspects of the environment impinge. Sound and vibration become intolerable and traffic noise, crowds and the general ambient hubbub of the streets cause incipient EH-sufferers to become reclusive and an agoraphobic homebound life-style is typical.

This, of course, makes matters worse, as they are never away from the hot-spot source that induced their symptoms in the first place. They develop a hypersensitivity to light, known as 'photophobia', and this reflects their sensitivity to other parts of the EM spectrum. Very short exposures to sunlight may induce a reaction in the skin, and one sufferer developed characteristic red dots on the arm which she rested out of the car window while she was driving for a short time. Some sufferers have to wear tinted spectacles constantly, and fluorescent light is also particularly bothersome. The flicker effect of long-life bulbs when they are coming on has been reported as being unbearable, and some sufferers have to be in total darkness before they can get to sleep. Strangely, thunderstorms seem to fascinate such people, especially the lightning, although this may be related to the change in the charge of atmospheric ions, to which they would be hypersensitive. Of course, the sensitivity to urban scenarios is related to their chemical intolerances as well, as it is gaseous media, e.g. volatile substances, which are the most potent in this respect. The hydrocarbons in car exhaust fumes are a contributory factor and exposure to cigarette smoke, aftershave and perfume during normal social contact also adds to the overall picture of avoidance because of sensitivities. Such a state of generally heightened sensitivity is known as hyperesthesia.

MICROWAVE HEARING

We are building up a picture of individuals who have become sensitive to the environment and, just as they are able to detect fields that are usually outside of human capabilities, their new sensitivities may include an unusual perceptual effect, known as 'microwave hearing', or 'radar hearing', whereby the microwave transmissions to which they are subjected in their hot-spot home manifest as a strange auditory phenomenon. Sufferers may begin to hear Morse-code-like signalling, or clicks, buzzing and chirping sounds, which seem to come from just outside the head or within it. This has been reported by a significant minority of experiencers, especially as a post-encounter effect. A report by investigator Andrew Collins on a major case in the UK – the Aveley abduction (Collins, 1974; Note 7), which involved a couple and children – provides a good example and is outlined on p. 142.

Microwave hearing has been studied by electrical engineers, and very thorough and detailed papers have been published which attempt to identify the mechanisms at work, although it is realized that the energy levels involved are very low, much less than those required for other biological effects. This is of course, consistent with the generalized hyperaesthesia of the EH subject:

> The microwave generated sound has been described as clicking, buzzing or chirping depending on such factors as pulsewidth and repetition rate. The effect is of great significance since the average incident power densities required to elicit the response are considerably lower than those found for other microwave biological effects ... This paper analyses the acoustic wave generated ... in man exposed to pulsed microwave radiation as a result of rapid thermal expansion ... We assume that the auditory effect arises from the minuscule but rapid rise in temperature in the brain as a result of absorption of microwave energy. The rise of temperature occurring in a very short time is believed to create thermal expansion of brain matter which then launches the acoustic wave of pressure that is detected by the cochlea. [Lin, 1977.]

I am a little surprised that James Lin, the author of the paper from which this extract is taken, has assumed that it is 'brain matter' which expands. I personally would have investigated the thermoelastic properties of the skull, or the 'stirrup and anvil' bones in the ear mechanism itself.

However, its robust appearance as a post-encounter effect contributes to our picture of hypersensitive individuals. Not only may they be hypersensitive to the sounds that we all hear, but they hear new ones which are inaudible to other people.

Related to this phenomenon is the ability of some experiencers to hear radio broadcasts or even telephone transmissions, and it would seem that such aspects as the skull plates, metal-amalgam tooth fillings or the deposits of magnetite in the sinuses are acting as transducers to convert microwave signals into auditory effects, due to their enhanced magnetic properties after an MEE. I have even had one case where a radio broadcast could be heard coming faintly from the head of the individual receiving it.

TASTE ANOMALIES

Hypersensitive individuals may also develop taste anomalies, especially a metallic taste, which has been described to me by an experiencer as 'like sucking pennies'. This is due to the action of the fields on the mercury-tin amalgam in their tooth fillings. This, in combination with saliva, which acts as a conducting fluid, or electrolyte, breaks down the amalgam in the mouth by a process called 'electrolysis'. This can cause the mouth to fill with mercury vapour.

All of these maladaptive changes, and more, register in the body but, usually, when individuals become aware of such symptoms, they take action and avoid the cause of them, or seek medical help to eliminate them. However, as stated on p.121, sufferers typically have no idea of the cause or significance of their symptoms, and I have found that, eventually, they just assume that everyone else is affected in the same way and they are no different. ('Yes, fluorescent lights do make me feel ill, but they do that to everyone.') This is partly due to the insidious nature of the development of such sensitivities. Eventually, as development progresses, the body finds that its usual warnings, i.e. unpleasant symptoms, are not acted upon, and a new phase and more radical strategy is implemented. The mind is drawn into the communications.

PSYCHIC VIDEO-RECORDINGS

Just as dreams reflect the inner workings of the unconscious, imagery is drawn from its image banks and is presented to the hypersensitive under suitable conditions. For dreams, the condition of sleep is imperative, but for the visions and hallucinations of the experiencer, the body utilizes EM fields, stress and chemical changes; in fact, all the factors which are already disrupting the body's systems. And what will it say in these symbolic communications to the individual? Basically, the message is 'Wake up! Things are going wrong with the way I am functioning, and I just cannot cope with all these different stressors from the environment'. However, just as the unconscious comments on the emotional life of the individual in dream imagery, these communications comment on the health of the individual in images. That is to say, the unconscious talks in pictures. Unfortunately, pictures are ambiguous and their meaning is not always clear. Dreams require analysis, or at least an interpretation, for their meaning to become evident and, most of the time, their meaning – what the unconscious is trying to tell us – escapes us.

Similarly, the content of these hallucinatory visions requires analysis but, once it is realized that the function of the visions is strictly biological, and that the overall theme is the welfare of the health of the experiencer, then many of the meanings become evident. However, like dreams, for most of the time their meaning eludes us but, as the body is urging the individual to act upon the information about it dysfunction, sensitivities are depicted dramatically.

However, it appears that this may be an extension of an existing function of dreams, and that they are already recruited to convey information about the health of the dreamer. Medical practitioners such as Dr James Le Fanu have carried out research into this. He comments:

> In contrast to the arcane world of Freudian dream interpretation, current medical theories on the purpose of dreaming tend to be reductionist and unimaginative. Dreams are auditory and visual hallucinations induced by signals from the brain stem, or designed to reinforce memories stored during waking life or like a computer dumping unwanted programmes, a means of forgetting useless information. Yet for doctors with time and interest to enquire, **dreams can provide fascinating insights into the lives of patients and their experience of illness** ... Dr Robert Smith at the University of Rochester, New York, has found that dreamers can equally reflect the severity of physical illness. He studied the dreams of 214 patients admitted to a cardiac unit for references to death featuring graveyards, wills and funerals. The greater the degree of cardiac disability, the more often were these death-related dreams reported, suggesting that they were in some subtle way warning the patients of their prognosis. [Le Fanu, 1994.]

If this 'welfare message' facility already exists with dreams it is not really surprising that experiencers receive similar messages about their sensitivities via their hallucinations, and it is interesting to note Le Fanu's comment about the brain stem initiating dreams, as it is the brain stem that is hardest hit during MEEs. So considering EH specifically, it is the 'dream centre', i.e. brain stem, which is most affected, and readily reactive to field exposure.

The hallucination of an EH/multiple-allergy sufferer was described as an old lady in a wheelchair holding a brandy glass aloft, from which pink sparkling particles of electricity crackled. It does not require a degree in psychotherapy to appreciate that, broadly, the message was: 'If you drink in anymore electrical energies, your body will become disabled'.

ATOMIC-DETONATION IMAGERY:
the radio-frequency connection

Examples of this imagery abound. One of the recurring images in alien-abduction experiences is that of atomic explosions, in which bright flashes of light are followed by spectacular mushroom clouds. In the drama of the experience, this scenario is often shown to the experiencer by aliens, on some type of futuristic TV screen. Of course, the extraterrestrial-hypothesis (ETH) enthusiasts have interpreted this as an indication that atomic weapons are threatening the stability of the solar system in some way, or that, similarly, the survival of the species is at risk. This latter interpretation does at least come close, and it is tempting to regard such imagery as a social comment. However, such images are *strictly personal* and pertain to the state of health and sensitivities of the individual perceiving them. For some time, I had regarded such imagery as a symbol of the ultimate energetic contamination that the environment could suffer. However, it is much more likely, in the light of the over-riding concern for the individual's physiology, to be a spectacular comment on their sensitivities. Consider the following information provided by a company who manufactures RE-shielding materials:

> ... the explosion of a nuclear device results in an intense burst of radio energy in the UHF [ultra-high frequency] band which, at distances beyond the likelihood of thermal blast damage, can cause temporary malfunction or permanent damage to electronic equipment. This is known as the EMP [electro-magnetic pulse]. [RFI Shielding Ltd, 1995, p. 257.]

Such imagery reflects the experiencer's sensitivities to a very common range of frequencies in the environment: RF fields. Such heavy-handed symbolism, i.e. a personal apocalypse, depicts a strong power surge rather than an atomic war, and throws up the question of from where does the unconscious get its information. The background of the individuals who have experienced this atomic imagery needs to be explored in order to determine the link, made in their body and/or unconscious, between atomic explosions and the RF/EMP. Obviously, watching a film of a mushroom cloud unfold on television may stock the image banks, but it would not allow the body to apprehend its EMP. It must be remembered, however, that we are dealing with people whose sensitivities to specific field frequencies can be extremely enhanced, and that an actual EMP would be a global phenomenon.

THE POST-ENCOUNTER HEALTH REVOLUTION

Other 'welfare messages' and embodied representations have been outlined. The abduction experience in which the experiencer felt that she was raped by an alien as a symbolic enactment of a vaginal fungal infection (candida), was also part of the allergy/sensitivities group. The same percipient saw female aliens drinking coffee, from which she was barred, and which reflected the development of a simple allergy to coffee. The abduction vision itself is derived from the destabilization of the body image; the involvement of aliens as a thematic response depicts the 'alien' nature of the fields irradiating the experiencer and are all variations on a theme. There is also a mixing and matching of imagery pertaining to developing clinical conditions, as well as the immediate sensations produced by the direct action of the fields on parts of the body, i.e. expressions of long- and short-term disturbances.

Such expressions of maladaptation are not confined to alien-abduction experiences and, in some cases it would certainly appear that the vision itself acts as a remedy. To understand this, it must be appreciated that it is the integration of the emotional and the physical that is involved in maintaining the body's equilibrium. Emotional stress adds to the load phenomenon and, in many cases, actually precipitates an experience. It does this partly because it induces adverse chemical changes in the body (see Note 8), such as the production of adrenalin, and also because it undermines immunocompetence, the ability to combat infection. Of course, long-term stress would be most effective in doing this, and can therefore be regarded in the same way as a progressive illness; both weaken the body's defence mechanisms and the body's ability to cope generally. The alleviation of such long-term emotional pressure would therefore act as a stabilizing cure, and sufferers have obtained self-help relief through the calming effects of meditation, yoga, prayer and other stress-reducing activities, including leaving their jobs!

This is the interface between the spiritual and the physiological, and this area, therefore, also relates to the load phenomenon. That is to say, life-situations can induce stress, and this can translate into adverse body chemistry; therefore, the introduction of an aspect which reduces or totally removes stress also reduces the load that the individual is coping with. Prayer, for example, can act as a safety valve, as it can have

Microwave beams emitting from a mobile phone relay pylon, made visible by atmospheric water droplets and magnetic field interaction (Heiligenschein). See page 59. Albert Budden

Examples of everyday sources of electromagnetic pollution. With the proliferation of electronic systems across the world, we are all now living in an invisible electromagnetic smog. Albert Budden

Investigator and author Albert Budden taking field measurements in his study using a TriField meter. Albert Budden

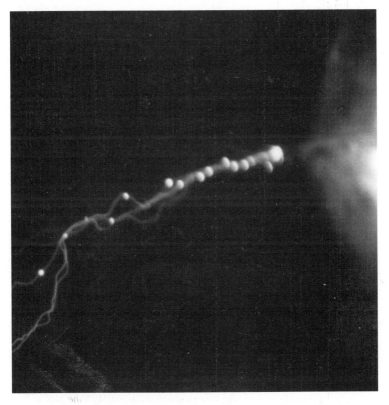

Electric fireballs generated by James and Kenneth Corum, USA, using Tesla coils to produce intermodulation effects. See pages 175–82. James Corum

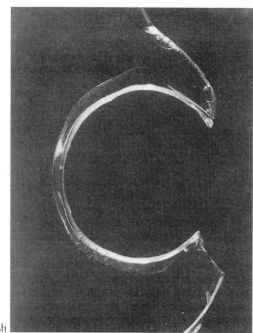

An example of a hole impressed through window glass by the thermos-electric energies of ball lightning.
See pages 175–82.
Courtesy of D.H. McIntosh

Bright unexplained light photographed emerging from the cloud and fog at Hessdalen, Norway, 1983. See page 183. Project Hessdalen

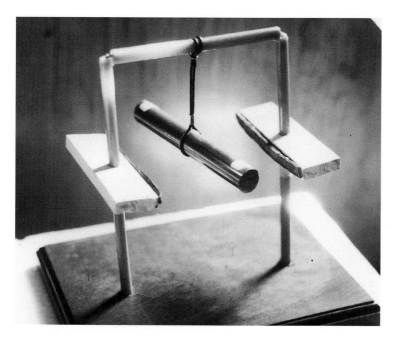

Nicholas Reiter's Magnetic Event Marker (MEM). Reiter distributed these devices through the houses of experiencers in the USA, as a means of estimating whether an atmosphere power surge had occurred within a specific time period, usually overnight. See page 88. Albert Budden

Self-made physicist John Hutchison reclining among a very small amount of his electrical apparatus at home in British Columbia, Canada. See pages 62–6. John Hutchison

Samples of some of the steel bars distorted by the Hutchison effect. See pages 62–6. Courtesy of the Max Planck Institute, Berlin, Germany

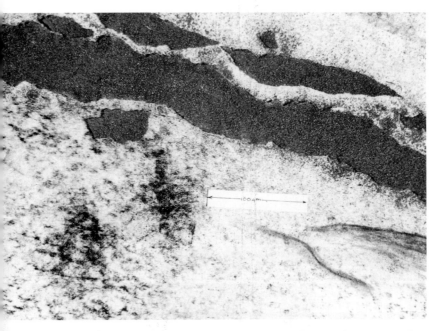

Enlarged microphotograph of a layer and associated deposits of magnetite in the human sinuses. See pages 80–6. Baker, Mather and Kennaugh, University of Manchester, 1983

Case 4: the Schillig's house in Ohio, USA. The photograph was taken from below a pylon that looms over the house. Peter Schillig

This ordinary looking house in north London was the site of the 'Enfield poltergeist' activity in the 1970s. Albert Budden

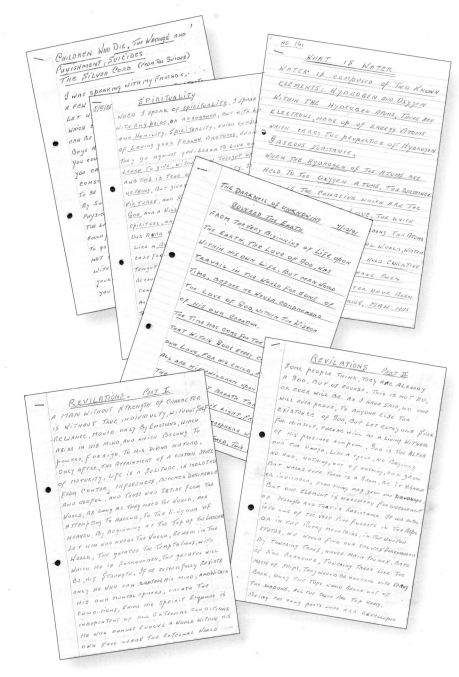

Examples of hypergraphic writing, which frequently develops after 'visitation/abduction' experiences. See page 119.

profound calming effects and, when coupled with belief, is even more potent to this end. Therefore, the production of a spectacular visitation experience, the content of which corresponds with a religious figure, would act as a powerful spiritual remedy and can form the basis for the genesis of a spiritual belief system.

In these cases, it is the visitation experience itself which acts as the remedy by producing an apparent and convincing supernatural reality. A good example of this is the appearance of guardian angels. To the highly stressed, such a phenomenon would act as a powerful agent of rescue.

While it would be only too easy to stray from the path of the medical/scientific model into the nebulous content of the spiritual, it must not escape our understanding that such physiological/spiritual aspects are, in fact, key concepts in our overall understanding of why and how these experiences take place. The validity of this approach is also supported in the type of changes that 'abductees' undergo after their experience, the content of which, (e.g. apparent firsthand knowledge of an alien realm) often becomes a basis for a belief system. That is to say, although there are physical changes, such as a dramatically revised diet and an altered chemical intake, this new metabolic purity usually goes hand in hand with a revision of outlook – a psycho-spiritual transformation – based on what they feel is real contact with real aliens.

Interestingly, a number of encounters are so powerful that 'abductees' undergo a nervous breakdown after their experience; a recovery and reformation, which has as its centre pieces a creative activity coupled with a new occupation in a caring profession of some kind, is typical.

The 'abductees' feel that these changes are endowed upon them by spiritually superior beings, with which they have had first-hand contact. Due to this flatteringly special selection, their sense of self-worth is enhanced, they have spiritual direction and, probably most importantly, they have their allergies and sensitivities under control (because they change their diet, stop smoking, drinking, avoid medications, perfume, etc.), which after all was the primary function of the experience. It must also be said that the effects of the experience can go the other way and may make the 'abductees' far worse; such encounters with electromagnetism precipitate a make-or-break situation, physiologically speaking. In fact, there are direct parallels with electroconvulsive therapy (ECT) which also involves an extremely close encounter with electricity.

PYROLURIA: a stress-induced disorder

As an example of the type of maladaptation that the body may develop due to stress, consider a condition known as *pyroluria*. It has been mentioned how the production of adrenalin during periods of stress is, for the experiencer, comparable to exposure to domestic gas, cigarette smoke, aerosols, etc., as it is just one more chemical suddenly introduced into the body. For such EH individuals who have acute chemical sensitivities anyway, such non-routine chemicals as those produced by stress would be like being exposed to an allergen. That is to say, in their case, emotional stress easily translates into adverse chemical exposure which exceeds the load-phenomenon threshold and leads to visitation experiences. With this in mind, consider another group of chemicals called *kryptopyrroles* induced by stress in the body:

> *Pyroluria describes the presence of an excess of chemicals called kryptopyrroles (KP) in the urine … When excreted KP removes vitamin B6 and zinc from the body producing a variety of physical and psychological symptoms … both are needed for adequate stress response … the result is an inability to cope with stress and often debilitating symptoms … This excess excretion of KP is brought on by stress. [Scarfe, 1997.]*

Dr Christopher Scarfe goes on to describe a patient who had developed pyroluria and accompanying alien-visitation experiences:

> *When Elaine came to me last February she had been suffering from depression and withdrawal since 1985 … She began to experience auditory hallucinations, even more severe depressions and was convinced that she was being controlled by an alien force. Elaine's KP levels were twice the normal range so I began by supplementing extra B6 and zinc along with manganese, B vitamins and plently of vitamin C.*

Interestingly, this treatment is comparable with the 'pure food/pure environment' ideology of post-encounter renewal, and is even more confirming of how closely pyroluria can be identified with the maladapted state, which brings on abduction experiences and similar consciousness effects. Its treatment involves exactly the same dietary revision whereby processed foods are replaced by fresh foods:

> *She was eating lots of processed foods, meat, cheese, chocolate and not fruit and vegetables, so I encouraged her to include more raw and vital foods so as to push out the refined fat and sugar-laden foods she was accustomed to … Now Elaine is a completely different person … outgoing and lively … studying for a course … [Scarfe, 1997.]*

This is exactly the sort of health regime that 'aliens' impart to those they have 'contacted' or, to be accurate, the regime the body expresses via the visitor experience. Therefore, we have here further confirmatory evidence of how stress is implicated in the physiology of the visitation experience, and how the 'welfare message' content duplicates the treatment otherwise prescribed by a doctor.

As the reader may now discern, I am drawing a line through a number of interdependent aspects and linking the latent physiological benefits of belief with visitation experiences. That is to say, as a post-encounter effect, experiencers are able to manage and make a strange sense of their sensitivities that previously ran amok; and they 'know' that this is because they have been chosen by an alien race which, they feel, has worked some kind of mysterious miracle on their physical and spiritual health. It was Dr Jacques Vallée, in *Passport to Magonia*, who stated that the UFO/alien phenomenon acted as a means to control belief. However, I wonder if he realized that this astute observation can also be applied to beliefs which, ultimately, can incur direct benefits to the health of the experiencer. That is to say, the phenomenon itself induces belief in aliens from another planet or dimension, and this provides experiencers with a way of making sense of their acquired sensitivities to the environment. Their state of health is translated into an ideology, and this acts as a means of integrating (if not elevating) their sensitivities into their lives.

However, it must be stated that such major experiences are really a close encounter with electricity, to which they are hypersensitive, and the outcome is a gamble. Many feel that their lives have been disorientated, or even shattered, by their encounters with 'aliens', and that they are now far worse off than before in terms of their health and mental state. In effect, they have undergone a massive seizure, not unlike being struck by lightning, but at lower field strengths and over a more prolonged period, e.g. through proximity to an electric fireball or UFO. In many cases, their sensitivities are triggered to more overt levels, whereas, before, they were subclinical, i.e. functional. These overt levels, of course, vary considerably and may or may not involve psychic effects.

The following catalogue of symptoms from EH patients (Choy, Monro & Smith, 1986) provides a range of typical reactions to field exposures, although it also contains extreme cases which, it must be said, are not especially uncommon:

1. LP. Age 15 years. Female. 'History of EM sensitivities. Overhead power lines produced unconsciousness when in a highly allergic state.'

2. HH. Age 19 years. Female. 'Since 1984, on the introduction of computers into her office she was quite unable to work, developing severe headaches and she also had to stop athletics at Crystal Palace [London, UK], where there is a high power TV/RF transmitter, because of loss of muscle tone, breathing and sudden fainting; she hears hissing noises when she is there. Her athletic ability is also affected by the power lines over the training track at Carshalton [near London]. She runs 3000 metres upwards and has done a 4-minute mile. A word-processor was recently installed at

her work place; her headaches became more severe, especially when she is near computer terminals.'

3. FR. Age 53 years. Female. 'When she travels beneath overhead high tension wires she gets pain in her glands in the anterior triangles of her neck; she also becomes mute (aphonic). Adverse effects also occur in humid and pre-thunderstorm weather characterized by weak pains in the glands in the neck. She had glandular fever in 1983. When passing near power lines in a car, she has the same symptoms if it is overcast; these symptoms persist, resembling glandular fever for three days. She has an electric cooker, but only uses the hob; she cannot tolerate meat cooked inside the (electric) oven … Use of electric toaster gives discomfort in summer when humidity is high, also hair driers and the iron give great discomfort. Fluorescent lights in shops cause symptoms. She finds that it helps to unplug all electric sockets at night.'

4. SR. Age 13 years. Male. 'Since 1984, electric light bulbs, computer games, television, electric car (toy), hand-held controls produced malaise, fatigue, severe headaches and hyperactivity. He reacts to lights in shops.'

5. PS. Age 39 years. Male. 'Gets ill when travelling south. Gets shocks from dictaphones; these were checked and found to have no leakage.'

6. JS. Age 61 years. Female. 'Lived under pylons for 25 years. She now gets severe attacks of migraine when exposed to some electrical equipment, especially overhead power lines and colour television sets. She had to move house when off-shore surveillance radar was installed near her home.'

7. ES. Age 41 years. Female. 'Extreme hypersensitivity to cold – and exposure resulted in headaches. These were more severe in the presence of electrical equipment, illustrating a cumulative physical load phenomenon.'

8. LW. Age 32 years. Female. 'A computer produced faintness and dizziness, headaches and nausea …'

9. HG. Age 61 years. Female. 'Since 1976, she has been sensitive to electrical appliances. Tinnitus and fatigue were her main allergic symptoms. A vacuum cleaner gave her a "prickles all over" sensation. Fridges, freezers and an electric cooker, made her lean over towards them(!), as did lamp-posts and transformers in the street; she went into a deep sleep after meals; she committed suicide in 1984.'

10. AH. Age 65 years. Female. 'Overhead wires near her home in Norway induced paroxysmal tachycardia. She developed this and panic reactions when in mountainous regions. Power lines descend down the mountains over a crest, and pass 500 metres from her cottage, which is entirely wooden.'

These are introductory summaries taken from the notes of practitioners, and patient identities, of course, have been altered. It is precisely such individuals who are susceptible to visitation experiences, although, as mentioned, the doctors concerned were not really interested in them and, understandably, were preoccupied with clinical diagnoses and treatments. However, throughout my own descriptions of how the experiences themselves are related to the environmental sensitivities which the sufferers develop, I have purposely referred to the body as an autonomous entity with its own aims and preoccupations. This is an integral part of the holistic ethos, and there is evidently part of the nervous system which monitors the state of the body. I could argue that this is an extension of the autonomic functions that govern breathing and digestion, or that the body could be seen as an evolving community of organs and cells. How widely this perspective is accepted I do not know, but what is evident is that the body's systems behave as if they have their own consciousness, or 'caretaker', which monitors the workings of its functions.

A book called *The Organism*, by Kurt Goldstein, echoes this holistic theory of the human organism (Goldstein, 1995, p. 422). Work with brain-damaged soldiers during World War One led Goldstein to view people as systems in equilibrium rather than as compartmentalized machines. He believed that, in order to understand recovery from brain damage, it was necessary to look beyond the damaged cerebral function and see the whole system as adjusting to a new norm of behaviour. It is evident that this 'body consciousness' is the intelligence which initiates the visitation event in all its many forms, including, of course, the alien-abduction experience.

FIELD STIMULATION INTO IMAGERY

An analysis of what goes on in alien-abduction experiences shows how EM stimuli are translated into the action within the drama, albeit as internal imagery. If the body is subjected to a power surge for example, the mind will comply and produce appropriate imagery. Consider the following extract about precisely this:

> *Betty was somehow floated onto one of the strange glass chairs, in that it had inlaid metal strips on its arms and on its seat.*

> ' ... *they're setting me down in that strange seat there. That different one from all the others, with those buttons and those steel things there. I'm sitting down in it ... And they're putting my hands – oh ... (sigh) ... They put my hands and my arms on that thing ... And they're looking at me with their eyes somehow, and for some reason, and – ah, oh-h-h-h!'*

*Betty's body jumped violently – once, twice! The dual convulsions star-
tled us. During a later debriefing, we asked her what had occurred …
On the fourth chair was something that looked like a button. One of the
entities touched it twice. Simultaneously, Betty had felt twin electrical
shocks course through her body. [Fowler, 1980.]*

This is a straightforward translation of an electrical stimulus into mental
imagery; events involving electricity abound in these experiences, and
are further testimony to their EM nature. Body consciousness *per se* is
preoccupied with expressing long-term malfunctioning or remedial
measures. For example, one scenario that regularly occurs involves some
kind of bodily cleansing procedure, and this theme is telling the experiencer that their body is polluted, reflecting the state of their personal
environment. Consider the following example:

*Next, Betty was directed to a platform illuminated from above by streaks
of dazzling light …*

*'Would you get under that please?' the entities asked. Well what is it
first? … 'It is just a cleansing thing' … Well, will it hurt? … 'No, it
is just to cleanse you' … And so they didn't touch me, but they held out
their hands as if to assist me. There seems to be a platform. The light's
above there. And it's bright-bright and it's got those streaks of light
coming out of it. It seems like it's moving me upward! … The light is
getting brighter and brighter. It's all engulfed in light. … It's just bright
white light … I'm just standing there … it's just white light all around
me, and on me … [Fowler, 1980.]*

This perception of being immersed in a bright white light occurs as a
single isolated effect when the visual cortex is irradiated and has been
nicknamed 'the exploding head syndrome' by some doctors. It cannot
be taken at face value as a remedy, but is a perceptual effect which has
been harnessed by the unconscious for its own expressive ends.

Another recurring scenario with a cleansing theme is one in which
the experiencer is depicted as being placed in a transparent casing,
moulded to the exact shape of a human body, and is mysteriously
cleaned. It is clear that the bodily systems of these experiencers need to
be cleared of some substance, effect or processes and, from experience,
such depictions are indicators of progressive conditions of which the
average general practitioner would be unaware, or at best diagnose as
some non-specific or idiopathic malady. These are frequently bioelec-
tromagnetically induced conditions which have long-term degenerative
or debilitating consequences, and are changes that are insidious, occur at
cellular levels and are certainly outside the awareness of the conscious

mind of the subject, e.g. masked food allergies. The body is aware of them, even when they are at subclinical levels, and issues warnings, one form being the 'alien cleansing scenarios'. A typical example of such an EM-altered cellular condition is called *electroporation*.

ELECTROPORATION

As implied, these visions may contain information of what is happening to the body at cellular levels, albeit in symbolic form, and, in fact, their analysis could be regarded as a diagnostic tool, just as dream analysis is used to this end in psychotherapy, in order to heal the disordered mind. Electroporation is an indicator of irradiation, and James C. Weaver, at Massachusetts Institute of Technology, USA, relates:

> *The essentially universal biophysical phenomenon of 'electroporation' occurs if an applied field causes the cell transmembrane voltage to reach about 0.5–1V in a time of microseconds to milliseconds. Ordinarily, the cell membrane is a formidable barrier to the transport of ions and charged molecules. However, electroporation results in a large increase in trans-membrane conductance, which is believed to be caused by ion transport through temporary membrane openings ('pores') ... Not only cell membranes, but also cell layers or even the stratum corneum of human skin can be temporarily altered by the electrical creation of aqueous pathways ... Electroporation is believed to be the rapid creation of aqueous pathways through lipid-containing barriers in cells and tissue ... This fundamental barrier to molecular transport is important to defining the intracellular region of a cell. The ability to use a physical stimulus – a strong electric field pulse – to compromise this barrier is of considerable significance ...*

And:

> *The basis of electroporation is believed to be an electrostatically driven structural rearrangement of the (cell) membrane, not heating. Pore forma-tion begins to occur extremely rapidly, before any significant temperature rise occurs ... some biological systems experiencing electroporation have clearly experienced negligible damage ... Electric field pulses that are too large or long are found to cause planar membrane destruction and are associated with cell killing. [Weaver, 1995.]*

It is, of course, highly unlikely that the experiencer would become aware of such altered cell reactivity, but it is this order of covert biophysical changes that register within the body and would be impli-cated in the 'cleansing scenarios' outlined. I am not suggesting that they are due to electroporation in every case, but that this is a good example of a latent on-going and potentially degenerative process induced by field exposure. Another is the formation of dangerous free radicals within the body, clinically identified by Dr Jean Monro and Dr C. W. Smith, which form due to the electrical decomposition of essential compounds in the body, known as electrolysis.

As all chemical reactions in the body take place in solution (forming an electrolyte), they are targets for such 'electrical splitting', where usually harmless compounds become the raw material for electrolysis effects. For example, if common salt (sodium chloride) in the body is segregated into the two elements which compose it, free metallic sodium and gaseous chlorine are produced. In solution, these would form minute amounts of sodium hydroxide (caustic soda) and hypochlorous acid (bleach). It is the cumulative effects of such biologically alien chemicals which register within the chemically sensitive system, and this eventually recruits the unconscious to communicate the unwanted presence of such 'chemical aliens' to the conscious mind via the cleansing imagery of the alien-abduction experience. It must be emphasized however, that, under strictly controlled conditions, electroporation could be used beneficially for the targeted delivery of essential drugs to previously inaccessible parts of the cell.

DREAM BABIES AND THE 'WISE BABY' MYTHOLOGY

An intriguing cross-reference on how physical aspects in the body are represented by imagery in the unconscious comes from Robert Van der Castle, a psychologist at Blue Ridge Hospital in Charlottesville, Virginia, USA. The implications of his work beg the question, 'Could the dreams of pregnant women hold clues about their unborn babies' health?' According to Van der Castle, the answer would be in the affirmative. He argues that dreams during pregnancy may predict such things as length of labour and even the likelihood of post-partum depression. His theory is based on the idea that any malfunctioning in the body usually doesn't register during the day. But at night, we are like a tuned-in radio. We can better process messages from our body without all the disruptive static that comes across during the waking hours.

To document this hypothesis, Van der Castle is currently soliciting dreams from pregnant women, and he has noted certain patterns. In the early months, expectant mothers dream of small animals, such as fish and kittens. But by the last 3 months, he has noted a seven-fold increase in references to the baby. Some women dream of rejecting or ignoring their new child – and that may prove to be a clue to the development of post-partum depression. While nightmares about unborn children usually indicate nothing more than common anxiety, some women have frightening dreams that certainly appear to be portents of danger. For example, one woman dreamed that her baby was floating on a cloud and waving goodbye. She suffered a miscarriage a few days later. Van der Castle reports:

> I've heard of many tragic stories from women who dreamed about their babies' deaths or about birth defects, and the dreams came true ... There seems to be some kind of internal communication. [Van der Castle, 1984.]

From this, it would seem that Van der Castle has also detected the messages from the body's consciousness and, while I would argue that such urgent systemic information is reserved for visionary experiences rather than dreams, this rule still seems to have been in force, as, again, there is a biological survival function at work, i.e. the welfare of the unborn child. Although the dreaming mothers may not be influenced by the intracranial fields necessary to initiate a visionary experience, the issue at stake is of sufficient survival importance to appear on the 'regular' channel of communication from the unconscious – dreams.

But there is another way to interpret Van der Castle's observations. Perhaps the mothers who dreamed of dangers to their unborn child did have more than enough access to EM fields, and their 'dream' was, in fact, field-driven. It has been mentioned how experiencers' dreams of aliens develop into visions of aliens, depending on their sensitivities and the levels of available electromagnetism. I would remind the reader of the extract from the report of the World Health Organization (WHO):

> There is increasing concern about the possibility that RF exposure may play a role in the causation or promotion of cancer, specifically of the blood-forming organs or in the central nervous system. Similar uncertainties surround possible effects on reproduction, such as increased rates of spontaneous abortion and of congenital malformations. [WHO, 1993, p.27.]

The implications suggested are that Van der Castle has also come to the conclusion that body consciousness is at work, which supports the ideas presented here; it also suggests that the mythology from American investigators about alien/human hybrids has, as its real basis, the sort of material that Van der Castle collected, and that this in turn is based on the dual irradiation of mother/experiencer and unborn child. In fact, the more one considers the Hopkins' complex of 'wise baby'/hybrid experiences in the light of this dual mother/foetus irradiation (and the WHO report), the more that a different picture entirely emerges.

THE FIELD/CELL INTERFACE

Without delving too much into the technical details of bioelectromagnetics, the literature from this exciting field constantly reveals aspects which unwittingly link up with those so far outlined as integral components of the biology of visitation experiences. As mentioned, the body can become aware of maladaptations to the environment at cellular levels, and these are translated into the action within the drama of the alien-abduction vision, as they can trigger the load-phenomenon threshold.

It is no coincidence that it is these latent microscopic and molecular processes which interface with the EM environment to produce either health or maladaptation. It is just such altered cellular reactivity that is involved in food allergies, EH and chemical sensitivities (see the studies by John Holt, p.42). Similarly, the presence of microscopic magnetite particles in brain and other organ cells (see Note 9) has been implicated in EH. The increased permeability of cells through electroporation also points to this cellular interface with EM fields. As if this was not enough evidence of the cellular sensitivity by which the body reacts to fields, the following extracts from a paper by W. Ross Adey, at the University School of Medicine, Loma Linda, California, USA, represents another indictment of EM pollution and provides leading clues as to the preoccupations of body consciousness:

> ... For as we have explored our inner universe, seeking to understand broad principles determining interaction of weak non-ionising electromagnetic fields with living matter, there has been a dawning awareness that we may indeed have opened a veritable Pandora's box.

And

> At the core of observed sensitivities to low-level EM fields are a series of co-operative processes. One such series involves calcium ion binding and release. Available evidence points to their occurrence at cell membranes and on cell surfaces in the essential first steps of detecting EM fields. Also, attention is now directed to newly defined roles for free radicals, that they may also participate in highly co-operative detection of weak magnetic fields ... [Adey, 1993]

Another passage links up with the 'aqueous pathways' and cell membranes involved in an earlier aspect – electroporation:

> In cellular aggregates that form tissues of higher animals (including man) cells are separated by narrow fluid channels that take on special importance in signaling from cell to cell. These channels act as windows on the electro-chemical world surrounding each cell. Hormones, antibodies, neurotransmitters and chemical cancer promoters, for example, move along them to reach binding sites on cell membrane receptors. These narrow fluid 'gutters', typically not more than 150 microns wide, are **also preferred pathways for intrinsic and environmental EM fields**,

since they offer much lower electrical impedance than cell membranes. Although this inter-cellular space (known as ICS) forms only about 10% of the conducting cross section of typical tissue, it carries at least 90% of any imposed or intrinsic current, directing it along cell membrane surfaces. [Adey, 1993. My emphasis.]

These channels, which act as conduits between cells, not only for the chemicals in the body, but also for EM fields from the environment, *are exactly the channels that would be physically dilated by an MEE*. From this it is easy to see why individuals who have undergone such an 'electrical initiation' would readily become EH, as their very tissue has become much more conductive to EM fields than before. If they are then irradiated through living in a hot-spot location, it is these widened 'gutters', as Adey describes them, which would allow the easier passage of induced body currents. Also, researchers working on other projects into how EM fields interface with the human body have come to exactly the same conclusion as Adey. In 1991, members of the Institution of Electrical Engineers (IEE) investigated this particular aspect and they too have concluded that it is the aqueous pathways *between* cells which are the conductive channels for fields from the environment to intrude into the human body. Consider the following extract from their Public Affairs Board Report:

*Electric and magnetic ELF fields induce currents in living tissue. At these low frequencies the dielectric barrier presented by the cell membrane confines the currents **almost entirely to the extracellular spaces**, as distinct from the interior from the cell. [IEE, 1991, p.5. My emphasis]*

From this, it is easy to see how the sudden and massive rush of high-energy fields from lightning or major electrocution would pass into these intercellular spaces [ICS], force cells apart and produce the physical effect of widening the spaces between them, thereby establishing permanently enhanced conductivity.

As another indicator of how an MEE and hot-spot activity are instrumental in enhancing the passage of fields through the tissues of the body, Adey enlightens us as to exactly how these in-coming fields interface with cells:

Numerous stranded protein molecules protrude from within the cell into this narrow inter-cellular space. Their glycoprotein tips form the glycocalyx, which senses chemical and electrical signals in surrounding fluid. Their highly negatively charged tips form receptor sites for hormones, antibodies, neurotransmitters, and for many metabolic substances, including cancer promoters. These charged terminals form an anatomical

> *substrate for the first detection of weak electrochemical oscillations in peri-*
> *cellular fluid, including field potentials arising in activity of adjacent cells*
> *or as tissue components of environmental fields. [Adey, 1993.]*

The IEE report also echoes these findings, telling us:

> *There is some experimental support for interaction models which involve*
> *specific membrane receptors. [IEE, 1991.]*

It would seem that it is this order of bioelectrical activity that the body consciousness monitors, and it is not difficult to appreciate how much of an alien intrusion severely modulated microwaves, for example, would represent to this harmonious and subtle system. However, to my knowledge, nobody else has published such bioelectromagnetic links with visitation experiences, and I am certain that vast tracts of researched data await, which, under the right direction, would reveal further aspects that would dovetail into information that I have gathered as an investigator into these bizarre consciousness effects.

Another key passage from Adey's paper will give the reader some idea of the bioelectromagnetic 'subculture' which exists in the biological and electrical-engineering sciences:

> *What has been learned about mechanisms of EM field interactions with*
> *living organisms and biomolecular systems? The answer depends on the*
> *level of organization at which the question is directed in a hierarchical*
> *system. In studies at cellular and subcellular levels, a spectrum of imposed*
> *EM fields, ranging from extremely low frequency to microwaves, have*
> *proved unique tools, not only revealing essential aspects of mechanisms of*
> *interaction, but also disclosing much new knowledge about intrinsic orga-*
> *nization of cells and tissues, particularly in normal and abnormal regu-*
> *lation of cell growth, including tumor formation. [Adey, 1993.]*

This is the extremely specialized scientific end of the EM pollution lobby, and this key concept of body consciousness is implied in such perspectives, and phrases like 'intrinsic organization of cells and tissues' certainly point the way towards regarding the body as an autonomous entity. However, another extract from Adey's paper comes even closer, and reiterates the EM nature of communication between cells:

> *Recent observations have opened doors to new concepts of communication*
> *between cells as they whisper together across the barrier of cell membranes.*
> *Regulation of cell surface chemical events by weak EM fields indicates a*
> *major amplification of initial weak triggers associated with binding of*
> *hormones, antibodies and neurotransmitters to their specific binding sites.*
> *[Adey, 1993.]*

Therefore, Adey does, in fact, specifically link the altered reactivity of cells and tissues to EM pollution, and presents a central concept of the holistic approach – that man's natural EM environment has been suddenly disturbed. It is a theme which permeates the symbology of alien-abduction experience and is responsible for the dramatic physiological changes experiencers undergo after such visitation events.

> *Is there a natural EM environment, and how has this been changed by man? All life on earth has evolved in a sea of natural low-frequency EM fields. They originate in terrestrial and extraterrestrial sources. Thunderstorm activity in equatorial Africa and the Amazon basin contributes huge amounts of ELF energy that is ducted world-wide between the ionosphere and the earth's surface ... Over the last century, this natural background has changed sharply with the introduction of a vast range of man-made devices and systems. These artificial fields expose humans in the home, workplace and environment to spectral peaks typically many orders of magnitude above natural background levels ... There are ELF peaks at power system frequencies and in the radio-frequency/microwave spectrum from AM and FM broadcasting, TV and radar emissions. [Adey, 1993.]*

It is this key concept – that man, in the course of evolution, previously only had to adapt to the natural EM environment and, in evolutionary terms, the proliferation of artificial fields has been extremely sudden – which is implicit in the ecological concerns that experiencers develop after an 'abduction' event. Humankind has not had time to adapt, and the body consciousness is evidently acutely aware of this abrupt disruption to the natural EM environment. Therefore, the body initiates visionary phenomena to the conscious mind via the unconscious, protesting and indicating that this is the cause of its own disruption; it does this through individual statements within the physiology of individuals, otherwise known as 'experiencers' or 'abductees'.

POST-ENCOUNTER PHYSIOLOGICAL AND ENVIRONMENTAL CHANGES

THE AVELEY EVENT AND SHARED EXPERIENCES

Probably one of the most well-documented examples of an apparently shared event was compiled by UK investigator Andrew Collins in his appraisal (Collins, 1974) of a 1974 multiple-experiencer event – *The Aveley Abduction*– and it is worth a short digression to comment on shared events generally.

As with all so-called 'shared experiences', once the logistics and background of the event are examined closely, the shared aspect collapses, the only truly shared factor being, say the sighting of the fireball which triggers it. The primary fracture in this collapse is the fact that the Aveley case did not come to the attention of investigators until 4 *years* after it took place, which gives the percipients plenty of time to discuss it and exchange information, not to mention develop a thriving belief system. This also applies to the famous Betty and Barney Hill case, where it was 2 *years* before the experience was investigated and documented. The Pascagoula dual experience in the USA is often held up as a valid example of a shared experience, but this case, now that it has gone into the history of ufology, has been subjected to a revisionist interpretation whereby it is maintained that the two percipients were immediately separated after the event and interviewed by the law officers. However, before Hopkinsesque 'abductology' and the advent of the subjective/objective debate, the very early accounts of this case in the literature simply relate how the younger of two men fell unconscious at the start, after a large blue light came close to them across a stretch of water; the weird aliens and 'examination' were only experienced by the other man, who *seemingly* remained conscious.

However, the details of the Aveley event that Collins unwittingly documents provide us with a clear example of post-encounter physiological changes that are typical, and these were accompanied by equally typical environmental phenomena caused by power surges through their home. The event took place in the autumn of 1974, as the group, referred to by Collins as the Avis family, were driving through a semi-rural area one evening. During their journey, as they travelled below and along the length of some power lines, they encountered a low aerial light which seemed to follow the car but could have been a corona effect on the lines themselves, as the road and the power lines ran parallel. Then, strangely, they suddenly entered a bank of luminous green fog, or mist, from which they emerged 3 hours later, according to their account, although the period may have been shorter. Their two young children remained asleep on the back seat. A third child, the mother and the husband, through hypnotic regression, later recalled a complex and lengthy encounter with at least two types of alien entity, an examination of their bodies and the interior of a huge 'flying saucer'.

However, we are concerned here with their revised post-encounter outlook and life-style, as reflected in their altered reactivity to the environment. This involved control of food allergies, chemical sensitivities and stress-management strategies, demonstrating how their load threshold was severely transgressed by irradiation, inducing a make-or-break situation. This physiological crisis was accompanied by, and embodied within, vivid symbolic enactments of the alien-abduction vision, induced by exposure to self-grounding fields from power lines, an electric fireball or corona discharge close above and prolonged enclosure in an 'electrical mist', which was also a type of unclassified atmospheric phenomenon (UAP). It must be remembered that such sensitivities must have been present before the encounter, but at functional subclinical levels, and that this was in fact the case is also evidenced by the changes which took place after the event. Significantly, in a private conversation with me, Collins told me that the mother *had been struck by lightning 3 weeks before this bizarre event*, but this had not been included in the report as its significance was not apparent until he had recently read my work several years later.

Collins's report relates:

After the incident, several notable changes occurred in all of the family. Although mostly in John and Elaine (parents), the children also went through changes. In addition to this, many odd events took place on the road and inside and outside the house ... Soon after the incident, John suffered a nervous breakdown for no apparent reason. He is not sure of the exact date but it was before Christmas (i.e. within two months of the encounter). Due to the breakdown, John had to give up his job and did not work again until September 1975. In September, a job 'fell into his lap', a job which he had wanted to do for many years, this being working with the mentally handicapped. He now felt much more confident in himself, but this could quite well have been due to him recovering from the nervous breakdown. He kept this job until July 1977 ... He is now working for himself and he is hoping to launch a career in teaching arts and crafts.

Elaine has also become more self-confident and since September 1975 has attended college – something she had wanted to do for many years. Kevin (the son aged ten years), who was backward in his reading at school, suddenly begun to get better and is now way ahead of his reading age ... John, Elaine (mother), Kevin and Karen (one of the very young children who were asleep throughout the encounter) all gave up eating meat and now cannot even stand the smell of it. John and Elaine now feel very strongly about this pointing out that animals should not be killed so that people can eat ... they both admit that on occasion they have tried to eat fish or meat but both freely admit that the taste makes them feel ill.

They are both very conscious of what they eat. No foods with any preservatives, colourings, flavourings or anything else unnatural are ever bought now. They do eat health foods to a certain degree. John and Elaine both now feel very strongly about conservation of the environment ... John feels that we are gradually destroying our lives by abusing our environment. His views are now very strong about cutting down trees, taking away hedgerows, taking oil from below the ground, pollution and other similar matters. Whereas both John and Elaine liked 'a good drink' before the incident, they hardly touch alcohol at all now ... Just before Christmas 1974 (i.e. soon after the encounter), John who had until then smoked up to 60–70 cigarettes a day, suddenly gave up smoking completely. Since then he has not wanted a cigarette and now hates the smell of them. Both feel that doctors are overused and that people just go for the sake of going and are prescribed useless medicines. Neither ever take tablets or medicine. The only tablets that are taken are biochemical (i.e. natural) tissue salts. Several other smaller changes can be seen in John, one of which I believe is a stronger personality and a more persuasive attitude. Also, he resents raising his voice to his children now. [Collins, 1974.]

Comment

To his credit, Collins has documented these changes quite objectively, with no bias towards an interpretation that explains them in terms of aliens monitoring the health of the human race. However, if this were the case, readers must ask themselves how it is that, out of all the aspects that could potentially interest ET visitors, they select the very aspects of environmental sensitivities and holistic medicine ethos that are also at the centre of the EM-pollution approach? It must be remembered that such environmental concerns would have been long before the present-day 'Green' movement began and anachronistically stood out in sharp relief, much to the bemusement of those who attempted to analyse the case at the time. It is no coincidence that these experiencers should alter their diet so dramatically, to the point of becoming vegetarian and avoiding food additives, and assume an ideology to accompany and support such changes. Similarly, the avoidance of tobacco, alcohol and medications is typical of acquired chemical sensitivities, and both food and chemical abstention is rationalized by ecological and self-healing concerns.

It is equally non-coincidental that these strategies reflect the holistic medicine ethos and the load-phenomenon concept quite independently. This revision of intake and acquired ideology are typical of post-encounter effects and, from the comments about a new emotional stability and increased educational performance in the case of the child, the newly acquired management of sensitivities has resulted in an improved performance overall. The removal of the sort of uncontrollable mood swings and inability to concentrate that coping with masked allergies brings would be typical. It has been found that many adults lose the ability to read and write during allergic reactions to food.

It does certainly seem that young Kevin was battling against masked food allergies which inhibited his performance at school. This is where an individual has become literally addicted to a specific food to which he/she is allergic and abstention from it induces such reactions as a depressed lethargy, 'zombie-like' states, panic attacks, inability to concentrate and trembling. Such withdrawal symptoms can be avoided at their onset by taking the food/drink again, which induces an elevated mood effect. However, once the body processes the food, a craving is set up, which usually cannot be satisfied by a child during school hours. Distinctive signs of masked food allergies include a pale complexion and dark crescents/puffiness under the eyes and/or a characteristic double wrinkle, known as Dennie's sign (see p. 20). To give some idea of the sort of symptoms that Kevin may have suffered, consider the points raised in a questionnaire designed to detect allergy-related behaviour and performance problems in schoolchildren. It asks:

> *Is the child: hyperactive/restless, clumsy, listless and tired, hostile and fights a lot, seems 'spaced out', talks too much or talks nonsense, good vocabulary but cannot read, cannot draw, print or write or has a short concentration span? [Rapp, 1979.]*

The incipient 'nervous breakdown' that John went through was symptomatic of a severely exceeded load phenomenon due to his exposure to fields during the encounter, which, it should be remembered, was really an encounter with electricity. It would have been during this period of systemic collapse that John was forced to confront and to begin to manage his sensitivities, whereas previously he had 'muddled through' them. The subsequent change of occupation also reflects the removal of the emotional load, with which John would have been coping, of being in 'a square peg in a round hole' job that frustrated personal expression. Such areas are not 'merely' psychological but have very real biochemical repercussions – as numerous high-blood-pressure/heart-attack victims in 'ulcer jobs' will confirm – and they again reflect the 'wholeness' of the individual, i.e. the holistic concept. It is not known to what extent this aspect played a part in John's life, but it must be remembered that it was evidently a contributory factor in a synergistic collection of undermining factors. However, even this new expression of self was later converted into an occupation with a directly artistic output, and the newly acquired poetic activities also reflect an unprecedented (for the individual) creative outlet. Also, incessant writing, especially poetry, is typical of the hypergraphia and enhanced temporal-lobe lability resulting from exposure to an MEE, which the encounter represents.

Sensitivities to medication certainly appear to be present, and antibiotics are often especially contra-indicated. Interestingly, both adults seem to have spontaneously adopted a holistic approach, to the point of becoming antagonistic to mainstream medicine! The inclusion of health foods in the diet and eradication of food additives, probably of the E-range, are also indicative of food/chemical sensitivities, and represent an area where the two overlap. Overall, it is apparent that the holistic/load-phenomenon aspect in conjunction with EH allows us to understand the biological function which these visitation experiences fulfil. It also shows how altered reactivity can lead to altered beliefs, as both govern the ability of the experiencer to adapt to an environment that, to a large extent, has become alien to them, or rather, to their body's physiology.

ENVIRONMENTAL EFFECTS

In Collins's report, environmental effects have been called 'strange happenings inside the house' and, although they are included here under the banner of effects in the environment, some of them belong to a category which includes perceptual effects. Collins's report relates:

> During the three years since the incident, several strange things have happened inside the house. Several items have disappeared from various rooms without a trace, or have turned up a few days later somewhere else. Objects that have been mislaid completely include pens, pencils, a roll of film and a hole puncher. Of course, with three young children around the house, it is quite possible that they had picked them up and mislaid them. [Collins, 1974.]

While there have been reports of objects vanishing in the vicinity of electrical generators, cases that have come to my attention so far have failed to convince me of the objective reality of this effect. However, I have found that experiencers do undergo periods of automatic behaviour in which they remove things and have no memory of having done so, sometimes hiding them in extremely inaccessible places. The lady with the knitting pattern mentioned on p. 121 is a good example of this. With at least two confirmed experiencers in a household, and three children, all of whom are evidently living in a hot spot, the chances for automatisms are greatly increased, as prolonged irradiation can induce epileptiform conditions. However, such apparent dematerializations can also be produced by the Hutchison effect, whereby objects are spontaneously relocated. Collins continues:

> One day, when Elaine was on the telephone ... the back door flew open wildly, crashing against the wall. This was very odd as she always kept the back door locked. This happened again under similar circumstances

during October 1977. This time John was present. He said that the kitchen was suddenly filled with a smell like lavender. John has also smelt a sickly sweet smell inside the house on numerous occasions. He explained that it usually seemed to suddenly waft across the room, and then fade away. [Collins, 1974.]

Here it is highly enlightening to repeat the passage by renowned EM researcher Anne Silk in Buckinghamshire, UK, who wrote:

*In the literature on psychical phenomena are reports of church bells that ring without human hand, doorbells ring with nobody present, **locked doors and windows fly open** ... pictures move on walls, people hear strange sounds, feel nauseous and fall to the ground. They hear footsteps, heavy lorry engines running and the heart may beat extremely fast ... there may be a wide range of light phenomena, spontaneous sensations of smell and auditory hallucinations of long-lasting periods of music as specific focal seizures in the brain which are triggered by geomagnetic and geoelectric fields in houses built over faults. In seismology, reports of such effects are collected as indicators of tectonic activity, and are known as diagnostics ... These effects may be recorded by the SPR [Society for Psychical Research], however, they are also listed in publications by the British Geological Survey such as the Mercalli and Principia Tables, Rossi Forel Intensity Scale and the MSK-81 Scale. Due to what are known as long-period motions, far distant earthquakes can produce effects up to hundreds of kilometres from the epicentre. Such felt effects are themselves graded. Earth waves or seismic waves, transmit energy by vibration. Low energy waves are known as elastic waves (P – primary, or push; S – secondary, or shear) and at an interface, Love waves are generated. At the surface of the earth are Rayleigh waves of special condition, which follow an elliptical path. The earth itself can generate eddy currents and in a near vertical sheet-like conductor these currents will flow in rotational paths and themselves produce secondary magnetic fields.*

The energies and wavelengths produced by such deep earth movements all traverse the known brainwave frequencies and can, in sensitive persons, produce kindling spikes in the brain from the ambient magnetic field. In the UK, magnetic fields over basalt dykes, sills and some intrusions can reach many thousands of nanoTesla. Over magnetite deposits 2 000,000 nT has been measured. When a human moves across, or lives in such a spot, his kindling reflex will be lower and, as the field traverses the brain, due to Lenz's Law, electric currents will be produced with ensuing biochemical change. All sensory modalities (vision, taste, hearing, touch and smell) can be involved.' [Silk, 1996.]

This *tour de force* of causative mechanisms independently provides information that certainly suggests that our experiencers are living in an area which is both rich in seismic diagnostics and an EM hot spot, albeit one which includes natural fields from the geology of the area. Sudden smells of lavender are typical of the olfactory hallucinations induced by focal seizures in the brain. Locked doors may fly open during micro-tremors that do not register as overt vibration, and the phenomenon that Collins mentions next is also indicative of hot-spot activity:

> *On several occasions, both John and Elaine have heard a humming noise from right outside the house. It is likened to a droning and is mostly heard after midnight, usually after they have retired to bed. The noise seems to start like a distant aircraft and then intensifies to a very loud level. It then seems to move across the top of the house. On each occasion it suddenly cuts out, it does not fade away. The humming has been known to last up to half an hour. Once John did pluck up enough courage to look outside, but saw nothing. Elaine's sister Anne often babysits for the family and she too heard the noise on one occasion. [Collins, 1974.]*

We are left to decide whether this sound is internally or externally apprehended and, as the sister heard it also and presumably is not an experiencer, I am attracted towards the conclusion that the house is situated on a fault which is subject to episodic tectonic strain, thereby inducing the phenomenon of *geosound*, which is produced by the combined effects of mechanical strain across rock masses and EM activity induced by piezoelectric processes. The roaring sound, which is compared to a jet engine in the report, is certainly typical of geosound. Collins continues:

> *Also a type of 'clicking' noise has been heard inside the living room on a couple of occasions. Anne, Elaine's sister was present when it was heard and described it as sounding like a rustling noise. On one occasion John went across to where he thought it was coming from, only to find that it seemed to move away from him towards another corner of the room. The 'clicks' are again only heard late at night, and are very sharp clear and loud. [Collins, 1974.]*

Readers will recall the Page effect (p. 48) which creates an auditory sound wave in ferrous materials when they are subjected to a strong magnetic field which suddenly drops, the 'click' being the point of demagnetization due to this sudden field cessation. Another perceptual effect induced by irradiation by microwaves is microwave hearing (see p. 124) and, in fact, Collins reports on a number of anomalous sounds perceived by the family, which are typical of hot spot locations:

On three occasions a kind of 'morse code' has been heard inside John and Elaine's bedroom. On the first two occasions this was only heard by Elaine. On the third the noise was also heard by John. On the first occasion, it was heard at 00.30 hrs. Elaine was in bed and John was downstairs. Suddenly 'morse code' started and it sounded as though it was coming from inside the bedroom. This only lasted for a minute or so, but was long enough for Elaine to remember a small part of the sequence. It did not make any sense to her. On the second occasion it was heard for much longer and again came from John and Elaine's bedroom. Some dots and dashes were scribbled down although again, no letters could be discerned. [Collins, 1974.]

This is typical of microwave hearing. However, considering the whole of Collins's report, especially the earlier section which describes dietary changes and life-style revisions, it quite independently (for it was written in the 1970s) illustrates the typical physiological changes that 'abductees' go through after their experience. We are considering individuals whose lives are, unbeknown to them, burdened with nutritional, chemical, EM and emotional loads, which they are coping with on an everyday basis. These individuals are then thrust into a physiological make-or-break situation by their exposure to an MEE, i.e. an electric fireball or some other UAP, which is 'identified' as a UFO and abduction by aliens from another world. The green fog has also been reported by others at the onset of their experience and is an 'electrical mist' that accumulates below power lines.

However, what is really at stake is the subjects' state of health, evidenced by the distressing physical symptoms suffered by experiencers when exposed to an allergen or an EM frequency to which they are hypersensitive. Because such sensitivities are thrown into sharp relief via the abduction experience, experiencers are forced to confront them, and an awareness and implementation of management strategies takes place. These are accompanied by beliefs which embody, somewhat implicitly, the holistic approach to health and well-being. It must be stated that other investigators/researchers have come to very similar conclusions about experiencers and their sensitivities. Professor Kenneth Ring, at the University of Connecticut, USA, wrote to endorse my approach, having discovered the incidence of EH in 'abductees' quite independently from me; he refers to experiencers as being 'psychological sensitives'.

Also, Dr David Richey (Brattleboro, Vermont, USA), following the same path, wrote of experiencers:

... preliminary indications are those who are psychologically sensitive are also likely to be immunologically, physiologically and/or environmentally

sensitive. They are people who have allergies or autoimmune disorders, who are unable to tolerate fluorescent lights, and/or are profoundly affected by changes in the weather or season. [Richey, 1994.]

This identification of environmental sensitivities by Dr Richey is independently confirmed by Dr C. W. Smith and his colleagues, who, in his list of questions for EH patients, asks:

Are symptoms brought on by weather changes, or by the electrical changes in the atmosphere that precede the arrival of weather fronts, thunderstorms, and desert or mountain winds? [Smith et al., 1986.]

However, the majority of those who dabble in the world of anomalies have developed no proper understanding of the fundamentals (i.e. environmental sensitivities) of the nature of these unusual experiences, and have certainly failed to grasp the *medical* implications of the changes that can follow alien-abduction experiences. For example, consider an extract by British spectator Kevin McClure:

More recently, physical evidence has taken a secondary role in providing 'proof' of the reality of the abduction experience. Greater dependence is placed on the apparent changes in the behaviour and lifestyle of those who claim to be experiencers, and in claims of newly acquired or remembered psychic abilities. This argument seems particularly weak. Many of us will know somebody who has been converted to a new belief or faith. They will know the vigour with which the convert approaches his or her 'new life', attempting to make amends for the 'old life', to live as their new faith demands, to demonstrably be a 'different' person. It happens to a degree with slimmers, with those successfully recovering from alcohol or drug dependency, or even with giving up smoking. It can happen when you fall in love ... We are currently moving into a 'post abduction psychicism' phase of seeking validation of claims of abduction. [McClure, 1995.]

It is especially ironic that McClure calls claims of post-abduction psychic enhancement 'weak', for he is evidently unaware of Dr Richey's and Professor Ring's conclusions regarding 'psychological sensitivity', which they have independently identified with EH, based on their empirical work with 'abductees'. The central thrust of McClure's argument *cannot have been borne out of firsthand investigation* because he fails to identify the *physiological basis* of these changes: the *physical symptoms* that are produced when these experiencers are exposed to allergens, including an EM field, or even EH itself, which becomes evident through even casual investigations of experiencers. Also, McClure appears unaware of the environmental sensitivities syndrome and its connection with the abduction experience, and seems to regard the post-encounter physiological revolution in these individuals as comparable with 'getting religion' in cases where an adoption of belief alone is involved. To compare such dramatic alterations in reactivity, diet, chemical intake and outlook with a slimmer's dietary zeal not only throws the baby out with the bathwater, but efficiently disposes of a whole kindergarten.

It also somewhat belittles the struggles of these experiencers, who are real people, not just pseudonyms in a book, and are victims of EM pollution. They are often battling against the odds by coping with not only their sensitivities, epileptiform sensations and bizarre visions, but also often the ridicule of those who dismiss these health problems as non-existent; among these, it would appear, McClure could be counted.

The 'alien/ghost' connection

Probably the most important aspect of the EM-pollution approach is that it provides a 'unified theory' for UFO-related events and the paranormal. That is to say, it has become virtually a truism for investigators to find that 'abductees' have a history of psychic experiences, often reaching back to childhood and often including encounters with other entities and apparitions. This is a factor that the extraterrestrial hypothesis (ETH) enthusiasts feel particularly uncomfortable with, because it suggests to even the most casual observer of alien-contact/abduction experiences that seeing 'ghosts' and encountering 'aliens' both fall into the same family of experiences, which is in fact the case. The ETH mythology would be stretched to breaking point in trying to explain how the same people have been plagued by both aliens from another planet and spirits of the dead. In fact, such EH individuals see formed figures (and other hallucinations) of many types, and it is my experience that apparitional experiences are a forerunner to UFO-related encounters, although this is not a rule set in stone and 'abductees' often continue to see ghostly figures on an episodic basis. Some division appears according to whether type A or type B EH is involved, i.e. whether an MEE is evident or not. Therefore, to round off the Aveley account, Collins records John's earlier apparitional experiences:

> *During his childhood, John had two experiences where a ghost-type apparition was seen. The first of these was whilst John was playing in a cellar of an old house on a bombsite. Looking round, he saw a small child standing in the cellar, covered in dust. On enquiring who he was, the boy turned round and just disappeared. The second experience was in a hall in which John was helping to arrange the scenery for a gang show. As only those helping were supposed to be in the hall, John was surprised to see a small boy standing near the stage. Suddenly, the apparition disappeared. [Collins, 1974.]*

The propensity to see such phenomena has been linked to EH by Dr C. W. Smith and Dr Jean Monro, who work with such patients, although it must be remembered that not all confrontations with apparitions involve fields, as some have a purely psychological basis. As if the consistent occurrence of such psychical phenomena among 'abductees' were not enough to indicate a common denominator, there are cases where 'ghosts' appear to the percipient actually *during* their UFO-related encounter, as I described in *UFOs – Psychic Close Encounters* [Budden, 1995a].

Place memories: a theory

Throughout this exploration of the EM-pollution approach, a distinction has been made between endogenous hallucination, i.e. imagery originating from the nervous system of the experiencer, and place memories, which have been described as 'recordings' imprinted in the fabric of a building, road, hill, quarry, etc. Such 'recordings' have been said to have been imbued into the environmental water of a location, because it has become evident to practitioners of environmental medicine (e.g. Dr C. W. Smith and Dr Jean Monro) that water can 'remember' frequencies; indeed, frequencies can be deliberately imprinted into it and it is such preparations that provide symptomatic relief for allergy and EH sufferers. [Smith & Best, 1989, Chapter 6.]

These same practitioners suggest that EH-status individuals are able to detect such imprinted fields by means of the EM fields which they themselves emit during their allergic reactions, and that they unconsciously scan an environment in this way, perceiving other fields as imagery, otherwise known as apparitions or ghosts. However, nobody seems to have emphasized how such ghostly 'recordings' could come about in the first place. I think it works something like this.

A building built above a fault is frequently irradiated by piezoelectric and piezomagnetic fields. The inhabitants eventually develop EH due to such prolonged exposure and every time they are exposed in this way they emit their own personal fields. In fact, it seems that they simply re-radiate the ambient field so that it is more coherent or 'beam-like'. Therefore, the geological field and the EH individual's own field are emitted simultaneously in the location and, at some point, the source-field emission is of a quality and amplitude sufficient to be filtered through the EH individual, whose body acts like a prism, concentrating the field which becomes encoded in the physical surroundings as a moving image. When the field drops, the 'recording' process also stops.

Later, new people come to live in the building and also eventually develop EH due to geological hot-spot activity; they react allergically to the geological field when it is emitted and emit a field themselves. This field scans the environment and the 'recording' from a bygone time is perceived not only as a visual image, but also in other sensory forms, e.g. accompanying sound. If any of the new inhabitants are EH when they arrive, they will experience the 'recording' as soon as there is a geological field emission. It may be that other stressors are needed for the 'recording emission' to occur; it is also my feeling that magnetic fields act as recording media as well, and, under optimum conditions, can be imprinted with sensory modalities from the human system. In such cases, an objective image appears whenever a field is present. Practical experiments to this end need to be devised and carried out – there is nothing so convincing as empirical demonstration. However, behind such 'haunting' phenomena are the aspects of EH that are dealt with in the more mundane clinical settings of the hospital environment.

ELECTRICAL HYPERSENSITIVITY AND ENVIRONMENTAL SENSITIVITIES
OBJECTIVE TEST CRITERIA

There is a range of biological effects and perceptual phenomena that may be either recognized in the descriptions of cases in the literature or gleaned from experiencers firsthand. It has been suggested to me that I should not take the testimony of experiencers as evidence of their sensitivities or sensations, and that I should use other methods which exclude subjectivity. There are a number of tests that the investigator can carry out. One is the 'magnetic response' (MR) discovered by Reiter, whereby intracranial stimulation with strong magnets in the 1000–2000Gs range (or much less in some cases) will produce characteristic sensations in experiencers but not in non-experiencers, as long as it is remembered that the elderly tend to have a reduced or non-existent response; I also suspect that anemic subjects may not be triggered because of the absence of magnetite in their system.

I have also found that the close presence of an illuminated fluorescent tube can have devastating effects on experiencers and, on occasions, they have run from the room as soon as I have switched one on. This is because such tubes emit electrical fields and RFs as well as light; testers should therefore make sure that the tube is full-spectrum lighting, as this tends to be more easily tolerated by EH subjects.

Another, somewhat ill-advised method of detecting sensitivities is to spray the room with an air-freshener aerosol, wear aftershave or perfume, or expose the subject to a small amount of domestic gas by turning the tap on for a few seconds. However, it should be remembered that all of these practices are potentially harmful and may produce an asthmatic attack, an acute mood swing, trembling, heart palpitations, sweating, or a drop attack through sudden unconsciousness. At least, the subject will feel 'weird', become distracted, complain of a headache, see flashes of light, feel weak and become unable to walk and may become mute. As investigations depend on interviewing the experiencer, this last factor is especially unwanted. I have also seen experiencers become rigid, tremble violently and throw their head back and howl hysterically for up to 10 minutes non-stop. Full-blown allergic reactions *can* be extremely dramatic and distressing, so be warned! However, Reiter's MR testing is safe as long as it is carried out in a graduated and controlled way, starting with exposure of the subject to weak magnets and working up gradually to stronger ones. I know one experiencer who can induce the sense of presence and the physical fear reaction with a novelty fridge magnet (see p. 244)!

The people who have suggested that I use such objective criteria are those who have no knowledge or experience of people with environmental sensitivities or of the holistic ethos. While I can understand their concern for objectivity, I also know from experience that if people with such sensitivities say they have them, they do. In fact, the very opposite is more likely to be true: 'abductees' who are aware of my approach usually want to maintain the view that they have encountered real aliens and deny such sensitivities, not wishing to be identified as EH. In fact, it is becoming increasingly difficult to obtain unbiased information due to subjects' reluctance to reveal that they fall into the sensitivity groups which I predict, and which have these experiences. However, I must confess that, at such times, I am tempted to get out the aerosols and I may also suddenly decide that the room needs the benefits of fluorescent lighting ...

Also, asking subjects about such seemingly obscure aspects as whether they ever experience a metallic taste in their mouth, or whether they have ever been struck by lightning, is not the same as asking them questions about their UFO encounters, because, usually, experiencers want to be identified as someone who has been in contact with aliens. That is to say, many are fully aware of the implications of questions about their 'alien contact', and welcome such an identification, because it raises their status within the UFO groups as at least someone interesting, and often makes them into 'special people' in the eyes of those who attend these groups. Many know only too well that 'coming out' as an 'abductee' can confer intrigued attention by investigators and others at the international UFO conferences held each year; it makes them sought after by radio and TV, on which they appear regularly, and basically provides them with a level of fame that others with greater talents may envy. While they may not fare so well with the press at times, this is now changing, as alien-abduction experiences are gradually gaining recognition. However, the point being made is that 'taking a history' from experiencers (in the medical sense of conferring a diagnosis or identifying their sensitivities) is in an entirely different league from asking them to describe their alien encounters. That is to say, they are completely unaware of the implications of the questions about allergies and EH (see Note 10).

Also, this concern for objectivity through non-reliance on testimony has become desirable in ufological circles due to the practices of certain well-known investigators/authors from the mid-1980s to the mid-1990s. It has become perfectly clear that, when vulnerable and attention-seeking experiencers are exposed to investigators with an apparently sincere, sympathetic and avuncular approach, who can also implicitly offer them stardom in their forthcoming books, they can be made to testify to almost anything, no matter how outlandish.

Returning to the objective criteria for environmental sensitivities, there are other less hazardous tests, but these have the disadvantage of requiring medical training and equipment. It has been found that contraction/dilation of the pupil of the eye can be detected when EH subjects are exposed to a field to which they are sensitive. This field, incidently, can be extremely frequency-specific rather than being related to field strength, and a specialized optical instrument (an *iridometer*) is used for this purpose.

CLINICAL DIAGNOSIS AND TREATMENT OF ELECTROMAGNETIC HYPERSENSITIVITY

Doctors C. W. Smith, Jean Monro and Ray Choy of the Breakspear Hospital have developed a medical protocol for diagnosing and treating EH. Their papers, published in *Clinical Ecology*, underline a number of intriguing aspects of this condition, and emphasize a fact that should not be lost on investigators: that its diagnosis is a medical procedure and not simply an investigative one to be carried out by the layperson. They comment:

> *Although [testing] is carried out using weak environmental electromagnetic fields, comparable to those which ordinarily leak out of domestic appliances, television receivers and personal computers, it must be regarded as a clinical procedure for such patients and should not be attempted without the immediate availability of facilities and staff medically competent to treat anaphylaxis (systemic shock). [Smith et al., 1986. See also Choy et al., 1986.]*

A review and an emphasis

The onset of symptoms of EH was described on p. 81, and exposure can precipitate unconsciousness and a drop attack; this is one way in which experiencers can undergo the 'time-lapse' or 'missing-time' experience so beloved of ETH enthusiasts. At this point, it is worth remembering that knowledge of the clinical procedures surrounding EH is not simply an unintended and digressive diversion into the dynamics of clinical ecology but also contributes to an in-depth understanding of the *unrecognized consciousness effects* induced by EM pollution, e.g. the alien-contact experience and other 'visitation' phenomena. Dr Jean Monro has spoken to me at some length about 'the visions', as she terms them, which her EH patients have experienced. In mentioning some cases she has treated, she related how patients 'expunged' these visions on their return to normal, i.e. saw them for what they were – vivid internal realities. She also told me how, very often, EH patients have their eyes open while experiencing visions, and often become mute. Others sometimes described their visions as they perceived them. As mentioned, the clinicians who treat EH are aware of such visionary experiences but do not appear to be very interested in them. They regard them as symptomatic of the condition which they are treating and no more, unaware that a whole mythology/industry around the world has been built upon these accounts of visitors from outer space or spirits of the dead.

CLINICAL PROCEDURES

On entering the Breakspear Hospital you are greeted by a prominent notice asking you not to go further if you are wearing perfume, aftershave, etc. This is, of course, to protect patients from adverse reactions to these volatile chemical products. Also, EH patients are separated by time and location within the building because of an effect whereby the EM emissions of one can trigger an allergic response in another. Sometimes patients can tell simply by entering the foyer that EH testing is being carried out somewhere in the building. This is because such testing involves exposing EH subjects to measured levels of fields, under controlled clinical conditions; the doctors' comparison of this with testing for food allergies underscores the interchangeability of the two conditions, as implied in the description of the 'relay mechanism' (p. 74). That is to say, both food and chemicals interact with the human biological system at EM molecular levels in the cells and, by reproducing the frequencies involved, patients experience the same symptoms as they would if exposed to a food or chemical; they may describe a particular frequency as 'a perfume reaction' for example. The doctors elaborate on this basic description:

The procedure for testing and treating electrically hypersensitive patients described here is based on provocation-neutralization therapy. It appears that increasing the frequency of a coherent electromagnetic oscillation has the same clinical effect on electrically sensitive patients as increasing allergen dilution on patients sensitive to chemicals and foods. Thus, it is usually possible to find certain frequencies at which the allergic reaction stops, just as neutralizing dilutions of the allergen bring a halt to allergic reactions. In the electromagnetic case, it is the frequency and its coherence which is important; the field strength is less important so long as it is above the particular patient's threshold. [Smith et al., 1986.]

The concept of masked allergies, in which addiction to specific foods occurs, was outlined on p. 26. If the 'relay effect' is a genuine one, and fields can become 'infected' by existing allergic reactions, we should therefore find cases of addictions to fields alone and, in fact, we do. An account of 'field addiction' comes from John Hutchison, the researcher who developed 'the poltergeist machine' described on p. 62. He writes this in a letter to me:

I would agree to the addiction of EM waves very strongly, and actually feel the need for regular exposures. After the Canadian government took my lab (it's a long story) I had one 30 kHz broadband generator left that I would turn on simply for the feel of it. [Private correspondence.]

Food allergies and chemical sensitivities

In the EH-testing procedures at the Breakspear Hospital, the doctors 'take a history', which includes searching questions about the patients' degree of sensitivity, so that field-exposure testing does not trigger a severe reaction. (If the results of these enquiries are regarded as being reliable enough for clinical procedures, then they are equally so for investigators exploring visitation experiences; after all, these are just another symptom.) This information is supplemented by examining the patients' records of food and chemical sensitivities, which have been previously determined by exposing them to serial dilutions (graduated from 1 to 10) of the allergens; if the patients react to foods which have been greatly diluted (i.e. over 6 serial dilutions), this strongly suggests that they are EH.

From an investigator's point of view, we have already seen how the existence of food allergies, and, particularly, chemical sensitivities in an experiencer is a strong indicator of EH due to the 'relay mechanism'. That is to say, the presence of these sensitivities is indicative of living in a hot spot and, it would seem that they develop before EH, acting as a base for it. Therefore, the presence of the EH condition is indicative of environmental sensitivities that are already well developed, i.e. EH comes about as a chronic end-state. In fact, if the sensitivities to substances are high, it is recommended that EH testing is postponed 'until the overall burden of allergens has been reduced'.

This is, of course, a reference to the load phenomenon. That is to say, these strange consciousness effects come about when EH is overlaid upon established allergies; if the individual has not acquired such multiple sensitivities, then EH does not develop as readily because the regulatory systems of the body are not under prolonged assault from these other stressors and can adapt to such irradiation. One reason why people in occupational hot-spot situations do not develop EH as readily as those in the home is simply because of their behaviour at work. If people feel unwell at work because of irradiation, or any other cause for that matter, they go home. However, if they feel unwell at home, there is no obvious place for them to go (except to bed perhaps), especially if they are unaware of the irradiation.

Non-linear and synergistic factors

The doctors testing for EH next require information about the patients' reactions to electrical appliances, and also the distances between the appliance and the patients at which reactions occur. During interviews with experiencers, and using a tape-recorder, I have often been told that 'even that makes me feel funny'. Another aspect that is directly relevant to the onset of visions is the 'latent interval between exposure and reaction'. An important concept to realize is that reactions to fields are *non-linear* (Smith & Best, 1989). That is to say, when dealing with a biological system, there is an intrinsic unpredictability about reactions to fields, as there are so many variables and the stimulus-to-response relationship is not always a simple one; it requires clinical experience to discern the dynamics of reactions.

As an example of this, a case I dealt with involved an experiencer whose reactions were especially prone to occur when she was exposed to fields and stress, while having her period. In her body, stress and menstruation released a combination of chemicals that enhanced her electrical sensitivities, and reactions to field exposure could take place several hours afterwards. On one occasion, she was suddenly recruited as wardrobe mistress in a well-known 'haunted' theatre in London, taking over from someone whose son had just died under extremely tragic circumstances. The theatre itself is built over an underground river – an off-shoot from the nearby Thames – which emitted unhealthy geopathic stress.

The sudden responsibility of dealing with a team of demanding actors was extremely stressful and, as with so many experiencers, she was extremely sensitive to 'atmospheres', a feature typical of EH subjects.

This was not helped when, quite coincidentally, as soon as she arrived at the theatre, a photo of the recently deceased son peeled itself off the wall and fluttered to the floor at her feet. This was at the very moment when I was speaking to her on the phone! Hours later, when she was thankfully back at home, trying to unwind but still in an overstressed state, her television did something it had never done before: it came on by itself, and then went off, then on, then off – and so on for over 30 changes, stopping abruptly after several minutes. It will be remembered that one sign of EH is the emission of coherent (i.e. beam-like) fields as a whole-body effect, and such weird effects to electrical equipment/systems are absolutely typical, but are often identified as poltergeist activity. This account is to illustrate the non-linear aspect of field exposure, which can induce symptoms or environmental effects hours, or sometimes days, after exposure, as implied in the case histories of EH patients.

Further enquiries

Another pre-testing enquiry relates to this emission of personal fields:

> Do electrical gadgets always go wrong when used by the patient? If they do, can this be due to the devices triggering allergic responses in the patient who then emits electrical signals which in turn upset the electronic circuits. Patients often say that they are inept with all things electrical, including TV and video-recorder remote controls. [Smith & Best, 1989.]

The close relationship between chemical sensitivities and EH has been emphasized and the doctors ask about this:

> Ask if the patient has ever been sprayed with a pesticide. There seems to be a synergistic effect between exposure to certain chemicals and the sudden onset of electrical hypersensitivities.

And:

> The testing room should be in an environmentally-clean area, otherwise it will not be possible to distinguish electrical from chemical triggers. [Smith/Choy/Monro, 1989]

This condition emphasizes the synergistic mechanisms at work when allergic reactions involving an EM component take place. That is to say, the emission, from the body of the EH subject, of fields that have the potential to disturb the environment is sometimes triggered by the subject's combined exposure to both a chemical to which he/she is sensitive and a field. A passage by Dr C. W. Smith describes this well:

> The problems which allergy patients have described are very wide ranging. One patient had a robotic system in a factory completely malfunction

everytime he stood near it. Another has had the electronic ignition system on successive new cars fail as soon as an allergic reaction was triggered by fumes from a diesel truck in front … The subject area in electronics which deals with such problems is Electromagnetic Compatibility. [Smith & Best, 1989.]

It would seem that, in some cases, a chemical catalyst is needed before the body emits a field, and this again underlines the importance of the load-phenomenon concept. At this point, it should perhaps be re-emphasized that the body re-radiates ambient fields, transforming them into a more coherent form, rather like the way that a prism concentrates a broad light-source. It is these 'beams' which interfere with aspects in the environment, often identified as poltergeist activity.

CLINICAL TESTING FOR ELECTRICAL HYPERSENSITIVITY

Under the heading of suitable equipment, the Breakspear doctors have this to say:

To set up a facility for testing electrically-sensitive patients, it is only necessary to acquire some ordinary laboratory oscillators such as those used in industrial, university or school laboratories. These oscillators should together provide continuous frequency coverage from 0.1 Hz to at least 10 MHz. Additional coverage to 1 GHz or even 10 GHz is desirable … If leakage of electromagnetic fields from the case of such instruments does not trigger an allergic response at a distance of one to three meters, it is unlikely that the patient has a major problem with electrical hyper-sensitivity. [Smith et al., 1986.]

However, for the non-medical investigator, Reiter's MR is reliable, although caution is advised and testing should start with a weak magnet and only gradually move on to stronger ones (see p. 88).

The test procedure itself is basically a question of producing EM oscil-lations in the patient's environment. (The doctors' paper provides a diagram showing how the field or signal generator, known as an *oscillator*, should be set out on a table near the power outlets.) The patient should be asked to sit on a chair or bed opposite the tester on the other side of the room, and should not be able to see the dials of the oscillators or tell whether they are on or off. An oxygen cylinder and facilities for treat-ment of systemic shock should be available, but out of sight. The testing is 'blind', both to the medical practitioner who observes the symptoms and to the patient. Neither knows which frequencies, if any, are in the environment at any given moment. The tester logs the symptoms, as reported verbally, beside the record of the frequencies and the time, but does not disclose the electrical status. The patient should not be wearing any metal objects e.g. necklaces, watch-straps, etc., as ungrounded metal can re-radiate fields and distort, i.e. enhance, exposure levels, as stressed on p. 36.

Electromagnetic feedback

Interestingly, the paper by Smith and his colleagues comments on how the EM emissions of the patients being tested can set up EM feedback between themselves and the microwave oscillators used, in much the same way as sound amplifiers and microphones/pick-ups can set up the characteristic electronic squealing of audio feedback:

> *The authors prefer the old-fashioned, vacuum-tube microwave oscillators ... they have more highly-resonant microwave cavities and emit more coherent oscillations ... However, such highly resonant electrical circuits are capable of a coherent response to any incident radiation ... It has been found possible to trigger patient responses by tuning such resonant cavities, connected only to an antenna and without the oscillator functioning. In such cases, **the patient must be the source of radiation in the microwave region**. These patients can probably emit enough EM radiation to excite any electrical resonance in their environment. This in turn reinforces their reactions ... [Smith et al., 1986. My emphasis.]*

In *UFOs – Psychic Close Encounters* [Budden, 1995a] I introduced the concept of the 'signal link', where I argued that EH experiencers became electromagnetically connected to electric fireballs in the atmosphere via their personal field emissions, which are their response to field exposure. This seems to support the idea of a feedback effect developing between patient and equipment (as these doctors found during EH testing) because the equipment, like an electric fireball, also emits fields. Another phenomenon that can result from this EM-feedback response has been called street light interference (SLI). This is where street lights are affected as the EH subject comes close to them, causing them to malfunction. A magnetostrictive effect takes place in the critical contacts of the mechanism, which are lost by distortions induced by the magnetic component of the feedback field; these return to normal once the field from the EH subject drops, allowing them to function again. The fact that this SLI phenomenon was reported by experiencer Whitley Strieber, who encountered ball lightnings (BLs) in his formative years, is an indicator of EH status.

Returning to the testing procedure, the signal to which the patients are exposed begins at a low frequency and is gradually increased until they report a reaction, or display a physical symptom, such as weakness, disorientation, unconsciousness, etc. Such levels are noted, and are used in the treatment of the patients' EH condition. It should be re-emphasized that this is a clinical procedure, not just an investigative one.

THE TREATMENT OF ELECTRICAL HYPERSENSITIVITY

The basic description of the treatment of EH gives an impression of almost ludicrous simplicity: water is placed in a tube and imprinted with a frequency; the patient holds it and feels better. It is precisely such cheap and effective field-oriented treatments which the drug industries appear to find so threatening. A doctor at the Breakspear Hospital related how a major international drug company paid $1 million to a well-known British TV documentary team to make a programme which effectively smeared the reputation of the Breakspear, who subsequently sued. The hospital received a public and published apology from the TV programme years later, but by then the damage to their good reputation was done.

As far as the treatment of EH is concerned, the doctors involved are able to alleviate the symptoms of EH sufferers. They describe a process whereby, once the frequency that induces an allergic reaction in the patient has been established, another can be found that neutralizes its effects; this can then be imprinted into tubes of water which the patients hold to alleviate their symptoms and desensitize them. These tubes can be frozen and sent through the post as a 'repeat prescription' if required, although the doctors mention that, if they are transported by rail, they may be exposed to electrical fields and their efficacy may be undermined. This neutralizing frequency is imprinted into the tubes of water by inserting such tubes into a coil and passing a field through it.

If I had not been married to someone with such sensitivities, I would not have been particularly convinced when reading about this procedure, just as I may have doubted the value of drinking boiled bark juice containing quinine for malaria if I had no knowledge of organic chemistry or tropical medicine. The real factor which convinces me of the value of anything is its widespread acceptance and use, and because quinine has passed this 'test' as a treatment for malaria, I do not question its value. Regarding imprinting water with frequencies, I find the procedure to be not only acceptable, but also confirmed by my own observations.

I have tried wrapping a bar of chocolate and a slab of wood in separate plain opaque packets of the same weight and offering them alternately to someone with an allergy to chocolate; I have then watched the recipient tremble involuntarily when handed the chocolate, even when blindfolded. There is no doubt in my mind that substances do emit something that can be detected by sensitives, and that what goes under the guise of extrasensory perception (ESP), in some cases, is really a highly developed electrical sensitivity; it seems that the two are often indistinguishable.

An EH patient may have several neutralizing frequencies, and these can be found by progressive tuning of the oscillator until levels are reached at which symptoms subside dramatically; the paper tells us that 'with some patients, it can take three hours or more'. The concept of a neutralizing frequency is echoed in Reiter's MR, where he found that experiencers' reactions could be suddenly quenched by the operation of a Tesla coil. Of the MR, Reiter tells us:

> *In at least one of these cases, the area of the volunteer's head where the sensation occurred corresponded to a location where the volunteers had recalled, under hypnosis, **'aliens' doing something to them**. Additionally, it was discovered that this sensation appeared to be temporarily deadened or nullified by the proximity of an operating Tesla Coil. [Reiter, 1994. My emphasis.]*

Significantly, both the Breakspear treatment with a neutralizing frequency and Reiter's 'quenching' seem to be describing the same basic mechanism.

This summary of EH diagnosis and treatment will be rounded off by a number of selected quotations that should provide additional insights into the clinical background of this unusual and fascinating condition:

> *[On testing] It is difficult to assess the response of patients at subhertz frequencies and this is still a research exercise. The response (meaning recovery time) for electrical sensitivities is likely to be about 15 seconds for reported sensation and eyelid movement, and about 45 seconds to regain muscle tone. It is possible to go through the whole range of frequencies and yet get no patient response; however, delayed allergic reactions may occur even a day later ... tests can conveniently be started around 1Hz and the frequency slowly increased while noting down the reported reactions ... it can take several hours to cover the full frequency range ... Although being challenged electrically, the patient may recognise allergic responses which correspond to chemical allergens: a 'perfume reaction', a 'beef or milk reaction', a 'ketone reaction', a 'man-made fibres reaction' and a 'thunderstorm reaction' have all been described ... We have challenged chemically-neutralized chemically, challenged electrically-neutralized chemically, challenged chemically-neutralized electrically and challenged electrically and neutralized electrically ... [Smith et al., 1986.]*

I also found that case notes, made by the Breakspear doctors on their EH patients' reactions during treatment and testing procedures, provided some intriguing background details:

> *Preliminary measurements on two patients (subjects J. B. and L. P.) have already been reported. These were remarkable in the extreme changes of mood produced with quite small changes in frequency within the audio frequency range. While subject J. B. was being tested, it was found that subject L. P. had become unconscious in the corridor outside the laboratory ... Subject L. P. was then tested and at the first neutralizing frequency*

found (105Hz) she regained full consciousness. No further testing was done because she was so sensitive. The electrical field at this subject (when outside the test-room – in the corridor) would have been in the order of 1mv/m. It appears that extremely sensitive subjects can respond to small signals in their environment even against the much greater background of the 50 Hz/60 Hz power supply frequencies usually to be found inside buildings. A similar specificity is found with chemical allergens. [Smith et al., 1986.]

This extremely specific frequency reaction is comparable to tuning in a radio to a specific programme, while being able to 'ignore' all others. The paper also comments on generalized irradiation:

Premature babies often remain in incubators for varying periods of their time in hospital; conventional incubators offer a 50 Hz/60 Hz environmental field. One wonders whether this increases a tendency to electrical hypersensitivities in later life. [Smith et al., 1986.]

Taking such pre-natal aspects as a cue, one of the questions I try to resolve as an investigator into visitation experiences is whether the mother of the experiencer, *while in an advanced state of pregnancy with him/her,* underwent an MEE, e.g. major electrocution or lightning-strike proximity. This may result in individuals being *born* EH and should be considered if investigators find an 'abductee' who shows all the parameters of EH type B but cannot recall an MEE. Alternatively they may not be aware of an MEE occurring, although they may recall a UFO encounter, when they were close to a ball of light, otherwise known as a UAP, otherwise known as an electric fireball …

5

Unclassified atmospheric phenomena: natural and artificially generated fireballs

INTRODUCTION

Scientific studies of unclassified atmospheric phenomena (UAPs) have had to disown the associations that the term 'UFO' carries with it, as it has been equated with 'alien spaceship' by the media; although a variety of alternative terms, e.g. 'transient aerial phenomena' have been tried in the specialist publications, they have not been generally adopted. This lack of a label for such phenomena has not helped them to become accepted as a legitimate area of study within scientific circles, and there even seems to be an inexplicable prejudice on the part of many physicists and other scientists against the reality of probably the best UAP candidate for scientific acceptance, ball lightning (BL). However, it would appear that indifference and rejection in many quarters are balanced in others by an intense interest amounting to little short of an obsessive passion for this fascinating electrical phenomenon. This is reflected in the extensive body of little-known scientific papers from around the world, especially the former USSR, on BL (see p. 187).

One of the valuable functions that UFO groups have fulfilled is the collection of reports of anomalous phenomena relating to atmospheric effects. The flying-saucer mythologists make use of such oddities, not real-izing (or caring) that they are unrelated phenomena. From a review of such collections, it is clear that many unclassified effects are the result of inter-actions between the weather, geology and the artificial electromagnetic (EM) environment – and some of them are very odd indeed. Consider for example, the following report from New South Wales, Australia:

22. 3. 76. Nemingha, NSW

A couple had stopped their car in front of a petrol service station when a bright, greenish-yellow light descended from the sky and enveloped a car approaching from the opposite direction. The light then disappeared. The car moved to the wrong side of the road, became enveloped in a thick ball of white haze and stopped. After about two minutes the white haze disappeared. (The car lights were assumed to be out at this stage.) A woman stepped out of the car and used a cloth to wipe the windscreen which seemed to be covered in a white substance. After a few minutes, she was about to get back into the car when its headlights came back on. The cloth, which she had thrown on the roadside was seen to burst into flames. As the car was re-started and driven slowly past, the witnesses noticed that it was covered in a thick paint-like substance. The couple were so concerned by the incident that they wrote a letter to the Tamworth 'Northern Daily Leader' newspaper seeking additional information from other possible witnesses. [Anon.]

Taking the proximity of the gas station into account, we might surmise that some type of petrochemical reaction took place around the car, where atmospheric electricity served to induce the precipitation of a hydrocarbon product. However, whatever we make of this, it is but one example which demonstrates the potential for unusual EM-hybrid UAPs. Another even stranger example, which took place at a small airport in eastern England, shows how UAPs also appear as solid objects:

Date: April 19, 1984. Time: 16.00

D, the senior controller at the airport since 1970 cannot be more specific about the location, but it is an airport with radar and air traffic control ... three witnesses were involved ... On duty were the deputy controller with an assistant ATC. It was a bright sunny day with no cloud at all below 5000 feet, wind 15 mph from the SW and visibility 10 Km. In view of these optimum conditions and the fact that only a light plane was on an approach, the radar was switched off. D heard the aircraft call that he was at 'base leg', which meant that he was turning into the approach several miles out. Idly looking out he saw a brilliant white glow, which he took to be an aircraft making an approach to runway 27. But then the aircraft called again and referred to runway 22, on which he was approaching. D said to B, 'You have something coming in on 27 also' and wanted simply to alert him about the possible traffic conflict as the two runways intersected on the ground ... D persisted in watching the brilliant object which looked like an aircraft reflecting the bright sun, although no shape was visible behind the glare.

Some seconds had now passed and the object had made a perfect approach to runway 27 and seemed to be landing on it! He grabbed binoculars to get a better look and could see it as a perfectly spherical ball shape that reminded him of nothing so much as 'masses of silvery paper crinkled up'. It reflected a tremendous amount of light in view of the daylight conditions. D was positive it was displaying controlled flight so he called out urgently to the two duty controllers. The UFO was now 'bouncing' off the runway at an angle of 80 degrees and 'rocketing' skywards. This angle of climb was out of the question for a conventional jet and its speed was considerable. It had reached 3000 feet in well under a minute. The other two operators now saw it, as it streaked away, and were shocked ... Both controllers said they would rather forget the incident ... B especially was very upset and shaken.' [Anon., 1984a.]

It is easy to see how such reports, under the influence of the UFO mythology, would be transformed into something alien. However, in fact, it was another UAP which serves to remind us of the freak possibilities at large. Even the apparent purposeful trajectory cannot be taken as 'intelligent', as nature abounds with precise patterns and regularities.

Of course, those UFO enthusiasts who believe in nuts-and-bolts flying saucers have no time for the UAP concept, and certainly not BL. I myself am actually a *lapsed* believer in alien-structured craft: in the early years of my career as an investigator, I believed the accounts in the many books on UFOs, and assumed that their existence was valid and that structured craft operated by an unknown and advanced technology were factual realities. However, after several years, I realized that I was really dealing with a powerful flying-saucer mythology, backed by economic-protectionist factions; i.e. flying saucers are a product which sells, and a belief system has been seeded into the population at many levels. As an investigator, I eventually found that the raw data I was getting from witnesses did not match up with the accounts in the popular books, and that something was seriously amiss with the evidence for solid craft of alien design – it did not stand up to critical scrutiny.

Probably the most damning aspect is the absence of physical evidence. Despite the fact that, over the past 45 years or so, during which there are supposed to have been hundreds of landings and contacts, *we do not have as much as the equivalent of an alien paper-clip.* One problem is that people whose occupation rests on selling popular books on UFOs are often the very ones who investigate them, or they are instrumental in organizing teams of non-writers to do so. They are also active members of UFO societies, promote an interest in UFOs generally, almost like a product, and are constantly on the look-out for new UFO 'angles' and material in order to satisfy their publishers. In short, they have a vested interest in the existence of UFOs.

The lack of physical evidence is fundamentally embodied in the fact that all of the groups, individuals and societies study not UFOs themselves, but reports of UFOs, and there is a wide range of stimuli to give rise to these reports: kites, birds, balloons, planes, meteors, stars, the moon and sun, temperature inversions, mirages, etc. Add to these the subjective perceptions of both common and unusual optical phenomena, straight hallucination and, of course, many hoaxes, and it becomes clear that *no overall identification of UFOs is actually possible* because the stimuli which give rise to reports of them are a mixture of unrelated effects, objects and phenomena. Also, if we add secret military devices, classified prototypes and experimental aeroforms, we get a good indication of the range of things in the sky that can be used in the formation of a UFO report. The Stealth bomber is a good example of a type of 'UFO' repeatedly seen in the north of England in the 1980s, and referred to as 'the mysterious manta-ray' or 'the Silent Vulcan' before it was shown to the general public by the US Air Force (USAF). I will also predict that the triangular craft (and other shapes) seen over Belgium in the 1990s will turn out to be another class of 'Stealth', perhaps designed to replace the helicopter, which has several disadvantages related to noise, range and load, and the physical clearance needed for landing. However, if there are no alien-structured craft, are there any UFOs at all? My answer to this is a qualified 'yes', and this chapter serves to expand on this position.

I shall begin with generalizations and then gradually focus on specifics. As an investigator into UFO-related reports of 16 years standing, and with an equal number of years exploring the work of others in the field, I can state that there is no doubt in my mind that there exists a range of unclassified EM light phenomena in the atmosphere which exhibit objective physical properties. They can be photographed and filmed, tracked on radar and observed by multiples of witnesses from different locations, and they can affect people and the environment. 'Close encounters of the second kind' is a classification created by Dr Allen Hynek, and refers to cases where a UFO has done exactly this, i.e. induced physical changes to the environment. Ground traces, burnt vegetation, broken tree branches, melted road tar, singed paintwork, broken car aerials, smashed glass, and more, have all been reported as the result of close encounters with strange lights in the atmosphere.

THE ELECTROMAGNETIC CONNECTION IN SCIENCE FICTION

It is interesting that fictional accounts of UFO encounters in films or on TV, almost without exception, show EM disturbance of one kind or another as the main effect of 'flying saucers'. Cars stalling, electricity supplies failing and static interference on radio and TV programmes are typical depictions; indeed, the 1950s' flying saucer classic *The Day the Earth Stood Still* actually shows alien technology bringing about a malfunction of the world's electricity supply! Quite unintentionally, such dramatic depictions do have a factual basis and, as will be shown on p.195, EM effects *do* occur in association with UAPs. From an examination of the reports compiled by investigators into situations where these lights have come close to the homes and vehicles of witnesses, it is evident that the lights can induce power surges great enough not only to cause malfunctions to electrical appliances, but also to leave lasting magnetic effects.

An event which took place in January 1979, at Rowley Regis (see Note 11) in the West Midlands region of England, involved a huge ball of orange light at least 1.5m (5ft) in diameter. This descended into the small garden of the home of Jean Hingley and hovered above the lawn just outside her back door. Although investigators have generally accepted that entities came from this object and interacted with the witness, the evidence suggests that these were smaller associated light phenomena which entered the house through the open back door; they were EM forms upon which hallucinatory figures were superimposed. Quotations from the original report compiled by the five investigators involved provide some examples of the persisting magnetic effects:

> ... the electric wall clock in the lounge loses time even after a new battery was fitted. This was checked and it was found that the clock mechanism was magnetised. We de-magnetised the clock mechanism with a de-gausser and the clock has since kept good time.

The television set had suffered from a severe loss of picture, and the mechanism for its production had also been subjected to the disorganizing effects of a strong magnetic field. The original report comments:

> The colour T.V. is now losing its image and this is due to the shadow mask of the tube being faulty. This can be caused by exposure to a high magnetic field.

The report also mentions the degradation of some tape-recordings:

> Three cassette tapes were on the sideboard during the encounter and these were later found to have been affected as the sound level was considerably reduced. Listening tests showed that there was an audible loss of signal and in places only low frequencies could be heard. Evidence showed exposure to a high magnetic field of some sort. The variation of signal strength could have been due to the angle of the tape cassette to the source of the magnetic field.

If cassette tapes that have been used for recording are subjected to high magnetic-field densities, there would be a disorganization of the ferric oxide particles impregnated into the tapes' surface. It is the magnetic patterning of this layer which produces the recording effect *per se*, as it has been organized by the magnetic heads of the recorder during the recording process. A randomization of these ferric-oxide particles by a generalized magnetic field would, in fact, produce a loss of sound as an audio play-back response, just as the investigators found.

Also, the recorder itself was affected, and the report simply states:

> ... the low performance of the previously well-functioning cassette recorder is also something of a mystery.

This is an example of just one type of UAP: an earth light, the origin of which is outlined below. However, when considering the broader picture, we appear to run into problems related to labelling and classification. However, by tracing the path of the argument involved, which acts as a vehicle for exploring a number of ground rules, the justification for referring to these atmospheric phenomena as 'unclassified' can be shown.

NATURALLY OCCURRING LIGHT PHENOMENA
CLASSIFICATION AND TERMINOLOGY

The term 'UFO' is problematic because it begs the question, unidentified by whom? It is common knowledge among investigators that all manner of objects and effects which they have been trained to identify, such as the planet Venus low down in the sky, are regarded as UFOs by witnesses unfamiliar with their appearance. To a small child who has no knowledge of a helicopter, it will be a UFO. The same labelling problem appears to beset the term 'unclassified atmospheric phenomenon' (UAP). Unclassified by whom? Scientists? Which scientists? Considering the prejudice against the existence of BL in some scientific quarters, they could be considered a poor choice as an authority.

Then there is the 'problem' of identification. If we consider BL again, is this a UAP? Strictly speaking it is not, because not only has it been classified, it has also been reproduced under controlled conditions, as this chapter will show. But, in many ways, it is the archetypal UAP. So what do we call those globes of light that can leave a trail of electromagnetic, thermal and mechanical disturbance in their wake? Investigators' nicknames abound: 'amber gamblers', 'shape-shifters' 'spook lights', 'ghost lights', 'phantom lights', 'flying oranges', 'bubble-balls', and so on. Or simply: the orange ball of light phenomenon.

The authors of *Earth Lights* (Devereux & McCartney, 1982) refer to them as 'light phenomena' and this is as good a term as any. However, it is difficult to determine the exact origin of a globe of light in the sky and I would argue that the existence of earth lights has even confounded the parameters of BL, as described in meteorological textbooks in the past, and has no doubt added to the difficulty of determining its true nature. In fact, as I shall also show, there are many types of light phenomena produced by different mechanisms, and these could possibly have confounded the descriptions of earth lights.

So we are left in the shaky position where we seem to be sure of BL and earth lights, which include earthquake lights, but are not really able to tell for sure which is which in every case. In addition, I have introduced other kinds of light phenomena, which originate through EM pollution and which I have termed 'electroforms' (see p. 47). The basic argument for electroforms is that, if BL forms in the transient fields of electrical storms, something like it must also form in microwave fields of radar and/or communication systems and voltages from power lines.

To add to this picture of uncertainty, I would also argue that both BL and earth lights can be altered and transformed by irradiation from artificial electrical and electronic sources, which increases their energy levels, and, conversely, electroforms can be altered and transformed by natural geoelectromagnetic energies. Furthermore, I suggest that some light phenomena are produced by intermodulations between artificial sources of EM fields (e.g. power lines or microwave repeaters) and natural sources (e.g. fault lines) and that these phenomena can be altered and transformed by fields from one or both of these sources, or by electrical storms, etc. The picture, potentially, is extremely complex and confusing.

Therefore, probably the best that can be done is to recognize a basic working model according to which natural atmospheric electricity can produce BL, tectonic strain at geological faults can produce earth lights, artificial EM pollution can produce electroforms, and there can be a mixing and matching between them to some extent. After all, for the purposes of exploring the type of disturbances to the human body and consciousness, as well as to the environment, we are really concerned with the EM fields that these phenomena emit. However, as will be shown on p. 183 we are also considering some extremely unusual properties of the UAP, which deserve equal attention.

Fireballs: real or imagined?

Individuals who have developed an epileptiform condition may hallucinate balls of light. These are specifically listed as a standard type of hallucination in the neurological textbooks (e.g. Gilroy, 1990, p. 71). That is to say, when a witness reports a light phenomenon, we cannot always be sure whether it is an internal or an external event. Incidently, there is no doubt in my mind that experiencers can also hallucinate a huge illuminated flying saucer, which is something that many extraterrestrial hypothesis (ETH) enthusiasts do not like to even consider.

TERMINOLOGY AND NON-LUMINOUS PHENOMENA

The astute reader may have noticed that the question about an alternative to the term UAP has still not been resolved here.

The problem with 'light phenomena' is that, as evidenced by many reports, not all are luminous. Some have a metallic sheen to them and the descriptions of BL include dark metallic-looking forms. Also, there are consistent reports of encounters involving a green luminous mist, as we saw in the Aveley case (p. 142), and this too is a UAP. I suspect that this mist or fog is an electrical phenomenon induced by power lines emitting grounding fields over water thereby altering temperature above ambient levels, thus producing an altered dew-point. If this proves to be right, it will no longer be unclassified, at least to those individuals who study these phenomena.

This point concerning the selective recognition of such phenomena may offer a way out of the terminology dilemma, because they are the province of 'ufologists', Forteans and independent researchers, such as myself. Present-day science has very little to say about them. If it scarcely recognizes BL in many quarters (and seems to refuse to accept its reality in the laboratory), and if earth lights have received limited attention and electroforms no attention whatsoever, we could fairly safely revert to the 'unclassified' label. We could answer the question 'unclassified by whom?' by identifying the source as 'conservative scientists' or 'certain scientific establishments'. However, we should remember that it was two scientists – electrical engineers James and Kenneth Corum in the late 1980s – who produced BL 90 years after Tesla, calling it 'electric fireballs', just as he did. Therefore, we have come full circle by finally accepting the term 'unclassified atmospheric phenomena' (UAPs) and, having done so, we have covered an essential argument and explored many factors that required clarification.

EARTH LIGHTS

In 1982, a book by Paul Devereux and geologist Paul McCartney was published, simply entitled *Earth Lights* (Devereux & McCartney, 1982). This provided in-depth evidence for a variety of light phenomena originating from geological fault lines (see Note 12). Basically, the authors stated that, during periods of tectonic activity and/or mechanical strain in faults, globes of light were produced which could be of various colours, last for considerable periods of time and had the ability to change shape. Orange and white were the two colours which predominated, and one of the mechanisms proposed involved piezoelectric and piezomagnetic processes, whereby vast rock masses, predominately silicates, produced such energies due to unreleased ground strain. Many different reports of light forms were collected from geological data around the world, showing that such terrestrial lights could take many different forms, e.g. globes, beams, multi-coloured points of light, discs, ovoids, etc. Devereux went on to do more in-depth research, thanks to sponsorship by the Fetzer Institute in the USA, and his work is now respected by many scientific institutions. He wrote an update of his work called *Earth Lights Revelation* drawing on the work of English researchers David Clarke and Andrew Roberts (Devereux *et al.*, 1989). My own investigations into fields emitted from faults show that it would be somewhat surprising if such light phenomena were *not* produced, as powerful intermodulations between radio-frequency (RF) pulses frequently take place. These, as we shall see, are intrinsically involved in the production of electric fireballs in the laboratory.

ELECTRIC FIREBALLS

Where science neglects an area of study, fantasy and mythology rush in to fill the void. This is why the consciousness effects induced by exposure to EM pollution have spawned the alien-abduction and haunting mythologies, and why UAPs have been the basis for UFOs and the flying-saucer movement. Such psychosocial phenomena have been superimposed over poorly understood or scarcely recognized physical EM phenomena. At the other extreme, there are the ultra-sceptics who think that there is no physical energetic basis whatsoever for these mythologies. Instead they trace them with a historical perspective, using the constructs of sociology, such as those involved in the social reality of religion. While whole illusory realities (such as a non-existent network of Satanic cultists) can be constructed and maintained by such psychosocial processes, it is a fundamental mistake to apply them so vigorously that physical mechanisms are ignored. The ability of psychosocial theorists to discount physical stimuli is as foolish and deluded as those enthusiasts who misinterpret EM phenomena as being the work of aliens from another planet.

A balanced perspective involves the realization that something extremely strange does in fact occur and, although it is not the work of exotic agencies such as aliens, spirits of the dead or interdimensional intelligences, there are, nevertheless, real physical mechanisms at work which provide the stimulus to drive such mythologies. This simple viewpoint took me about a year of investigation and research to appreciate, and a further 15 years of investigation and research to confirm through field studies. When considering BL, the multitude of scientific papers from around the world, accumulated across decades of research into this phenomenon, presents an odd contrast to the trite sentiments of many physicists and meteorologists which effectively say that BL is merely imaginary. The following extract expresses this well:

> Ball lightning may, or may not exist. Many people, including some meteorologists, think it is all imagination, and are possibly influenced by the fact that such fireballs cannot be explained, and have not been artificially produced in the laboratory. [Holford, 1977.]

I have found that scientific specialists sometimes react absurdly to things which they cannot understand or identify. As a 14-year-old mineralogist, I took an unusual crystal which I had found in a chalk quarry at Leatherhead, in the south of England, to the mineralogy department of the Natural History Museum in London. I could not identify the brown ferrous crystal and, to my surprise, neither could the Scientific Officer who saw me. However, I was even more astounded when, in his frustration, he 'accidently' crumbled the specimen hard between his fingers, reducing it to powder, with a look of 'problem solved' on his face. Also, I used to work in a biological laboratory where the Senior Scientific Officer had a reputation for ramming the objective of the microscope into the glass slides of specimens he could not identify. There seems to be a similar arrogance at large when considering the existence of BL, especially when books and papers are published linking it to psychic effects. The following resumé of a volume on Hungarian BL observations expresses a number of relevant points:

> Ball lightning is one of the most intriguing natural phenomena on Earth. Its physical nature is still unknown despite attempts to understand its guiding principles. Experimental simulations to reproduce ball lightning have failed so far. The only way to learn about it is by eyewitness accounts ... Ball lightnings do pose a serious challenge for conventional scientists, because of the large number of unexplained features, such as high energy density yet limited damage on impact, penetration of closed spaces and paranormal effects on metals and electrical appliances without heating. Mysterious psychic effects are noted concerning those humans who were in touch with ball lightning ... [Egely, 1994.]

The last sentence of this summary, concerning 'mysterious psychic effects', refers to the sensitizing effects of a major electrical event (MEE) and represents an interesting cross-reference. Earlier, it reflects how information on the Corums' work has not reached the author and, judging by many other reactions of surprise and interest, nobody in the

UK has heard of it either. Therefore, let us examine the production of
BL in the laboratory, via the re-interpretation of Nikola Tesla's *Colorado
Springs Notes* of 1897, by Kenneth L. Corum and James F. Corum. For
readers who are not familiar with the technical aspects, I do recommend
perseverance, as terms will be explained as they occur.

THE LABORATORY PRODUCTION
OF BALL LIGHTNING

*The electromagnetic conditions required for Tesla's production of ball light-
ning have remained as an intriguing riddle for serious investigation for
almost a century. The large-scale ball lightning discharges observed in nature
are stable (observers declare that they maintain their physical structure for
durations from a few seconds to as much as a minute) and spheroidal (with
diameters from a centimeter up to thirty centimeters or more). Over the past
156 years, a remarkable family of theoretical models for electric fireballs has
appeared. Nevertheless, as with the study of General Relativity, the ratio
of significant experiments to theoretical papers is a very small quantity.*

*Until the summer of 1988 it was not known that open air, laboratory
generated artificial ball lightning could be successfully achieved on
demand. In fact, it was commonly believed that this technology would not
become available for several decades. [Corum & Corum, 1989.]*

The authors continue:

*Last summer, during the 3rd International Tesla Symposium at
Colorado Springs, while walking around Tesla's Laboratory site ...
Leland Anderson made the comment, 'I don't understand why we don't
all see fireballs. The way Tesla described them, they just seemed
to bubble from his machine.' We had been discussing the 'missing'
Chapter 34 (of Tesla's notes recently published) ... It was a puzzle
to us. While flying back to Cleveland, we continued to compare
Chapter 34 with the photographs in Tesla's published notes. And then
it struck us. We just weren't using the circuit configuration which Tesla
shows us. When we got back, we re-arranged our apparatus ... [Corum
& Corum, 1989.]*

When the Corums had done this, they later reported:

*Recent low-power experiments performed in the U.S. with average
powers of only a few kilowatts exhibit mobile fiery electrochemical (RF
generated) plasmoids capable of trajectories of several meters into the air.*

And:

> *While the physical chemistry of these structures is certainly complex and presently not well understood, the mode of their generation is elementary ... (As Conan Doyle once wrote, 'Any mystery is simple, once it is explained to you.') [Corum & Corum, 1993a.]*

The Corums can be regarded as the foremost authorities on this electric-fireball generation and, as a result, on the nature of BL itself. I say this not just because of their successful experiments, but also because they have evidently collected, reviewed and absorbed the most promising and progressive scientific literature in the field, from the late nineteenth century of the present day. However, astoundingly, in a small, somewhat home-made booklet sent to me by James Corum, there to the following statement:

> *Perhaps one of the most obvious conclusions of our work is that Tesla's apparatus and method of fireball production requires rather modest equipment. Now a host of experimenters may carry on fireball generation and experimentation under their own controlled conditions. Best of all, the required apparatus is readily available in a multitude of existing laboratories around the world. [Corum & Corum, 1993a.]*

Receiving a generous collection of papers, photographs and information from James Corum after a long-distance phone conversation, I wrote to the physics departments of six British universities in order to gauge the level of interest in this 'new' approach to the artificial production of BL. I did not receive one reply ... The relevance to my own post-ufological, EM-pollution approach is that, among other considerations, their method of BL production involves that potent and ubiquitous process in EM-anomaly research – *intermodulation* between two or more fields. As shown on p. 85, it is the intermodulation of magnetic fields in the brain which induces the seizures that give rise to many hallucinatory sensations and perceptions, and it is via intermodulation effects that Hutchison's 'poltergeist machine' produces its many phenomena, i.e. via interactions of fields from clashing technologies. Similarly, Tesla's electric fireballs are produced by intermodulations between two RF fields. Tesla states:

> *I have succeeded in determining their mode of formation and producing them artificially ...* **it became apparent that the fireballs resulted from the interaction of two frequencies**, *a stray higher frequency wave imposed on the lower frequency oscillations of the main circuit ... [Tesla, 1897. My emphasis.]*

Kenneth and James Corum boldly relate:

Our laboratory in Ohio [USA] has developed equipment that will produce electric fireballs that will last after the external power is removed. We have been able to produce electric fireballs that will fit the conditions and circumstances that are frequently seen in nature (i.e. fireballs passing through window glass, inside airplanes, traveling along fences, etc). [Corum & Corum, 1989.]

The first question that people ask when they learn of the Corums' work is about the size and duration of the fireballs. This is rather like asking, 'How long is a piece of string?', i.e. it depends on the power input and its delivery within the apparatus. The Corums' report on their early experiments mentions 2.5cm (1in) fireball diameters, but:

Tesla, of course, was running about 100 times the power which we could produce with our rather modest equipment ... [Corum & Corum, 1989.]

And, qualifying this statement:

Concerning the physical size of the fireballs obtained at Colorado Springs [where Tesla had his laboratory] Tesla wrote:

' ... the balls produced with the apparatus experimented with are probably up to one and a half inches in diameter and possibly more ...'

During our last trip to the Tesla Archives at Belgrade (in the Fall of 1993), we had the opportunity to examine the large glass plates from which the Colorado Springs photographs were made. To our astonishment, fireballs could be easily distinguished on the originals in Photo IX, where a 12-inch diameter fireball can be plainly seen issuing toward the viewer from the tip of the pointed wire, and in Photo XII ... a six-inch diameter fireball can be identified over between the wall studs. [Corum & Corum, 1993a.]

Also, during their later experiments, which produced larger fireballs with greater lifetimes after the power had been switched off, the Corums obtained some unusual variations:

We were able to produce other interesting features. Often we had pulsating fireballs. These would appear and then shrink. When they were hit by [high voltage] streamers, they would grow in size and then shrink again. This would occur a number of times and then they would fade away. Another feature was that some had the appearance of a doughnut [i.e. ring-like]; bright circles with darkened centres. Others appeared to the observer as white, red, green, yellow, blue-white and purple. [Corum & Corum, 1993a.]

So what apparatus was used by the Corums (after Tesla) to produce artificial BL? They tell us that it is relatively simple and already present in many colleges and universities around the world.

EQUIPMENT
POWER SOURCES

This section, by its nature, is directed towards those readers with technical knowledge and interest, although such information will be mixed with aspects of direct relevance to the study of UAPs generally. I will begin by stating that the size and duration of the fireballs, i.e. robustness/stability, is determined by the accuracy of the power input in terms of delivering high field amplitudes as short bursts, or 'power spikes'. According to my conversations with James Corum, it is really a matter of *quality of delivery* within the apparatus rather than quantity of power (i.e. a pulsing regime of 'high pulses but short bursts') and some experimenters, using overly high field strengths, have swamped the fireball discharges with electrical sparking so that they are difficult to detect. The Corums relate:

> *We rewired our apparatus as two synchronously pulsed high power RF oscillators, the first at a frequency of 67 kHz and the second at 156 kHz ... the exact frequencies are not critical. The basis for the apparatus was first conceived and patented in 1897 by Nikola Tesla ... The apparatus can be seen in dozens of photographs and circuit diagrams in Tesla's Colorado Spring Notes. [Corum & Corum, 1989.]*

And:

> *... it is clear that very little power is actually required to attain extremely high voltages ... It is no wonder that Tesla would say:*
>
> *'With such coils, I found that there was practically no limit to the tension available ...'*
>
> *Similar remarks are made throughout the Colorado Springs Notes. [Corum & Corum, 1989.]*

THE APPARATUS

The apparatus, which is described in technical detail by the Corums, is shown opposite. Precise details of its operation would mean little to the lay-reader; suffice it to say that:

> *The apparatus consists primarily of two one-quarter wave length, slow wave helical resonators above a conducting ground plane. Both of the resonators were magnetically coupled by a common link to a spark gap oscillator, of peak power (approximately 70 kW), operating at a frequency of 67 kHz. The actual average power being delivered to the high voltage electrode was of the order of 3.2 kW (2.4 megavolts RF). [Corum & Corum, 1993b.]*

AN INTRODUCTION TO THE TESLA COIL

It is not an easy task to convey the nature of Tesla coils to the layman without presenting a lengthy technical treatise starting from basic principles and working up to an increasingly complex description; it is also perhaps unnecessary as long as the concluding import concerning their function is emphasized. However, as a basic description (and may Tesla coil afficionados forgive me), Tesla coils may be described as an electrical apparatus consisting of two coils of copper wire, one tall and one short, in which the taller (called the 'secondary') is placed inside the shorter (called the 'primary'). They are not physically connected to each other and the tall secondary receives electricity via a magnetic induction effect from the outer primary (see below). This energy is boosted by the many

Demonstration of a Tesla coil
(Mechanics and Handicraft, 1935)

turns of wire that make up the tall secondary and is emitted from it as discharges of long electrical streamers from the copper- or brass-ball terminal at the top, and functions to produce high-voltage RF fields. The short outer primary is connected to a powered circuit in which a unit, called a 'spark gap', is placed; this emits high-voltage RF sparking between two heavy-duty terminals. For uninitiated readers, this simplified outline should serve as an introduction to the world of the Tesla coil and whet their curiosity to learn more; it should, however, be supplemented with reference material.

OBSERVATIONS ON FIREBALL PRODUCTION

The Corums report:

> Initially, we thought that the fireballs were 'born' in the streamer near the high voltage electrode. They sometimes start out as a 6 mm sphere, which appears to glide up to a knot in the streamer, and then begins to grow. The ball seems to then sit still, floating in space, while the streamer fades out. The floating ball is then struck by the next streamer and begins to grow larger. In one sequence, the ball is struck by six separate discharges, growing in size each time. One fireball grew from an initial 6 mm sphere into a 5 cm diameter fiery red globule, over a 1.0 second time interval. Some fireballs appear to spin, with moving dark patches (like sunspots). Some appear to change colours as they evolve and eventually explode like Novae. As hypothesized above, placing a wax candle on the low frequency resonator clearly enhances fireball production [being a source of carbon]. The phenomenon is quite similar to the fireballs often seen in the regions above volcanic activity. The relative ease of electric fireball generation by high voltage discharges in the presence of carbon films, smoke, ash and dust is consistent with its frequent natural observation in and around chimneys, where carbon is deposited in great profusion. [Corum & Corum, 1993b.]

The Corums describe two methods of fireball production, the first described in principle, using Tesla's words:

> ...it became apparent that the fireballs resulted from the interaction of two frequencies, a stray higher frequency wave imposed on the lower frequency oscillations of the main circuit ... This condition acts as a trigger which may cause the total energy of the powerful longer wave to be discharged in an infinitesimally small interval of time and at a proportionately tremendously great rate of energy movement which cannot confine itself to the metal circuit and is released into surrounding space with inconceivable violence. It is but a step, from learning how a high frequency current can explosively discharge a lower frequency current, to using the principle to

design a system in which these explosions can be produced by intent. [Tesla Tries to Prevent World War II, J. O'Neill, 1988]

MORE EVIDENCE FOR INTERMODULATION EFFECTS

Tesla comments:

> *Parasitic oscillations, or circuits, within the main circuit were a source of danger from this cause ... Even when the principal oscillating circuit was adjusted for the greatest efficiency of operation by the diminution of all sources of loss, the fireballs continued to occur but these were due to stray high frequency charges **from random earth currents** ... From these experiences, it became apparent that the fireballs resulted from the interaction of two frequencies, a stray higher frequency wave imposed on the lower frequency oscillations ... [O'Neill, 1988. My emphasis.]*

It has been argued that electric fireballs, or UAPs, are generated accidentally as a side-effect of EM pollution where intermodulations occur. The statement by Tesla certainly supports this, as it virtually describes the field interactions I have proposed, whereby natural and artificial fields combine to generate fireballs in the environment. It is precisely such 'random earth currents' that would be involved in intermodulations with microwave RF fields from the powerful transmitters of TV and radio stations. In fact, Paul Devereux and his colleagues, in *Earth Lights Revelation* (Devereux *et al.*, 1989), describe many observations of aerial lights around and travelling back and forth from transmitter masts; this is also covered in *UFOs – Psychic Close Encounters* (Budden, 1995a).

METHODS OF FIREBALL PRODUCTION

A number of interesting features arise during the production of these energetic sources, which link with case details regarding close-encounter conditions, i.e. EM effects. The Corums comment on the first method they used:

> *Using the high-frequency coil to arc to the low-frequency coil, the latter would then release its energy rapidly, in a burst. The burst of energy released manifests itself in the shape of a ball or 'bubble'. [Corum & Corum, 1989.]*

And in the second method they state:

> *A second method of fireball production includes the use of microscopic vaporized metal or carbon particles. We used the low frequency coil alone*

and deposited a thin film of carbon particles on the high voltage electrode. The current passing through the carbon film tended to rapidly heat the carbon particles. This dissipation of power also tends to quickly reduce the impedance and subsequently release all the power rapidly into this heated micron size 'resistor'. The same results may be gotten by using 'the tip of rubber-covered cable or wire #10' to 'facilitate the pumping of the spark' [Tesla's words from Colorado Springs Notes, pp.173–174] Old fashioned rubber is loaded with soot ... The relative ease of electric fireball generation by high voltage discharges in the presence of carbon films, smoke, ash and dust is consistent with its frequent natural observation in and around chimneys, where carbon is deposited in great profusion ... Readers familiar with Michael Faraday's famous Christmas Lecture, 'The Chemical History of a Candle' will recall his glowing remarks about the presence of smoke and solid carbon particles in a brilliant candle flame – they give us glorious colours and beautiful light. If you cannot get the 1 or 2 MV that ... is required ... you can place a wire-wrapped plumber's candle on the side of the small Tesla coil and get an idea of what can be seen on a larger machine.' [Corum & Corum, 1989.]

From this it is clear that electric fireballs are composed of a layered bubble enclosing an energetic centre, and this bubble-membrane is composed of vaporized carbon or metal produced by electrothermal processes. Subsequently, it will also be shown that other products, e.g. water and ozone, are involved in the production of this 'bubble'.

However, we are now considering a UAP which is, in fact, 'made of something', albeit a particulate shell of micron thickness. In *UFOs – Psychic Close Encounters* (Budden, 1995a), I described a case which occurred in 1979 and in which a police car in Warren, Minnesota, USA, was in collision with a large atmospheric light and sustained physical damage. The light was spotted by Val Johnson, the officer in the car, at a distance of about 4km (2½ miles) and was low in the horizon and near some trees. He drove towards it and, after about 1.5km (1 mile), the light, which seemed quite large, hurtled towards him, covering the remaining 2.5km (1½ miles) or so instantly. As it hit the car he heard no sound from the light, and it appeared as a blinding glare. Johnson lost consciousness at this point but did recall the sound of breaking glass. It transpired that one headlight was smashed, a small circular dent was found on the bonnet, the windscreen was shattered, a red light on top of the car was punctured and two radio antennae were bent backwards. One can only speculate on the physical nature of the UAP, but the combination of a rapidly moving magnetic field and associated physical particles is a feasible mechanism for causing such damage.

ANALYSIS OF UNEXPLAINED LIGHTS SEEN AT HESSDALEN, NORWAY

In 1983/84, a study was made of unexplained lights which appeared regularly over several months in a remote snow-covered valley in Hessdalen; this research project involved tracking them on radar. It may be assumed that an atmospheric body consisting of a shell of carbon and/or metal particles will produce a robust radar return, which is what the Hessdalen investigators found. However, this does not explain why these lights could not be seen. That is to say, at times they appeared on radar, but could not be seen optically. Some of these lights reached mean speeds of up to 9000m/second (9850yd/second) from a standing start. Others pulsated, just as the Corums described their fireballs, but the Hessdalen investigators shone lasers at the pulsating lights and found that their rate of pulsation changed. Strangely, the scientific team recorded an incident where a light shone a red laser beam back at them! The lights took several forms: simple globes, bullet shapes with the point downwards, upside-down 'Christmas trees', small flares near the ground, or groups of lights moving together as if on a dark body. Many colours were seen: white, yellow, blue, red and orange, which is comparable to the range that the Corums obtained. Bearing in mind the Corums' description of how fireballs faded and grew in size whenever they were hit by streamers from the high-voltage terminal of the Tesla coil, consider the following description of an unknown light observed at Hessdalen:

> A strong light, just over the horizon in the east. Slowly moving horizontally to the south. It was slowly flickering: It was strong and it gradually became weak. Again it became strong and weak and then strong ... This happened about five–six times. Each time we managed to take a picture. [Strand, 1984.]

The Hessdalen investigators used spectrum analysers and magnetometers, and found that high-frequency power spikes occurred across the whole frequency band from time to time in the valley. The source of these power surges was not identified, but it would appear that they acted as high-voltage streamers and boosted fading fireballs/lights. Such power spikes would also have generated intermodulation effects. From the Corums' experiments, it became evident that the presence of soot/carbon greatly assisted the formation of the fireballs, i.e. the Corums found that, if they supplied a source of particulate carbon, the fireballs would form more readily. It should perhaps be considered therefore that the Hessdalen Valley was subjected to elevated levels of atmospheric particles, e.g. smoke pollution, for a short period, which then fell, causing the lights to cease as well.

There is an important and fundamental aspect of UAPs that many researchers and investigators, surprisingly, seem to overlook, and that is simply the many different types of UAP at large in the atmosphere, ranging from the differing behaviours of BLs to different types of this specific form of UAP:

> *There may be more than one type of ball lightning. For example, the ball lightning that attaches to conductors may be different from the free-floating ball lightning; and the ball lightning that appears near ground level may be different from the ball lightning that hangs high in the air or the ball lightning that falls out of a cloud. [Uman, 1969, p. 245.]*

To use the mode of appearance alone as a means of classification does not seem to be very sound, and it should perhaps be supported by identifying the means of production, e.g. tectonically produced or storm-related. But then, what do we call a light produced during an earthquake and a thunder storm? There is no doubt, that, as it is not possible to definitively pin down atmospheric lights in terms of origin, some quarters of science have tended to ignore them, as scientists prefer phenomena that can be measured and UAPs are notoriously transient. However, this makes the work of the Corums even more of a break-through, because BLs can be produced to order and used in experiments. To consider the variations of BLs, such factors as whether carbon or a metal is involved in the shell of the 'bubble', the proportion of water to ozone, etc., all contribute to its forms and parameters.

CONDITIONS FOR FIREBALL PRODUCTION

Concerning the fireballs that they have produced, the Corums have determined a sure-handed set of conditions which are ideal for their production. They are:

> 1. *Generate a lot of carbon or vaporized metal particles in a small region of space.*
>
> 2. *Create large electric fields in the same vicinity (of the order of 1–2 MV/m).*
>
> 3. *Rapidly elevate the temperature of the particles. [Corum & Corum, 1989]*

They tell us:

> *Video tape easily documents the results of meeting these three conditions. From this, fireball lifetimes are deduced to be 1–2 seconds and dimensions are 1 to 3 centimeters in diameter. Also, these are in agreement with Tesla's observations and conclusions. For example, in one place he attributes fireballs to the presence of resistively heated material in the air. (Colorado Spring Notes, page 333). [Corum & Corum, 1993b.]*

THE PASSAGE OF BALL LIGHTNINGS THROUGH WINDOW-GLASS

The Corums made a video-recording of fireball behaviour in their laboratory, which shows fireballs after striking a sheet of glass. (This was one of the experiments that the Corums undertook to see if they could reproduce the effects reported by observers, i.e. passing through windows.) The experimenters describe what happened when the high-voltage streamers which emanate from the Tesla coils or resonators, operating simultaneously, struck a sheet of glass mounted in a wooden frame:

> ... What was observed by the operator of our apparatus was astounding! The streamers went from the high voltage terminal and struck a window-pane. There were many fireballs present between the electrode and the window. But where the streamers hit the glass, there were many fireballs emanating from the opposite side of the glass. The fireballs would then travel slowly horizontally 12 inches or so and flare up. Some would travel out a bit further and explode ... These results are reproducible on demand. Try it! [Corum & Corum, 1989.]

From this description, it would seem that the presence of the glass as a barrier had little or no effect on the progress of the fireballs, and probably one of the most important discoveries made though performing this experiment is that, in some cases, the observations of BL passing though glass is an illusion. The Corums quote Powell and Finkelstein, who have described a mechanism for how fireballs may appear to pass through a glass window intact:

> Initially electric lines of force pass freely through glass. Positive ions from the ball follow force lines and pile up on one side of the glass while electrons from the room accumulate on the other. When the ball approaches, the glass is heated or broken down enough to become slightly conducting. It then becomes an electrode, and a ball is formed inside the room; the ball then floats away from the window. [Finkelstein & Rubinstein, 1970.]

The Corums comment on this and go on to relate:

> And from repeatable laboratory demonstrations, they give the appearance of passing through ... metal apertures. They have even been shown to explosively ignite wooden boards. [Corum & Corum, 1990.]

Their comments on the effect of fireballs passing through window glass are fairly technical, but they also contain more accessible information:

> The actual physics may be somewhat different, but the sequence of photographs support the general idea ... We believe the phenomenon that

manifests itself when the coherence time is cut short could indeed be the same phenomenon that occurs in nature. Instead of having a short helical resonator being the transmission line, the natural lightning strike could be the full quarter-wave transmission line with its own coherence time shortened by small streamers at one end of the lightning strike. According to lightning specialists, most of these small streamers occur at the top end of the lightning strike. This would account for the infrequency of ball lightning on the ground side of the stroke. Dust, soot, ashes and other pollutants in the air near lightning strikes would, of course, produce similar results.

Our conclusion is that these fireballs are primarily radio-frequency (RF) in origin, and not nuclear phenomena. Consistent with Tesla's observations, they can be produced either by a high current dump into hot air or by the presence of resistively heated material particles. The latter would account for 'engine room fireballs' produced by high current switches and relays ... In our literature research on the topic over the past 26 years, we have read through hundreds of technical articles, papers, reports and books ... we believe that Tesla's is the only apparatus that has been developed that can address and reproduce on demand the many descriptions of ball lightning in nature. [Corum & Corum, 1990.]

These conclusions support the proposal that a BL-like phenomenon can be produced accidentally, through the intermodulations of the RF fields used in electronic communication systems, radar, etc., as EM pollution, i.e. 'electroforms' to distinguish them from natural BL. However, as we are considering intermodulations between RF fields, as used by the Corums after Tesla, and as RF fields are also produced via subterranean piezoelectric and piezomagnetic processes, we may begin to consider the probability of earth lights also being produced in this way. That is to say, a form of electric fireball could seemingly be produced underground, or just above the ground, by the RF intermodulations present during geomagnetic storms, or through ground strain at fault lines, thus giving rise to a geologically originating electric fireball, otherwise known as an 'earth light' (Devereux & McCartney, 1982).

COMPOSITION OF FIREBALLS
FRACTAL CLUSTERS, AEROGELS AND FIREBALLS

In their article, in a section entitled 'Recent Soviet Advances', the Corums relate:

> *In June 1989 we became aware of the significant advances in ball light-*
> *ning theory which have been published in the Soviet scientific literature*
> *... there is a remarkable thread of publications which we believe, describes*
> *the Tesla method of ball lightning formation with surprising accuracy ...*
> *This theoretical approach has been developed to a mature and scholarly*
> *level through the dedicated efforts of B. M. Smirnov and his colleagues*
> *at the Institute of Thermophysics, Siberian Branch of the Academy of*
> *Sciences, USSR, at Novosibirsk ... At the outset of his work, Smirnov*
> *recognised the futility of all ball lightning models that did not incorporate*
> *chemical energy storage. He also possessed a clear understanding of*
> *aerosols, aerogels, filamentary structures, plasma chemistry and dust*
> *particle combustion. [Corum & Corum, 1991/92]*

We may wonder where this encouraging fanfare for Soviet research into
BL, with its underlying elements of smoke, dust and other micro-
particle knowledge, may lead. In fact, the descriptions presented bring
us closer to understanding not only what some UAPs are 'made of', but
also the structure of the 'bubble', or 'shell'. In fact, for the first time, we
may have genuine insights into what is really up there in the sky,
behaving in such remarkable ways and, of course, being reported as
UFOs. I am not suggesting that all UAPs are BLs, or that all UFOs are
UAPs (95 per cent of UFO sightings turn out to be mundane
objects/stimuli). However, what the Corums have uncovered from the
former USSR in the work of Smirnov and his colleagues, provides
models which, we may reliably generalize, are involved in a variety of
other forms. Therefore, in as much as we may recognize the anomalous
behaviours of UAPs, e.g. incredible accelerations and speeds, so we may
begin to realize just what sort of structures we are dealing with in all
their various permutations. The Corums relate:

> *With the advent of the concept of fractals and the physics of diffusion*
> *aggregation in the late 1970s to mid 1980s, Smirnov was able to exten-*
> *sively develop an aerogel analytical model in which the active substance*
> *of ball lightning is in the form of an electrically charged structure of inter-*
> *woven submicron filaments − i.e. a porous fractal cluster of great internal*
> *chemical capacity. Almost the entire envelope filled by such an aerogel*
> *structure is occupied by vacant pores ... Energy release from a chemically*
> *charged fractal can be described as a multistep combustion of a charcoal*
> *(carbon) fractal dust cluster, in ozone absorbed by a model process in ball*
> *lightning ... [Corum & Corum, 1991/92]*

In more everyday terms, we are considering a 'bubble' of electrically
charged filaments of carbon with a condensed form of the gas ozone as
a binding 'glue'; however, most of this filamentous 'bubble' consists of

vacant space! Fractals can be regarded as self-accumulating clusters of particles which condense out of an electrothermally produced carbon aerosol (in this case) or dense metallic vapour. If we picture steam (which actually consists of tiny water droplets) as being made up of carbon particles which have been physically altered at the atomic level, and which swirl in heated ozone and condense around hot incandescent air, we may get close to the structure and dynamics of the formation of the physical parts of electric fireballs, or UAPs. Talking to James Corum in July 1996 provided a further insight; it would appear that the carbon 16 isotope is involved, which naturally forms into the 'Buckyball' spherical form of 'Buckminsterfullerine'. This closely resembles the structure of modern-day soccer balls, which consist of five- and six-sided plates joined along their edges to form a sphere, and it may be a clue as to what occurs on the macro-level.

POROUS FRACTALS AND
THE EARTH-LIGHT/FIREBALL LINK

Other important researchers, such as Forrest and Witten, who produced a dense gas of metallic particles that condensed and formed chained aggregates, also found that fractal structures form after the thermal explosion of materials – something which occurs in the formation of BL. When Tesla electrothermally vaporized a piece of rubber-covered copper wire in order to 'facilitate the pumping of the spark' on the coil, it seems that, in some cases, copper vapour was produced, as copper oxide can form fractals/aerogels. Surprisingly, the Corums mention that silicon dioxide (otherwise known as silica, quartz, flint, etc.) can also form into the fractal/aerogel 'bubbles' of electric fireballs. Significantly, this links with the earlier proposal that earth lights are produced by similar RF modulations at subterranean depths within faults, which find their way to the surface and out into the atmosphere. After all, it is the silica-based rocks which seem the most potent candidates for inducing piezoelectric/piezomagnetic fields under the physical stress of tectonic activity.

Ergon W. Bach studied BLs of volcanic origin and provides an intriguing picture of fault/fissure-bound fireballs and their expansive release into the atmosphere:

> The fireballs may have crept upward through crack-like vapour chambers, then raced … at sonic or supersonic speeds, having expanded 3000 times from 10 kilobar pressure. A 100 metre sized ball will fit into a crack 1 cm wide, but 130 metres long and deep. Such cracks interlace down to a 5–15 km depth … [Bach, 1992.]

This physicist draws an intriguing picture of how geologically originating fireballs are contained within subterranean fissures, and the extreme malleability he describes is certainly consistent with the 'shape-shifting' behaviours of the ball-of-light phenomenon in the atmosphere.

OZONE AND OTHER REACTANTS IN THE FORMATION OF FIREBALLS

Ozone has been cited as being the 'glue' which stabilizes the delicate fractal 'bubbles' of the fireballs, but it would seem that other chemical reactants are also involved. The Corums comment:

> *Now, as Smirnov points out, merely creating the porous fractal bubble would not be sufficient to result in ball lightning with lifetimes in excess of a few milliseconds – fractal formation occurs in the soot in Faraday's candles. But other ingredients are necessary for the production of ball lightning lasting several seconds or more. We noted that the Tesla apparatus was a copious generator of ozone and other reactants. We believe that these reactants, and perhaps other chemicals, are quickly absorbed into the charged porous fractal bubble. The plasma temperature in the discharge region where the structure is formed is sufficient for the multistep combustion process to initiate. [Corum & Corum, 1991/92]*

Also, the work of Forrest and Witten, who experimented with the production of metallic vapours by electrothermal means, has implications for the dynamics and structures of fireballs:

> *Forrest and Witten's apparatus consisted of a tungsten filament electroplated with either iron or zinc. When the filament was rapidly heated by a short-duration high-current pulse, the plated material vaporized off the filament and formed a dense gas (metallic vapour) which was diffusion-limited in the surrounding atmosphere ... The hot particles rapidly moved outwards from the hot filament, came to rest in the ambient medium, due to collisions, and formed a spherical halo about 1 cm from the filament ... [Corum & Corum, 1991/92]*

From these extracts we may begin to apprehend a process in the formation of electric fireballs, in which substances such as carbon and metals are vaporized by electrothermal processes and form a spherical container, or 'bubble', enclosing a gaseous plasma of extremely high temperatures. It would seem that, depending on the substances which are involved and subjected to this process, a variety of UAPs is produced, with differing densities, colours and other properties. These objects are energetic in the extreme, and are therefore unstable and may release their energies explosively or as heat and/or EM emissions; they may also leave chemical deposits and, in fact, just such unusual metallic deposits have been found after so-called 'UFO landings'.

However, before we explore what proximity and contact with BLs and other UAPs can bring (especially in terms of effects on the human consciousness), there are a number of extracts and quotations from Tesla and the work of the Corum brothers that are both interesting and insightful.

ELECTRIC FIREBALLS: METHODS OF ARTIFICIAL GENERATION – A SUMMARY

A compilation of Tesla's *Colorado Springs Notes* edited by Marincic summarizes the methods of artificial generation thus:

> *There are presently three experimental methods by which electric fireball objects bearing serious resemblance to natural ball lightning may be formed:*
>
> *1. Engine room (high current) fireballs.*
>
> *2. Ignited fuels and chemicals.*
>
> *3. Tesla's (high voltage) fireballs.*
>
> *The principal difference between 1. and 3. is the mode of their predischarge energy storage. There are, of course, a whole host of other ways to make plasmoids, bouncing sparks etc., but because of their short lifetimes and energy requirements none of these are serious contenders for the manmade generation of actual ball lightning. It is required that the fireball exists while the external source is not visually supplying power. [Marincic, 1978.]*

THE DESTRUCTIVENESS OF FIREBALLS

Tesla comments:

> *When working with these powerful electrical oscillations the most extraordinary phenomena take place at times. Owing to some interference of the oscillations, veritable balls of fire are apt to leap out to a great distance ... a ball of fire may break out and destroy the support or anything else in the way ... [Marincic, 1978.]*

ANIMAL 'MUTILATION' AND THE ELECTRIC-FIREBALL CONNECTION

Examples of extreme fireball damage are, thankfully, fairly rare. Following on from this post-Corum/Tesla round-up, there is another major area of study regarding the destructive powers of electric fireballs: the range of physical traumas inflicted on grazing animals. This other area, which I have explored, shows that animals such as sheep, horses and cattle have been electrothermally damaged by unidentified lights in the sky, especially in the USA, although this may reflect differential reporting patterns. That is to say, in the USA, there seems to be an inclination to attribute such physical traumas and deaths to aliens in UFOs rather than to close encounters with electric fireballs. However, my own study project, based on experiments by Australian researchers, who subjected anaesthetized sheep to artificial lightning bolts, shows that such fireballs are attracted to the body apertures of animals (Dayton, 1993). These act as wave guides, inducing the fireball into the interior of the animal and causing death and severe electrothermal damage; there is little blood loss due to the cauterizing effects of the heat produced. Case studies have shown that such atmospheric lights are closely associated with such animal traumas (see Note 13).

THE EFFECTS OF FIREBALL PROXIMITY

Investigations by Bach into volcanic fireballs (see p. 188) offer some relevant insights into how they may be contained within the geology, although it is the interaction of UAPs with the more commonplace human environments of town and country which is the main focus of my investigations and research. In addition, it is their effects upon the human physiology that concern us. To a large extent, this has already been addressed (p. 21) when we considered physiological responses to EM fields, as it is, of course, this energetic component of UAPs which intrudes upon the nervous system. In fact, it may be difficult to separate the two – field and fireball – when exploring cases in which individuals have come close to a UAP of some type, because, as we have seen, the UAP comes into existence due to the presence of fields in the first place. However, it is evident in many cases that the UAP brings unique EM disturbances along with it, as opposed to the usual ambient field effects. Another effect, which only rarely results from field interactions, is the electrothermal aspect and this does seem to be almost exclusively UAP-centred. Although there is a possibility of thermal phenomena (diathermy) being induced by RF fields, microwave exposure or the Hutchison effect, the energetic effects of heating on individuals and the environment have been often associated with proximity to electric fire-balls or other UAPs. However, this will be considered along with the other consequences of proximity to aerial light phenomena.

A KEY CONCEPT – FIREBALL PROXIMITY

It is often thought that progress in understanding the close-encounter experience will come about when more data has been collected in terms of measurements. However, such hard data is directionless without a conceptual framework in which to interpret it; therefore, the impor-tance of conceptual development cannot be overestimated. It was the realization that close encounters could be divided into two distinct cate-gories – the physically real fireball on the one hand and the effects of their EM emissions on the witness on the other – which revolutionized the thinking of many researchers.

This simple concept of dividing such events into two distinct areas – objective-physical/subjective-consciousness – introduced a whole new approach to the close-encounter experience. Here was a way of under-standing such events which retained a physically tangible UFO which could be photographed and seen by multiples of witnesses from different locations, which registered on radar and could be seen to induce phys-ical effects on witnesses and the environment, but which could also induce perceptions of alien entities and their apparently associated envi-ronments. Simply put, the fireball is real, but the encounters with aliens are hallucinatory episodes which are induced by the EM fields that the fireball emits.

It has frequently surprised me how many intelligent and experienced investigators have failed to take on board this model of understanding. I have received letters from some which tell me that the idea of shared hallucination cannot account for how a brilliant UFO was seen by witnesses many kilometres apart. I remember waiting to deliver my contribution to a BBC World Service programme on the UFO phenomenon at Bush House, London, and listening to ETH enthusiast Roy Dutta tell listeners how the Linda Jones case (see Note 14) could not have been the product of EM pollution because three witnesses saw a mysterious luminous object. It is frustrating to be confronted by such objections which result from a failure to understand this simple concept. Therefore, it is clear that information on what an electric fireball is like, and what happens when witnesses get close to one, is essential for our understanding of the UFO experience.

It must be remembered at the outset that we are dealing with several different variants of UAP, even if we consider BLs alone. The permu-tations of interactions of field and fireball have already been pointed out, and it is clear that the effects on the witness and the environment created by one incident may not apply to another. We are looking at a family of phenomena as opposed to a single type and, as a result, predictions of what to expect can only be extremely broad. Some fireballs induce heating effects while others do not. Some cause power failures; some cause power surges. Some affect the the witness adversely; some have been downright beneficial. Some witnesses fall apart physically and mentally after getting close but, for others, it is a new beginning, heralding an unprecedented era of creativity. It may be noticed that similar variations apply to being close to a lightning strike, or actually being struck by lightning. Thus one of the first aspects that we should appreciate is that UAP proximity has very close parallels with a close encounter with lightning – it could be extremely dangerous.

The clinical aspects of how the human body reacts to a lightning strike were covered on p.83, and UAP proximity both shares and contrasts with these aspects. Another parallel could be drawn between UAP proximity and electroconvulsive therapy (ECT), whereby an electric current is deliberately passed through the brain of a clinically depressed patient. Sometimes the treatment is beneficial and sometimes it is not. However, before individual cases are examined, it should be emphasized that a close encounter with a UAP, BL included, is extremely likely to constitute an MEE; for someone who is already hypersensitive to EM fields, such an encounter could precipitate a make-or-break situation, physiologically speaking. As described for the Aveley event (p.142), this typically includes a vivid hallucinatory episode that represents a fundamental turning point in the experiencers' life, in terms of their health, outlook and emotional well-being. For those who are not electrically hypersensitive (EH), close proximity often involves unconsciousness and a consistent range of mental and physical after-effects.

It was American folklorist Dr Edward Bullard who examined the alien-abduction phenomenon across populations, and who subsequently marvelled at the consistency and orderliness of the experience (Bullard, 1987). This is, of course, exactly what doctors tracking a discrete condition in the open population would expect and rely on to identify it; i.e. it is the human nervous system and its response to prolonged field exposure, including the development of environmental sensitivities, that gives the abduction vision its consistency. The human body reacts in the same way to the same sort of stimulus across populations.

When considering instances of close exposure to UAPs, it would seem that we are regarding unique situations which involve periods of irradiation longer than those that occur with proximity to lightning strikes; the latter are obviously over in an instant but are of higher inten-

sity in terms of field strength (amplitude) than those found in environmental hot spots, e.g. power-line proximity. MEEs to which the
individual may be subjected, e.g. major electrocution through
physical contact with current-carrying circuitry, do not involve the
particular conditions of prolonged high-amplitude irradiation. Fireball
proximity seems to bring with it not only a singular form of irradiation
(involving, for example, whole-body exposure, thermal aspects, etc.), to
which the human biological system reacts uniquely, but also visual
cues that add a particularly potent aspect in terms of the UFO
mythology.

Professor Michael Persinger at the Laurentian University, Ontario,
Canada, found that, if he magnetically stimulated the temporal lobes of his
subjects in a chamber where quasi-religious imagery decorated the walls,
the sensations induced were largely interpreted in mystical/spiritual terms.
If, however, he replaced this with planetary and space-travel imagery, the
experiences induced were interpreted in quasi-cosmic/alien-communi-
cation terms (Ruttan et al., 1990). It is clear that context strongly influ-
ences how percipients identify their experiences, and it is not difficult to
imagine the impression which a large sphere of light, suddenly swooping
down to settle on the ground nearby, would make on a witness; this is
exactly the circumstance of several close encounters I have investigated.
Such unusual events certainly mimic the landing of spaceships.

UNCLASSIFIED ATMOSPHERIC PHENOMENA: families and hybrids

UAPs have been differentiated according to their mode of production,
although even this seemingly foolproof method of identifying types has
its problems. BL may be produced in the electrical fields of a thunderstorm but, once formed, it could be irradiated by artificially produced
fields from microwave transmitters for example or enter the home-field
of the earth light and become caught up in geomagnetic fields emanating
from faults. In the experiments of the Corum brothers on the laboratory
production of BL (see p.175), fireballs which were struck by high-tension
streamers from the Tesla coils were altered in that they increased in size
and duration. Comparable alterations by exposure to environmental
fields are quite feasible and, with altered parameters, the original, naturally produced BL could be transformed into something quite different.
In fact, altered aerial phenomena such as exotic light forms have been
consistently reported for decades. This hybridization of usually recognizable UAPs, such as BL, through continued irradiation must be one of the
most feasible mechanisms for the production of unusual 'lights in the sky'

(LITS). Consider the following report of an encounter with a UAP:

> At about 9 p.m. on the night of March 4th, 1968, the witness was
> driving his 1967 Triumph Spitfire Mk. 3 sportscar along a narrow
> country lane in the district of Higher Chisworth, situated on the
> Cheshire/Derbyshire border [in the UK]. The night was dry but very
> dark. As the witness, a Mr Burnell, neared the T-junction with the lane
> from Holehouse to Ludworth Intakes, a small golden object, travelling at
> high speed, suddenly appeared ahead of and to the right of his position,
> from the direction of Cown Edge Rocks. At the same instant the car's
> headlamps were extinguished, the radio was silenced, the engine stopped
> and the car lurched to a halt. Within approximately 2 seconds, the object
> travelled without noise on a very flat trajectory across the valley to the left
> and diminished before disappearing beyond the Longendale spur to the
> north. The car's headlights re-lit as the object passed to the observer's left
> after crossing his path. After the object had been lost from view the engine
> was re-started without difficulty, but it was discovered the radio would not
> work. [Lockwood & Price, 1979.]

Such accounts as this, which is entirely typical, show how deserving
such phenomena are of their 'unclassified' label. BL does not behave like
this, and it cannot be identified using the undefined parameters of earth
lights. Interestingly, the report continues:

> In the vicinity of the object's apparent path over Longendale spur,
> numerous electrical supply pylons are prominent features of Shaw Moor
> ... A small radio mast surmounts a 900 ft mound called Harrop Edge
> ... Mr Burnell indicated that the object had appeared to arc downwards
> slightly as it disappeared in the dip between these two features.
> [Lockwood & Price, 1979.]

This witness was lucky, as such a fireball encounter may constitute an
MEE and an an extreme exposure. However, the radio in the car
showed that it had malfunctioned because of either a heating effect or
an externally induced reversed current direction in the electronics.
Other witnesses have not been so fortunate.

From the rare accounts I have investigated personally, and from the case
reports of others, there is little doubt that getting too close to a large electric fireball is potentially dangerous. However, people usually live to tell the
tale, and such an encounter does, of course, constitute an MEE. A firsthand
description of what it is like to undergo such a close encounter with an
electric fireball is fairly rare. Usually, when witnesses get close to fireballs
they fall unconscious or exhibit epileptiform symptoms or behaviour.
Such individuals have frequently related how at one moment they were
looking at the UAP and then, with no sense of transition, they have found

themselves somewhere else, doing something different from their last memory. This sudden jump in reality is a hallmark of automatic behaviour, and the following description is typical. In this, the witness had been observing a light in the sky which seemed to have been following him:

> *Half way across the field he saw a bright light hanging in the sky … WP rushed off the fields and onto the lane that leads directly to the pub. He noticed that it was unusually deserted. But the object was now close above him, between him and the pub, and was a structured device surrounded by a greenish mist. It was perhaps 100 feet from him. He estimates that the object was 20–30 feet wide and six to ten feet high, like an elongated oval in shape. It seemed to be made out of a sort of 'gunmetal' but was silent. The mist rolled around it and seemed to be fluorescent and glowed on the surface of the object. WP also realized that the ambient sounds he would have expected to hear had gone. Everything was strangely quiet … WP had only seconds to take this in. For suddenly (with no sense of transition) he was inside the men's toilets, adjacent to the pub, staring at the outer wall as if he were ready to walk out. He had no idea how he got there! [Anon., 1984b.]*

Typically, when WP did go into the pub, the landlord told him that there had been a power cut. This account is a good example of UAP-related automatic behaviour. The strange eerie silence reported is another epileptiform symptom produced by the electrical stimulation of the reticular portion of the mid- and forebrain (Thompson, 1976). Therefore, after the induction of at least two epileptiform hallucinatory perceptions, it is entirely consistent to identify another, i.e. to experience a visual seizure. The solid appearance of the UFO, complete with fluorescent mist swirling around it, is a typical choice of simple UFO imagery by the brain, cued and irradiated by what began as simply a weird light in the sky, seemingly following the witness.

Other 'classic' cases, once they are taken out of the ETH mythology, become candidates for UAP encounters, because of the epileptiform symptoms which are associated with them, e.g. the case of Alan Godfrey. This British policeman sat in his car, sketching the apparently structured object which confronted him, and then, to his surprise, instantly found himself driving down the road, once again, with no sense of transition; this is another prime example of automatic behaviour. Interestingly, this took place in Todmorden, which is one of the most EM-polluted locations in Britain. It surely follows that another effect of such destabilized electrical activity in the brain must also have manifested – visual seizure or hallucination *superimposed on a physically real UAP.*

Appendix

Investigations and case-file studies:
in-depth examinations of events
from the UK, North America
and Australia

THE UNIFIED THEORY

It has been stated that the consciousness effects known as alien-contact/abduction experiences are basically extensions of perceptions of other psychical phenomena, including ghosts, apparitions and numerous other entities, or formed figures. It must be remembered, however, that some apparitions are 'place memories' and therefore objective phenomena, and a mechanism for these has been presented (see p.152) It soon becomes a truism among investigators that percipients who have alien encounters also have a history of psychical experiences, and one frequently shades imperceptibly into the other. Both are symptomatic of electrical hypersensitivity (EH) and multiple allergy and, once the investigator becomes sensitive to the primary parameters invariably involved, they 'jump out' from the assortment of information on a case, as they are extremely robust. As one investigator put it:

> There is nothing 'airy-fairy' about these characteristics. They are the blunt instrument with which to hit the ETH [extraterrestrial hypothesis].

Even Dr C. W. Smith and Simon Best, in their epic text book on health, and electromagnetic (EM) pollution, *Electromagnetic Man* (Smith & Best, 1989), comment in passing that EH individuals tend to have a history of paranormal experiences. Likewise, individuals who do not have on-going periods in their lives during which all manner of unusual sensations and strange episodes occur, including 'paranormal' events and apparent spontaneous intrusions of aliens of various types, do not exhibit the primary parameters. That is to say, such anomaly-free controls do not have the combination of major electrical event (MEE), environmental sensitivities and continuous hot-spot exposure. For some unknown reason, those who have doubted the validity of the

EM-pollution approach, automatically seem to assume that I have not carried out any controls and that I have arrived at my conclusions lightly. However, those people who wish to hold on to the idea of aliens from outer space, or those who think that all the complexities of these experiences can be reduced to sociological phenomena, will just refuse to see the correlations and identifications which I have made. I would draw the reader's attention to the quotation by Max Planck at the beginning of this book.

I remember the first lecture which I gave when I launched the environmental health approach in 1994, and told the audience that I had carried out 19 in-depth investigations of alien-abduction experiences. One pro-ETH lady stood up and smartly pointed out that there were hundreds of such cases on file and I had only looked at 19! She had failed to realize the import of my straight 19, i.e. I had not picked and chosen my cases, throwing out the ones that did not fit, but had looked at 19 consecutive cases *just exactly as they passed into my hands at random* from the grapevine, and all of them exhibited the same cluster of primary parameters. If this were due to chance, it would be like winning an accumulator bet spread across 19 separate races – extremely unlikely, if not impossible!

I have now looked at over 80 cases and they all share many of the basic parameters and, even as I peruse the basic details of further cases, I sense continued consistency. So what are these primary parameters? They have already been set out in the blueprint on p.19, although I shall remind readers of them as we progress through the following cases. Basically, however, I am predicting MEEs, hot-spot exposure and a range of signs, symptoms and environmental effects induced by such energies, many of them already examined. The consistent occurrence of these aspects constitutes a fulfilment of such predictions and it is generally agreed in science that the correctness of any theory *rests on its power to predict*.

The following cases are a mixture of 'alien', apparitional 'haunting' and other entity events, and, as an investigator faced with a percipient who has experienced both 'ghosts' and 'aliens', it appears somewhat arbitrary as to which to focus upon. It is ironic that psychical researchers do not investigate cases in which the percipient encounters aliens, and ufologists do not consider the incidence of ghosts as being within their area of study, and that both are influenced by the redundant conventions of these labels. The rigidity of establishment conventions was brought home to me when Dr John Beloff, editor of the house journal for the Society for Psychical Research (SPR), returned a paper that I had submitted for publication which was entitled 'Preliminary identifications of alien contact/abduction experiences as hallucinatory states induced by prolonged exposures to electromagnetic pollution in the environment.'

His comment was to the effect that, whatever implications EM fields may have for alien-abduction experiences, they had none for psychical phenomena in general, i.e. he failed to appreciate that alien-abduction experiences are, in fact, psychical phenomena. Such an absence of awareness was frustrating, especially as, at that point, I had been investigating psychical phenomena (including apparitions and poltergeist activity) in identified hot-spot locations for 3 years or so. Belloff later went on to challenge whether the Hutchison effect was involved in poltergeist activity, such as that at Enfield, north London, a well-known case in the UK; his objection rested on the fact that 'the Hutchison device could not have been present at such suburban locations'! For some strange reason, Beloff had not made the comparative link in his thinking between the effects which occurred due to the low-power fields generated in Hutchison's laboratory and those at large in the environment at hot-spot locations. This, of course, was the whole point of introducing the Hutchison effect into the equation in the first place.

However, not only do 'alien' and 'ghost' categories mix and match, so that the same percipient may report seeing both, either as consecutive experiences or *together in the same experience* (See Note 15), but physical poltergeist activity may also occur with the same percipient and/or location, i.e. *in the same case*. In the past, investigators may have considered this as further evidence of a 'haunting', but it does not sit easily with encounters with extraterrestrials (ETs), and poltergeist activity and ghosts are frequently found in such cases. However, this embarrassing incongruity is conveniently ignored by the ETH fraternity. This alien/poltergeist association occurs because the effects of EM pollution can be divided *for convenience only* into the three categories mentioned earlier, i.e. health, consciousness and environmental effects.

THE ARRIVAL OF THE LITMUS TEST: HOAX OR REALITY?

The approach presented could usefully be described as a 'unified theory' because it provides commonalities which link UFO/alien-encounter experiences, ghosts and poltergeists. However, it is also a radical step forward in terms of the identification of such experiences as genuine (i.e. the authenticity of a report) because, before the EM-pollution approach, one of the quite legitimate criticisms that scientists could level at reports of these experiences was that there was no way of telling a genuine case from a hoaxed one; this potentially made all accounts and associated data suspect (see Note 16). Now all this has changed and investigators have a set of major diagnostic tools at their disposal in terms of the EM hardware in the environment, field measurements with conventional field-meters, and the signs and symptoms of the clinical conditions which are an intrinsic part of alien or other entity encounters (including Reiter's response) and which can be predicted.

'Abductees' have allergies, chemical sensitivities, EH and epileptiform symptoms, and I have yet to find one who has not experienced the sense of presence on an episodic basis. They all exhibit the same cluster of signs and symptoms, which number at least 25, as well as a number of other environmentally induced conditions that are intrinsically associated with hot-spot exposure. In addition, there are the objective measurements taken by instrumentation: the readings of field-meters are objective facts that cannot be denied. Also associated with 'abductions' or 'visitations' is a well-defined cluster of health effects and, where one is found, the other is not far behind.

Linda Brown, from Troon, Scotland, telephoned me in the spring of 1995 after hearing of my investigations into the adverse health effects of EM pollution. She heads a local support group for sufferers of myalgic encephalomyelitis (ME), simply called 'Search Me', as there had been so many cases of this post-viral fatigue syndrome in her area. She related how her local area had been investigated by leading British figures in EM-pollution research: Drs C. W. Smith and Roger Coghill. Measurements had shown high field levels in and around Troon due to a combination of a major surface fault, a military base and Prestwick airport. Coghill had noticed a repeated association between EM hot spots and cases of ME and, from my own investigations, it would certainly appear that sufferers never fully recover from this post-viral fatigue syndrome because of the stress put on their physiology by environmental fields. Our conversation began with aspects relating to health effects, but eventually I sensed that she had something unspoken on her mind. She hesitantly mentioned that, in addition to ME, local sufferers also have 'mental effects' and, eventually, and somewhat sheepishly, she told me, 'Well, we are getting aliens ...', meaning 'visitor' experiences. This was welcome independent testimony, supporting my conclusions, from a group of people who were initially preoccupied with dealing with the outbreak of a clinical condition, but who now, quite spontaneously, found the consciousness effects I had predicted.

But there is more. In addition to these health effects, there is a recognizable set of accompanying environmental effects. This secondary diagnostic cluster is due to the direct effects of EM fields upon the domestic environment and these range from, for example, the short life of light-bulbs to the appearance of micro-voids in polymers, including contact lenses. Any investigators who take on the EM-pollution approach as a means of identifying and understanding their cases will soon begin to recognize these recurring clusters and, by using 'The 25

Questions' (see p.28), will develop a feel for cases and be able to recognize the effects of field exposure. That is to say, unlike so many investigators at vigils in 'haunted' locations, they will know precisely what they are looking for and why. They will begin to sense the robust consistency behind the bizarre accounts they explore, to re-assess cases they have investigated in the past and to recognize the significance of a number of details that previously had no particular meaning.

In a way, I am reluctant to disclose many of these details because, at the moment, experiencers are unaware of their significance (i.e. that they are indicative of environmental sensitivities) and so openly admit to them. Many experiencers prefer to retain their status of being real alien contactees, as opposed to suffering from environmentally induced illnesses. Therefore, as they became increasingly aware of the situation, they may not admit to a hypersensitivity to light or to volatile chemicals, such as perfumes, cleaning products or aerosols, in order to guard against such a diagnosis. I have in fact found it increasingly difficult to obtain unbiased information on their sensitivities because some have learned what and what not to admit to, from reading my books or attending my lectures. They do not want to let go of their aliens.

However, there is a simple and devastating way of getting around this, which I would not necessarily recommend, and that is to expose them to such chemicals and EM fields. On a few occasions, in my inexperienced days, after being given information that I suspected was false, I have sprayed the room with an aerosol air-freshener while the subjects were out of the room. Their return has been most instructive; despite telling me that such chemicals have no effect on them, I have witnessed them collapse with an overwhelming weakness and loss of muscle strength and have to be escorted from the room into the fresh air. However, I would like to emphasize that this is not a practice that should be adopted as an investigative ploy because, potentially, it is clearly hazardous.

There are some experiencers with no chemical sensitivities or food allergies who have developed temporal-lobe lability, which is triggered by field exposure, and these will be described subsequently. Such people display a different consistent cluster of recognizable systemic effects related to this heightened sensitivity, which has been induced by encounters with electricity in formative years. Similarly, switching on a radio-frequency (RF) signal generator in their presence may be probative, but it is grossly irresponsible because it could precipitate systemic shock. It has been emphasized that such procedures are not only an investigative protocol but also a clinical one. It would appear therefore, that Reiter's 'magnetic response' (MR) is the safest objective test, although this should be adopted cautiously, beginning with weak magnets, and it does not really overcome the problem of the unco-operative experiencer or hoaxer.

Of course, one objective environmental test is the presence of raised levels of fields in the subjects' homes, and these can be detected by a field-meter. Eventually, investigators with an open mind will begin to realize that, in tracing these aspects, they are dealing with symptoms of a medical/environmental syndrome that has hallucinatory episodes as one of the symptoms, as opposed to encounters with aliens from other worlds or spirits of the dead. In a way, this latter section is intended to act as a revisionary handbook for investigators, so that they may recognize the natural history of these experiences as being bioelectromagnetic phenomena and so that the way such accounts are recorded and related is fundamentally revised. Raw anecdotes need to be supplemented with information on the sensitivities of the experiencer, the geology and some indication of the EM-pollution profile of the area concerned. It is essential to use instrumentation and *no investigator should be without a field-meter*, preferably one which detects magnetic and electric fields separately, as well as those in the RF/microwave range.

CHILDHOOD ABUSE

There is another factor that runs through 'abductee' populations which has not been emphasized so far, and that is the incidence of childhood abuse. This trend is not an iron law, but a recurring aspect that is difficult not to notice when the histories of such experiencers are taken. Professor Kenneth Ring, in *The Omega Project* (Ring, 1992), also outlines this trend, which he found in his American samples too. So what does it mean, in terms of the experiences that are the subject of our study?

It would appear that children who are subjected to prolonged abuse, which, remember, occurs during their formative years when their basic psychological elements are being laid down, may develop a particular defence mechanism whereby they are able to shut out unpleasant realities by the construction of a powerful and stable inner fantasy life. That is to say, they develop what has been termed *disassociative entrainment*, whereby they are readily able to 'switch channels', as it were, so that their outer world takes on a lesser reality status than their inner imaginative domain (see Note 17). This ability is a biological survival mechanism, enabling them to deny their immediate situation, which is so stressful that it would destroy them emotionally, spiritually and, by evoking repeated traumas, physiologically. Therefore, they reach a developmental position where, under semi-conscious control, they are able to 'flip' and live in a self-constructed world.

It would seem that this ability has fundamental implications for the alien-abduction vision because this disassociated state involves a powerful and stable visualization process in which the subjects are able to interact with the contents of their internal drama as if it were an objective reality. They may 'flip' into this internal world automatically, with little or no sense of volition on their part, because this response has been imprinted into their make-up as a regular strategy for dealing with the world, through the prolonged reinforcement of classical conditioning. It was the English occultist Graham Fletcher who once told me, during a discussion on hallucinatory realities, that, as far as the experiencers are concerned, it does not matter whether the entities they encounter originate internally or externally because they behave, and the experiencers react towards them, as if they have an external objective reality. As an investigator, one soon becomes aware of the 'trippers', who play videos in their heads more readily and vividly than we more mediocre day-dreamers.

In my investigations I have not explored such childhood traumas in any detail, but I have become aware that they exist in the backgrounds of many experiencers. Also, I have noticed that such early trauma, especially if it is sexual, is reflected in other aspects of the experiencers' lives. There is a trend for female 'abductees' to marry or partner someone who is much older or younger than they are. This could be because, in adult life, either they need the paternal support and reduced sexual demands of an older man or they feel that they supply a maternal, and therefore asexual, relationship for an equally needy younger man. One experiencer in her late thirties, based in north London, married a 16-year-old boy, and another, in Kent, also in her early thirties, married a man in his sixties. Of course, such partnerships with non-experiencers take place without the developmental conditions described, and many experiencers are more equally matched with their partners in terms of age; nevertheless it is a trend that is difficult not to notice.

Case 1

Ian of Peckham

Location: London, UK

Time frame: 1993–94

Description

Ian is a young man in his mid-twenties, living on his own in a small bedsitting room on the third floor of a large Victorian house. At one time he worked for the Post Office and then as a bus-driver, but, at the time of investigation, he seems to have given up looking for work and spends many hours a day writing, having filled many thick A4 pads. He freely admits that this has become an obsession with him. His outlook on life and his motivations have been totally transformed by his dramatic experiences, which have taken place episodically over the past year or so.

A couple of months after moving into the bedsit, in January 1993, during the early hours of the morning (between midnight and 3 a.m.), he began to be visited by tall humanoid figures made of dazzling golden light; one by one, these slowly emerged through the wall of his room. Sometimes as many as six of these figures filled his small room, and the light which emanated from them was dazzlingly brilliant. Nobody else has seen them.

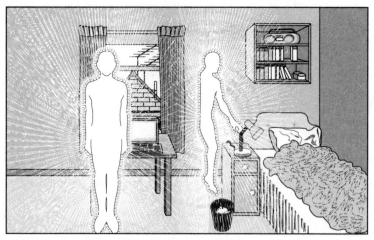

The experiencer's perception of luminous humanoids entering his room. Note the radio antennae outside his window.

He has held conversations with them and has 'learned' that they came from another galaxy and that he has been chosen to communicate their message to the world via a book that he must write. He feels that he has been given a vast amount of information by them, and that he must finish and publish the book within 2 months. He relates that he has been told that, once the information in the book is released, there will be a social upheaval and conflict; therefore, he must be prepared for this and, as he will play an important part, he must keep strong and healthy. In short, he feels that he has been given a supreme mission by these aliens, and he is extremely suspicious of 'the authorities' who, he believes, know what is going on and sometimes follow him in the street. He has painted a picture of the planet that the aliens come from, which bristles with weaponry.

The 'humanoids' (a word that he uses) communicate with him through normal speech, and also with words in his mind, which can intrude into his thoughts anytime and anywhere. They know all about his personal history and once reviewed his life. However, because he has been chosen by them, he receives instructions on how to maintain his health; they monitor his diet and insist that he eats only fresh meat and vegetables, which he now buys regularly. He once broke these dietary rules and relates how they severely admonished him, showing him a horrific vision of his own death by heart attack, to emphasize how he must not eat 'junk food', sweets, canned food, biscuits, etc. After this vision, he bought an exercise bike, which he now uses daily, as the aliens instructed him to lose weight. His appearance is of a healthy young man, and he does not smoke or drink alcohol.

The aliens, he relates, 'are friends with God, and can control the weather'. He was once saved by them, as they mentally told him not to step into the street, which was then struck by lightning a metre or so away from him. He knows that they colonize the bodies of others as he has seen these beings of light emerge from people in the street. On occasion, he has seen dark shadowy figures in his room, which he identifies as spirits of some kind, and he often feels a presence as if they are watching him, although he cannot see them. He has out-of-body experiences (OBEs) occasionally.

SENSATIONS AND SYMPTOMS

When he is sitting down writing, Ian sometimes finds that his whole body 'jolts like an electric shock', after which his vision is blurred and misty. He also suffers from severe headaches in his temples and gets shooting pains in his head. He often gets an all-over tingling sensation when he is in his room at night, and sees small lights about the size of a large coin flitting about the room; these are green in colour with a reddish aura. Episodically, he suffers from severe dizzy spells and an overwhelming weakness that is unrelieved by rest or sleep. He also suffers from a numbness down one side of his face which can last for up to an hour. In addition, he complains that his memory has deteriorated and suffers from headaches.

Observations

Although Ian was very nervous at first when I interviewed him, his mood throughout was calm, rational and, at times, humorous. He was aware that what he was telling me was incredible and, when he had finished, asked me directly if I believed him. He seemed relieved to learn that I did, and that I believed that he had in fact seen the things which he described.

I initially spoke to him for about 2 hours, sitting in his room, which was packed with electrical appliances, e.g. video-recorder, two midi-systems, word-processor, fridge, radio, television set, etc. As soon as I switched my miniature tape-recorder on, I noticed that the light-emitting diode (LED) did not light up as usual. About half-way through the interview the recorder stopped for no apparent reason; the batteries were flat. As a standard procedure I always check that equipment is functioning normally before leaving home and record a short message, which I had done on this occasion. I changed the batteries for new ones and wrapped the recorder in aluminium foil to shield it, as it is typical for EH-status subjects to emit fields that cause electronic equipment to malfunction, which is what happened in this case. The recorder reluctantly began to work again but soon stopped altogether. Ian then remembered that he also wanted to record the interview and switched on his mains-operated cassette-recorder, which seemed to function properly throughout the remainder of the interview, although I did not hear the recording it made. My mini tape-recorder worked normally the following day at home, just as it had before I left to travel to Ian's location.

On testing with a field-meter, I found that Ian's body was emitting an electric field at a frequency above 60Hz. A girlfriend of Ian's was also present; she was tested too and did not emit a field. Ian told me that he builds up static easily and often gets shocks from metal. He has on occasion put his hand on the casing of the video-recorder and 'it has started by itself'. He related that he was told by the aliens that they were adapting his body and mind and, in a few months, when this process was complete, he would be able to energize circuitry on a regular basis. At the moment he gets small shocks when plugging in electrical appliances.

OTHER DETAILS

Near the end of the interview, Ian said something quite revealing:

When I was seven years old, I lost control and rammed my head into a wall.

Also, he 'loves lightning' and recounted:

Once when I was out during a storm, I was crossing the road on a zebra crossing and lightning just missed me. It went phew! into the ground just in front of me. Then there was a roll of thunder. I went ahh! [putting his hand on his chest]. It really took me back.

FIELD SOURCES

At one point I asked Ian if the aliens came through any wall or one in particular, and he indicated the wall with the only window. On looking out of the window I was astounded to see, about 9m (30ft) away, three RF-transmitting antennae mounted on a neighbour's roof: two yagis and a dipole. The neighbour is a radio ham and Ian would have been irradiated in his room at point-blank range.

A field-survey of the room when no transmissions were taking place also revealed that his bed was against a wall that constantly emitted an electrical field of 55.0V/m, while the wall that the bedhead rested against emitted a constant electrical field of 104.16V/m! I later learned that such high points are common in older Victorian houses where the circuitry is often poorly insulated with oiled paper and the water content in the plaster acts as a conductive medium. Also, due to the many appliances, there were magnetic-field-density high points, e.g. 56.65nT. Note here, that the term 'high point' is used to define raised field levels emitted by appliances and circuitry inside a building; 'hot spot', on the other hand, denotes the intrusion of fields into the building from the environment outside, e.g. from RF transmitters. Of course, all homes have high points, but it is their number and distribution within the rooms which contribute to the ambient field levels; these, in Ian's room, were very high.

Analysis

EPILEPTIFORM SYMPTOMS

Ian, through prolonged irradiation from the field sources mentioned, has developed an epileptiform condition and suffers from focal seizures. These manifest as a variety of sensations and perceptions. The sense of presence and intense feeling of being watched are due to temporal-lobe stimulation. The coloured lights he sees flitting about the room are magnetophosphenes, which can also be induced in the upper left quadrant of the visual field when the temporal lobes are stimulated. However, Ian may also have epileptiform tendencies due to minor trauma to the brain in childhood, when, as he says, he 'lost control and rammed my head into a wall'. The profuse writing activity is clearly hypergraphia. More serious focal seizures occur from time to time, and Ian does complain of his body suddenly 'jolting like an electric shock', especially as this is followed by blurred and misty vision, which is a typical after-effect of seizures, or syncopes, as they are now referred to. Ian also mentions that, sometimes, time seems to stand still for him, although everything else carries on normally. This is an effect called desynchronization, and, again, is caused by temporal-lobe stimulation.

ELECTRICAL HYPERSENSITIVITY

The tingling (somesthesia) and numbness (paresthesia) are typical symptoms of field exposure, and are due to the sensitivity and over stimulation of the nerve endings. The loss of muscle strength which is unrelieved by rest is also a typical symptom of exposure. However, even more typical and probative were the field emissions from his body, which interfered with the functions of my tape-recorder, causing it to stop altogether. Similarly, he is able to activate electrical equipment by touching it, and these personal field emissions registered on a gaussmeter (a Coghill Fieldmouse). Also, power loss from batteries is an effect which occurs repeatedly in the presence of EH-status individuals. I wondered how he fared with the word-processor and saw that his writings are by hand. To conclude, Ian would have already acquired a temporal-lobe lability, as he had undergone an MEE via his proximity to a lighting strike, which seems to have been repeated during the period of his hot-spot exposure.

THE HUMANOIDS AND THEIR 'WELFARE MESSAGE'

Ian's physiology has been destabilized by prolonged irradiation from the RF transmitter close by and from the electrical fields which emanate from the walls close to his bed. It is no coincidence that the hallucinatory humanoids he encountered were depicted as being concerned for his health, their 'welfare messages' acting as compensatory measures. It is not difficult to regard these perceptions of luminous formed figures, who emerged through the wall, as alien personifications of the constant stream of microwave fields, which, in real physical terms, did penetrate the walls of his room.

In the light of the link between such field exposure and food allergies in the clinical literature (see p.74), it is also no coincidence that the humanoids were depicted as imparting strict guidelines about his diet, banning 'junk food' and foodstuffs with additives, sweeteners, artificial colouring, E-rated flavour-enhancers, etc. From a personal perspective, after living closely with someone with food allergies, I am only too aware of the instantly adverse effects that precisely such chemicals will induce in someone with sensitivities to them. Such people have to maintain a daily diet of fresh meat and vegetables, and it is not coincidental that this was also exactly the diet prescribed by the humanoids for Ian. Nor is it a coincidence that Ian does not smoke or drink, and that he is preoccupied with exercise and keeping fit, which is a pattern that I have noticed among many EH-status/allergic individuals.

Conclusion

This is just one of many cases to be described in which concerns for the purity of bodily intake are the practical consequence of these strange experiences, reflecting the holistic medicine ethos, which the experiencers unwittingly enact. It is interesting to note that, in Ian's case, such a strict dietary regime was held in place by a belief system imposed upon his perceptions. He felt that he had been given a unique mission which could influence the destiny of mankind and which was little short of a religious command. Certainly, past visionaries have founded complete apocalyptic religious movements on less, and Ian's profuse writings are concerned with the cosmological/theosophical issues so typical of hypergraphia. However, such apparent significance is only a tool, employed by the irradiated body, to influence behaviour, so that the body can reach a new state of equilibrium and counteract the effects of constant irradiation. This is to ensure that the individual is metabolically well adjusted, and that destabilization, malfunction, and failure of the regulatory systems are avoided. In fact, this is exactly how allergic responses have been defined. Once again the mind and body in concert provide a strategy that has no consequences for anything except the highly personalized welfare of the individual undergoing these experiences. That is to say, these visions and associated belief systems are purely personal.

It is difficult to imagine how it would feel suddenly to witness something so completely strange and unrelated to our previous life, and then to receive information and instruction via that phenomenon which tells us to carry out a mission that will affect the destiny of mankind. In many other cases there are similar personalized belief systems in place and, in a way, it is essential that the experiencer continues to be deluded by them and acts in terms of them, while being completely unaware of the body's hidden agenda that creates them as a biological survival mechanism. It is difficult not to become aware of an intelligence at work in these cases but, instead of entities from another galaxy, such effects come about through the interactions between environmental fields and the part of the consciousness of the human organism concerned with the welfare and health of the body. In this way, we could regard 'body consciousness' as our own personal 'caretaker', who monitors our health as biological organisms and communicates with us via these strange visionary episodes when things go wrong.

As I have investigated case after case, I have been struck by how people's lives have been totally taken over by their experiences and associated belief system. As implied by the identification of these visionary episodes as a biological survival mechanism, these strategies by the 'body consciousness' to regain a measure of metabolic equilibrium in the face of destabilizing irradiation have not previously been recognized. However, this is what these experiences are all about. On p.133, the view of Kurt Goldstein was quoted because he too, in his work with brain-damaged soldiers, came to the conclusion that the whole biological and spiritual system comes to the rescue of such physically traumatized sufferers. There is a direct parallel with the occurrence of these strange experiences but, instead of mechanical brain damage, the brain (and body) is disturbed by irradiation and responds. The person, true to the spirit of biological evolution, adapts to produce a new norm of operation, just as Goldstein's patients did; it is just that this adaptation has consequences in terms of a belief system. In order for the operation of the body to be kept intact, food and chemical input must be controlled. This is mostly self-regulating, as allergic people become ill if they transgress the dietary rules. But the irradiated are not consciously aware that they must counterbalance the accumulating load with dietary restraint, and the symptoms produced are not linked with food allergies in their mind, so that hidden or masked allergies occur. Therefore the 'body consciousness' must step in and recruit the mind via the fields which irradiate the brain and produce visions and an associated belief system.

One well-documented epileptiform symptom in which the individual may obsessively adopt a religious outlook is known as becoming *religiose* (p. 122). It would appear that this is harnessed to induce a belief system in alien visitation, which in turn causes the experiencer to act in terms of it, i.e. to conform to healthy living routines.

RANDOM CASE SELECTION AND PRIMARY PARAMETERS

This and the following case have parallel parameters, and readers could be forgiven for wondering if the cases presented here have been specially selected. However, once the surface narrative of so many cases is scratched, these recurring characteristics become evident and an underlying pattern is found to repeat itself. As stated earlier, there has been no process of 'picking and choosing', i.e. selection, at work here. One of the things that convinced me of the validity of this approach in the early days, as I tested it myself, was that, of the cases that came my way at random, all shared the same primary parameters, and many of the secondary parameters too. In contrast, the control interviews, which were carried out with non-experiencers, were, in their way, equally revealing.

After exploring one case in detail, the reader is advised to look again at the primary parameters, listed on p. 25, before considering further cases. These parameters are the primary characteristics that will segregate experiencers from non-experiencers, although there are other less robust aspects that will be identified as they arise. These aspects can be regarded as secondary parameters and include, e.g., low blood-sugar levels and diabetic tendencies, as the pancreas often seems to be the organ that displays a sensitivity to irradiation and, therefore, shows an altered reactivity. Readers may judge for themselves the extent to which this case, of 'Ian of Peckham', complies with the parameters listed. The following case-catalogue will become moré complex as it progresses, although the same underlying aspects underpin all of the cases presented.

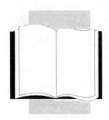

Case 2

Ally-Pally Woman (APW)

Location: Alexandra Palace, North London, UK

Time frame: 1963 to the present-day

Description

In many cases, experiencers do not link the occurrence of their MEE with the onset of experiences, and this is one such case. This electrical initiation took place during the percipient's early years, when she was 13 years old, and heralded a life-long history of psychical events. At the time of interview, September 1993, this experiencer was in her late thirties. Her experiential history was as follows:

When she was almost 13 years old, APW was a very keen supporter of the Tottenham Hotspur football club. One afternoon, she went with a group of other fans to meet one of the team members, John White, who was also accompanied by his wife. The group went for a walk across a golf course and, after they had reached an open area, the sunny weather began to break and storm clouds gathered overhead. As raindrops began to fall, it was White who ran ahead and sheltered under a tree, followed by other group members. However, as soon as White reached the tree, slightly ahead of the others, there was a flash and a roar as he was struck by lightning, killing him immediately. APW was barely 3.5m (12ft) away, and she reports:

> I heard a crack and I thought the tree had split in half ... I felt a vibration of some kind, and I felt that I suffered a mild electric shock ... my hair went up ... I had a pain in my arm ... the pain went up my arm, and I also got like a crick in my neck, which I couldn't get rid of for about two weeks afterwards.

Soon after this account, I asked her how long she had been having 'experiences' and, unequivocally, she told me that they had been on-going since the age of 13. However, as mentioned, no connection with the lightning proximity had been made:

> AB: Can you start to tell me what the first thing was that happened to you? What sort of age were you and everything?
>
> APW: The first thing I remember was at the age of 13; I had a visitation.
>
> AB: Was that before or after the lightning strike?

APW: I've got to think about this now ... Well it would have been afterwards. It would have been about 6 or 7 weeks later. Er, I never gave it much thought. I mean it's not very nice to see someone die.

The giant luminous humanoid

About 2 months after her MEE, APW began to experience a most extraordinary sequence of complex hallucinatory events, which must be appreciated within the context of a life of violent abuse from her father. APW was evidently a most difficult and disturbed child, and constantly truanted from school. When she did attend, she was openly defiant and fought with both teachers and pupils, receiving very little education as a result.

APW had been truanting for some weeks when her father found out and she was sent to her room. She was not allowed to have the light on but, ever-defiant, read comics under the bedclothes by torchlight. She comments: 'If my dad had known, he would have killed me. Literally.' The time was about 6 o'clock in the evening and, as it was winter, it was already dark and cold. The only heating came from a single-element electric fire, mounted high up on the wall of the small room, which she had to switch off before getting into bed.

After reading beneath the bedclothes, APW suddenly felt that someone had come into the room and, thinking that her father had crept in to check up on her, lay there frozen with fear. She lay there for a minute or so, all the while feeling that a strong presence dominated the room. She could not hear any sound at all, and she cautiously peered over the bedclothes. She was startled when, without warning, the electric fire on the wall began to radiate sparkling blue light which quickly seemed to fill the room. It stopped as suddenly as it began, although the sense of presence could still be felt. She began to wonder if someone was looking at her from outside the window, as the curtains were slightly drawn, but then her attention was drawn to a plate-sized circle of shimmering light on the ceiling, in the corner of the room. It reminded her of the reflection of sunlight on a glass of water and, after a few seconds, began to turn blue. She did not think of it as being particularly unusual until it began to drip what looked like blue liquid, with a silvery sparkling glint to it. Gradually, as it fell, it formed a human male figure about 2.4m (8ft) tall, completely blank with no features or detail, and luminous blue in colour.

As APW looked on at this huge figure with a sense of awe, she found that she was completely paralysed, even to the extent of being unable to blink, and her eyes were filling with water. Then a voice boomed through her head:

Don't be afraid. I'm not going to hurt you. I'm here to teach you. You have not been going to school, have you?

It crossed her mind that this was some kind of trick that was being played on her to get her to go to school regularly, but was surprised to hear the voice in her head say:

No, this is real. You are different, and whether you like it or not, you have got to learn.

APW noticed that the humanoid figure was hovering upright and motionless very near the circle of light on the ceiling, and she formed a question in her mind, asking him where he came from. His answer surprised her:

There'll be a time for you to ask me questions, and there will be a time for me to ask you questions, but that is not now. You have to listen to me. I'm going to show you something.

As soon as he said this, the dimensions of the room altered; the bed got smaller and was positioned differently, at right angles to its usual place, and the room appeared much bigger. (This is an epileptiform distortion of spatial perception known as *micropsia* and *macropsia*.) Then, a large light, about 1.5m (5ft) across, appeared on the floor in the middle of the room and a dome appeared, covering it. As she looked, she could see tiny people walking around inside the dome, with vehicles and buildings, like a complex miniature city full of activity. This was evidently just too much for this 13-year-old child to take and she tried to scream, but nothing would come out, no matter how hard she tried. Then, as if it had just been switched on, a broad beam of light came from the dome, spanning its width and shining out at an oblique angle. APW commented how solid this beam appeared in contrast to the blue humanoid, who seemed insubstantial and made of light.

As she mused on this difference of solidity between the two, the huge figure slowly and deliberately tilted and revolved, as if by remote control, so that its head was lower and it seemed to be looking out of the window, through the gap in the curtains. Outside the window was the large radio mast which transmitted for the BBC from Alexandra Palace, and she heard questions booming inside her head: 'Is there power there?' followed by 'What is that place for?' At this time, she seemed to find her voice and she told him, 'That's Ally Pally. That's where I go roller-skating on a Saturday.' APW then described how the humanoid suddenly seemed to be intensely interested in the transmitter, asking, 'What is the power? What is the power?' over and over again. She eventually replied that she did not know, as she was quite unaware of the transmitter anyway, and he ended by saying something to the effect that it did not matter.

APW's next memory is of waking up in the morning with the room looking normal. However, the following night, another visitation experience occurred, and the night after that, and so on for the following 3 weeks or so. After that, the experiences were less frequent, but still occurred on an episodic basis. Then APW began attending school again, although her defiant behaviour continued, including many fights in the playground. There is strong circumstantial evidence to indicate that APW's behaviour throughout her teens was governed by a fundamental underlying allergic state, and a textbook on childhood allergies specifically lists fighting and aggression as being well-established allergic responses. As a child, she reports that she did not trust the information that she was taught and failed to see how the teachers could really know about such historical figures as Napoleon if they had not been around when he was alive. She demanded 'hard evidence' for everything in the textbooks and challenged the teachers on the authenticity of their knowledge. This radical misconception of education, which continued throughout her teens, did nothing to integrate her back into school life. However, it must be said that such apparent quest for knowledge was really an aggressive displacement activity, covering up what must, at that stage, have been poor performance levels.

However, APW rationalized that her formal education was unnecessary, as she was being given her own private home tutorials from the huge blue humanoid each night. Apparently, his opening statement about answering questions was a reference to the role that he would play in APW's life. When he appeared, she could ask him any questions she wished, about anything she wished, although it had to be done in simple and unambiguous language. His answers were verbal, unless elaboration was needed, and then they took the form of animated models, maps, diagrams, etc., inside the luminous dome, which she enjoyed seeing. After this period of question and answer, he would 'make twenty statements to me', but she received no further help if she did not understand them. Although APW was a 13-year-old child at the time she recalls:

> I asked him if there was really a monster in Loch Ness. And if there was really a man in the moon. Silly questions like that. But as I got wise to him, I started asking him questions that I knew he could not answer simply, so he would have to give me more visual lessons.

However, APW became aware that the humanoid was tutoring her on how the world was changing in terms of the deterioration of the environment and this again relates directly to her acquired sensitivities. He also seemed to be concerned and curious about issues to do with energy or power, which is also a reflection of her field sensitivity. APW wanted to ask why her electric fire shone with the brilliant blue light, but there never seemed to be the right opening. Also around this time, she began to 'put poetry together' and to write things that she did not fully understand. This was usually in the small hours of the morning, on awakening. This is a typical symptom of developing temporal-lobe lability (see p.119).

APW recounts how, as a teenager, she found that, by going right up to the Alexandra Palace transmitter and sitting in the grounds of the building itself, she would feel a distinct sense of calm, 'as if I were protected in some way', because 'I didn't feel anything there'. This is an interesting comment to make, because there are 'dead zones' around an omni-directional transmitter, known as 'side nulls', where the signal cannot be picked up, especially at close range. Someone hypersensitive to RF fields would feel their absence because they act as ambient stressors on the body's regulatory systems.

APW's 'supernatural' tutoring continued, although it apparently began to wane as time went on, and she gained a sense of being different from her peers because the mode and content of these lessons was so very strange. However, they seemed to have consisted of the usual cosmological/destiny of mankind preoccupations that so many hypergraphic experiencers adopt. It is difficult to describe how life-long experiencers integrate into their lives events and phenomena that many would regard as exceptional. After a while, so many strange anomalies take place that experiencers become blasé about them, but, after listening to their experiences, it is quite clear to me that they feel and see the world very differently from non-experiencers. As an adult, APW had certainly developed an extremely eccentric outlook, although it is absolutely typical of those whose lives have been shaped by their encounters with electricity and electromagnetism.

Background

SENSITIVITIES AND RAPID HEALING

Tellingly, APW also reported that she had become allergic to a lot of 'stuff that wasn't natural', and related how she could not bear to wear make-up, like most young girls, as it used to irritate her skin. She could not tolerate perfume, tobacco smoke, after-shave or domestic gas, which she could detect when others could not. These are classical chemical sensitivities so often closely associated with EH. Also, she noticed how cuts and abrasions seem to heal very quickly; she showed me a small scar on her finger that only very recently was a gaping wound, caused by an accident with a carving knife and really requiring stitches. However, her medical aversion caused her to forgo such treatment, but nevertheless healing took place

rapidly. There are well-established treatments of wounds and bone frac-
tures using EM fields and Dr Roger Coghill, in his book *Electrohealing*
(Coghill, 1992), includes an extensive section on this. This may be the
only positive aspect to field exposure, in terms of the well-being of the
experiencer. In addition, APW would sometimes talk for extended
periods of time in her sleep, apparently in a foreign language, according
to her husband's testimony. Her speech functions were disturbed during a
stroke and this may have produced a brain lesion that affected Broca's and
Werninke's areas, which are responsible for speech. I have found a
substantial minority of experiencers feel that they have the ability to 'speak
in tongues', although I feel that such involuntary performances are due to
EM stimulation of the language areas of the brain.

A COMMON FEVER

Also around this time (1988), APW underwent an acute period of
illness, with symptoms similar to those independently described by many
other experiencers, who, of course, also live in hot spots. Also like other
experiencers, APW had developed an antagonistic attitude towards
doctors and medicine in general, which echoes the general cold war
between holistic and conventional approaches to health. However, this
seems to be an unconsciously motivated attitude, as APW was not
consciously familiar with the holistic ethos at all. The same anti-medical
attitude existed with the experiencers in the Aveley case (p. 141).

It is certainly ironic that such an outlook should be prevalent because,
as a general statement, experiencers are unwell on a more or less permanent basis and are often coping with their conditions at subclinical levels.
I have found that many experiencers have gone through a period of
illness where their temperature soars and they develop an acute fever
similar to malaria. In fact, one of the first questions asked by the medical
personnel who attend them is whether they have been abroad and have
had the chance to contract some form of tropical disease. The transient
nature of the attack belies its seriousness and, as in other cases, APW felt
that she was going to die, although her condition subsided 5 or 6 hours
after admission to the emergency ward of the local hospital. The clinical
evidence for the destabilization of body temperature by irradiation of
the hypothalamus by Frey and Wesler was given on p.000, and the incidence of such fevers are reported by experiencers quite commonly, as
we will see from other cases. They are certainly something that I have
noticed consistently during my investigations.

ELECTRICALLY INDUCED STROKES?

Another recurring condition that experiencers undergo may be somewhat more serious in its consequences. No doubt many critics will

accuse me of being irresponsibly alarmist when I state that strokes are a common pattern; nevertheless, I can only report what I have found. Unless such attacks are completely unrelated, and this association occurs by chance, it would seem that another outcome of prolonged irradiation by EM fields may be that, eventually, people have strokes. Of course, this conclusion has been arrived at from studying only a handful of cases and an in-depth survey of the population would be needed to establish it as fact. My viewpoint is based on individual case-file studies, as opposed to epidemiological or statistical surveys, and, of course, the impression I have gained may be only that – an impression.

ALIEN-ABDUCTION VISION AS A PRELUDE TO A STROKE

APW felt unusually exhausted one afternoon and fell asleep for several hours. She was surprised when she awoke to find that it was 9 o'clock at night and, after an hour or so, she returned to bed and slept the whole night through, waking 3 hours later than was usual for her. She felt a bit nauseous and dizzy, and decided to take a bath. When recounting this, interestingly, APW said:

> I don't have hot water. I'm not allowed to have hot water – so my water is just tepid really.

This, I was told, was by order of the 'humanoid', who advises her and insists on various practices to do with her health and well-being, which APW tells me, he monitors. However, on this occasion, she found that, after contact with water, she felt a burning sensation and the skin on her arm and stomach became enflamed with lines of raised blisters. She describes these as 'burn blisters', which were 'very lumped up' and 'were burning on the inside, as well as the out'. Further descriptions elicited that 'it was like a microwave burn, it burns from the inside' and, revealingly, 'I've got a microwave oven, and I'd taken something out of it, and it had a funny feeling to it, more than just hot-burning, but tingling … it was like that feeling'.

ELECTROSLEEP

It was evident that APW had been subjected to RF fields which induced a condition known as *electrosleep*. Practitioners have induced this state in patients by using ultra-low frequencies (ULF), thus inducing deep sleep without the use of drugs. However, when such frequencies are abroad in the environment, they can induce comatose-like conditions in EH subjects, and those witnessing a family member in electrosleep often become aware of their unnatural state and are somewhat disturbed by the deep unconsciousness it produces. The phrase 'as if they were in a coma' is not uncommon. Previously, we have noted the tendency for

EH-status subjects to undergo drop attacks when exposed to field frequencies to which they are sensitive. This would certainly explain how APW's sleep period was so much longer than usual, and it was during this extended period of immobility that she suffered microwave burns, as evidenced by the blistering of her skin. A look at the map shows that APW was in range not only of the ground-reflected signal from the Alexandra Palace transmitter, but also of another local transmitter. It was the WHO report (WHO, 1993) which issued warnings about intersecting microwave beams from multiple transmitters producing high-amplitude hot spots, especially when they are in phase, i.e. at right angles.

A study published in 1972 by the US Army Mobility Equipment Research and Development Center, entitled 'Analysis of microwaves for barrier warfare', examines the feasibility of using RF energy in warfare situations. Researcher and author Paul Brodeur relates that:

> ... the fact that a microwave beam with the power density of twenty watts per square centimetre can produce third-degree burns on human skin should come as no surprise. [Brodeur, 1977.]

Interestingly, APW also reports that she was extremely thirsty on awakening, which, as we have seen in other cases of irradiation, can occur due to volatization. But perhaps more startling was the fact that she recalled a medical examination by small men who took her to another realm. This memory only began to come back to her gradually but, when it did, her account provided some interesting details, which for her, explained how she received the microwave burns:

> I started to remember ... I was laying on my bed, and a figure appeared through the middle of my bed. A figure appeared standing through the centre of my bed, around where my knees were, and then there were two. They were sort of featureless and shrouded, and I looked up, and I said, 'Who the hell are you?' ... The answer came back, 'We have to take you. You've got to come with us now.' And I said, 'I ain't going nowhere' ...

The entity then extended a long arm and, grabbing her by the hand, pulled her out of bed and walked through the wall and part of the window-frame, with APW in tow, telling her, 'We have to go now.' She was concerned because her room was on the third floor, but she seemed to be floating through the air with the gardens some way below her. She remembers wondering if the neighbours could see them and then, with no sense of transition, she found herself in a white room, which she describes as being 'like an igloo'. It was domed like an upturned basin and was lit up inside, although 'you couldn't see where any of the lights were'. She then found herself stretched out on a table, and two beings with large heads and skinny bodies came over to her. They had large black glistening eyes, and APW stared into them, trying to see her own reflection, but could not. Their faces and demeanour were expressionless as they took positions on either side of her; she had the impression that one was male and one female, although they looked alike.

Then something happened that seemed to inject some humour into the vision. As APW craned her head forward, trying to look closer into the eyes of one of them, he mimicked her by suddenly poking his face up to hers – 'like he was saying – this is how silly you look!' The other then approached her with an instrument about 30cm (1ft) long, with three long sharp prongs on it, like a miniature pitch-fork. The being turned it over in her fingers and held it like a pen, and calmly pushed it into her abdomen. APW was paralysed as a sharp jagged pain rippled through her stomach and she found that she was unable to cry out. The instrument was removed; and the other being approached with what looked like a long silver pencil with a slim blue flame shooting from the end, somewhat like a gas jet. APW was still reeling from the pain of the prongs and thought, defiantly, 'No way are you going to touch me with that thing!' As the flame got nearer to her stomach region, close to where the holes from the prongs were, she summoned all her strength and managed to push his arm away, so that the flame caught her with a glancing contact across the stomach, which left a burn mark there. APW comments:

> It kind of shrivelled – like dead skin. It was awful, you know, it hurt on the inside, like a microwave type burn … I had a microwave burn once.

APW then saw the two beings huddle together and heard them say, 'She's not supposed to be here. We have to take her back. This is not right. She does not belong here.' The next thing APW remembers is waking up in bed at 9.00 p.m. and then taking a bath, which seemed to have brought out the burns as a row of blisters and scarred area.

From this description, we can see how microwave irradiation has been incorporated into the abduction vision as an aspect of the alien surgical procedure; this left a physical trace that would certainly seem to indicate alien intrusion, if the EM-pollution approach is not implemented. Many such marks and physical skin traumas have been presented as physical evidence for alien abduction but are, in fact, systemic reactions to fields by the hypersensitive individual with this 'electrical allergy'.

The following 3 weeks were not pleasant for APW, as the high fever seemed about to return; it seemed to have peaked when she awoke to find that she could not lift her head from the pillow. Her family were very concerned and, despite their home nursing, she did not improve after a few more days. But when they insisted on calling the doctor, APW strongly resisted, telling them 'I hate all doctors!' This is exactly the anti-medical ethos displayed by experiencers in other cases and seems to be an unconscious embracing of the holistic ethos. APW lay in bed for another 3 weeks, with her condition deteriorating, until she found that she was paralysed on the left side of her body, and had painful seizures whenever she tried to lift her limbs or head. Her speech was slurred and she finally reached a state of collapse on attempting to walk, as she had no control of the left side of her body. However, she still resisted all medical help, but, when the fever returned, her family became so frightened that they called for emergency medical assistance at 2.00 a.m. She was diagnosed as suffering from a stroke. APW fully recovered but, from the information she gave, it appears that she still suffers from the inexplicable fevers on an episodic basis.

Analysis

THE ENVIRONMENTAL HEALTH ISSUE

From an examination of this and other cases, it has become evident that such alien-contact/abduction experiences are closely linked to electro-magnetically induced illnesses, and that these visionary episodes are hallucinatory expressions of such conditions. We may wonder if the abduction experience just described contained any 'welfare messages' which may have served to warn APW of her imminent stroke. It seems that it is only too easy to forget that the occurrence of a vision depicting painful tamperings with the body by alien beings is a vivid and dramatic enactment initiated by the psyche. By harnessing the harmful and intrusive energies from the environment, the psyche then sends a message effectively saying that these energies are now actively burning the skin and that something is seriously amiss with the way that the body is functioning. Because we have been exposed to so many such accounts in the literature, press and television over the years, we have become blind to the fact that, for each experiencer, it is a new, unique and traumatic occurrence. There may be many such experiences on record, but for the individual biological/perceptual system that experiences the enactment of a surgical operation by aliens, the event is exceptional and often shattering. To quote Marshall McLuhan, 'The medium is the message.'

However, when we consider the content, things could hardly be spelt out more clearly. The aliens were depicted as saying, 'She is not supposed to be here ... This is not right ... She does not belong here.' Very often, visitations are so frightening because they are saying, in a very direct way, 'You are very ill; the body is malfunctioning.' Many of us have heard of the hallucinations people get when they are feverish or delirous; as a child I remember seeing the wardrobe swarming with filthy-looking rats during a period of high temperature after contracting measles. Alcoholics undergoing delirium see snakes or a multitude of grasping hands reaching for their throat. Of course, in other cases, the vision may act on the stress or load directly, and its content used to calm the experiencer. I had one case in which the experiencer was suicidal, so great was the stress she was under, but the appearance of a beautiful guardian angel, who exuded a sense of peace and calm, literally saved her life and triggered a religious belief which then acted as a support system after the immediate crisis was over. Once again, with such events, we are considering a survival mechanism, quite literally in this case.

Alcoholics in withdrawal experience quite peaceful visions at some stage, which is also the mind trying to calm the chemically stressed body. One such sufferer, during a period of alcohol withdrawal in the early hours of the morning, watched as a triangle of light, formed by intersecting curtains, detached itself and floated down as a luminous glass arrow, until it silently 'stuck' into the surface of the window-still. This was during a period of self-induced detoxification and the subject felt that he was on the brink of finally losing his mind, when he became aware of a light in the middle of the room that gradually filled it completely, penetrating every cell of his body. An overwhelming emotion consumed him, which he could only describe as feeling totally and unconditionally loved; this, he felt, saved his life. While not all hallucinations are aberrant, those associated with allergies and other environmental sensitivities act as indicators of systemic dysfunction because people are generally unaware that they have developed such conditions or, of course, that they are being irradiated on a full-time basis.

Conclusion

I was not able to carry out a field survey of APW's house, although conditions would have altered over the years, but I did detect power surges consisting of magnetic fields of over 100mGs and from 0.2 to 0.5mW/cm^2 in the RF band in the street outside her house. As a general rule, I have found that fields are actually enhanced inside buildings due to reflections, re-radiation, 'beats', high points, etc. To conclude, it hardly seems necessary to point out how many of the primary and secondary parameters are satisfied in this case, e.g. MEE, hot-spot exposure, food allergies, chemical sensitivities, psychical history, childhood abuse, hypergraphia.

To conclude this case examination, there is one important aspect which has not been covered and which the astute reader will probably have considered: the connection between APW's truancy and the 'supernatural' home-tutor. I can do no better than to quote from a resumé of the case in *Allergies and Aliens*:

> *The blue giant (humanoid) and the dome appeared to APW frequently after the first episode, and it was made clear to her, she felt, that this was a programme to learn and gain knowledge – an educational process. It is no coincidence, that for years prior to this hallucinatory event, APW had been a chronic truant, and could not cope with school life at all. This eventually resulted in a battle of wills between APW and the education authorities, who put intense pressure on her to conform and attend school regularly for the sake of her developmental and educational welfare. This was the quite legitimate reason that they gave to APW to explain the pressure that they were putting her under, recruiting her father's influence also, of whom she was extremely fearful. Therefore, it is entirely understandable, if not extremely appropriate, for her unconscious, given the right electrical stimulation, to provide a supernatural home tutor from whom she felt that she could learn. She did this by asking questions and then have them answered via maps, diagrams, scenes, etc. as luminous holograms inside the dome.*

> *The guilt and genuine concern that she must have felt as a confused 13-year-old child confronted with the issues of her own welfare was relieved by the appearance of this 'alien tutor'; reducing her load-phenomenon threshold, this to some extent defused her internal conflict about this major life issue. APW could ask any questions she wished, as long as they were phrased in exacting language, and the answers would be shown to her as images in the dome, courtesy of the luminous giant 'tutor'.* [Budden, 1994.]

This was a complex hallucinatory construct that was eventually replaced by a recurring feature of such experiences: messages in the mind, which must be distinguished from the auditory hallucination of psychosis. These EH people are not insane, but have developed an acute EM sensitivity and resultant sixth sense.

There is strong clinical evidence to suggest that APW's educational and behavioural difficulties were the outcome of her allergic condition, as even many educated adults lose their ability to read and write on a temporary basis while under the influence of an allergen. These bizarre events, therefore, are evidently an unusual compensatory measure, enabling APW, who, unbeknown to herself, was disabled by her allergic condition and traumatized by a violent home life, to cope with her situation. It is a salutary lesson about the human spirit's will to survive, even in extremely adverse circumstances.

Case 3

Lori and the Marlbro Power-line

Location: Marlbro County, Ohio, USA

Time frame: Early 1960s to the present day

Introduction

The pioneering work of investigator Nicholas Reiter, of Gibsonburg, Ohio (see p. 87), has echoed my own, with the link being made between magnetic fields and the alien-abduction experience. Reiter has provided us with one of the most useful and probative tests for such experiencers: the magnetic response (MR), which I feel should be known as 'Reiter's response'. It was Reiter who placed magnetic-field detectors in the homes of experiencers across the USA and found that they were triggered when experiences occurred. This case was investigated and donated by Reiter and focusses upon another female experiencer: Lori.

Description

Lori seems to have experienced unusual sensations and events, associated with an unusual reactivity to light, since early childhood. This concerned her parents enough for them to take her for a brain-scan before the age of 5, but no abnormalities were found. At around the age of 10, Lori recalls play activity with her foster-sister in which, together, they took delight in pulling balls of fibre out of their chenille bedspreads with their teeth! To keep these bedspreads out of the way, because they were by then sopping wet with saliva, they placed them beside a dresser and were amazed to see them defy gravity by sliding up the side of the dresser and then start to glow in the dark. By her early teens, Lori began to suffer from paralysis on awakening in the early hours of the morning and, on one occasion, she was totally immobile for over 90 minutes and experienced great difficulty with physical movement throughout the following day. During her early to mid-twenties, the death of her grandmother coincided with an intense period of electrical disturbance in her home, during which radio and TV sets, as well as the house-lights, would spontaneously activate. By her late twenties, she would be jolted awake in a state of fear, to be dazzled by a bright white light and feeling that someone or something was in her room, although nobody was present.

Understandably, Lori evidently began to be influenced by the recollections of well-known author and experiencer Whitley Strieber, as she wrote to him about her own experiences, but received no reply. The type of detail which she feels is significant and has chosen to record is reminiscent of the 'hallmarks' of latent phobia, paranoia and trauma that author Budd Hopkins links with abduction experiences: she recalls fairly typical nightmares and selects certain dreams; she mentions a fascination with owls (whose eyes are supposed to be like those of aliens) between the ages of 12 and 14; she mentions her grandmother's UFO sighting, and that she could smell a cardboard odour at night, which is another Strieberesque feature. In fact, she states flatly:

I began to suspicion [sic] the alien phenomenon ...

Of course, I regard such details as totally irrelevant and note quite different EM aspects as being significant, e.g. the fact that she was very close to a lightning strike at the age of 2 years (which she felt). Also, she was again close to a lightning bolt, which struck her house, damaging it slightly, when in her early twenties, just before the period when the electrical disturbances occurred. That is to say, such disturbances went on because of her newly enhanced EH status which resulted from this second MEE. No doubt readers will be able to identify other features mentioned so far: the sense of presence and paralysis due to temporal-lobe stimulation; bright light on awakening; the 'exploding head syndrome' (visual cortex stimulation); the photophobia which followed the lightning proximity when Lori was 2, which concerned her parents enough to warrant a brain-scan. Ironically, such a procedure, which uses coherent magnetic fields focussed into the brain, would have constituted an MEE for such an extremely young child, and would have also greatly contributed to her sensitivities. By this stage, readers will be aware that, for this case to follow the patterns predicted, the incidence of these MEEs should be followed by prolonged hot-spot exposure.

Observations

THE INCIDENCE OF HOT SPOTS

Throughout her life, Lori has lived in four locations, two of them about a kilometre or so (less than a mile) from a major radio station (Alliance). However, more probative, today she lives just 120m (400 ft) from two major power lines, which snake their way across Lexington and Marlbro townships in Stark County, bisecting Portage County from northwest to southeast.

Interestingly, we might here recall that this conforms with the data by Canadian researcher Lorne Goldfader, who published an article

(Goldfader, 1993) stating that the majority of his 'abductees' lived close to power lines; this is also the case with Bill Chalker's 'abductees' in Australia. In Lori's case, however, there is also a powerful radio-transmitter *actually in her home* – and we have not yet even begun to consider any geological/geophysical data ...

From the age of 20, Lori lived in two locations quite near to each other, both about a couple of kilometres (about a mile) or so from the vast Walborn Reservoir to the northeast and a huge quarry to the south-west. Such features serve to destabilize surface faults, because the weight of water on one side of the fault and the removal of stone on the other gradually result in a loss of equilibrium between the masses of rock on either side of faults that settled into their resting positions long ago in geological time. Such a sudden tipping of the scales, as it were, brings uplift on the lighter quarry side and subsidence on the weighty reservoir side. This brings piezoelectrical stress, creating both intense RF fields and light phenomena from the fault, and transforming it into a natural EM hot spot and an active earth-light/electric-fireball area. Another contrib-utory factor is the ubiquitous presence of underground water in the area: Lori's land does in fact have a well, like many dwellings in the locale.

Incidently, the account of the weird poltergeist-like behaviour of the saliva-soaked chenille in Lori's early years is a tell-tale clue which reveals that she was living in a hot spot even then, because such strange envi-ronmental events are typical of the way that the rules of reality can be temporarily altered at such charged locations. However, Lori would have been subjected to RF fields from the Alliance radio station trans-mitter, as opposed to the extremely low frequences (ELF) fields typical of power-line emissions, and she now may have become sensitized to two distinct frequency ranges from either end of the non-ionizing EM spectrum. As a coincidence, her present situation involves both RF and ELF fields, as well as geophysical features usually associated with minor tremors and earth lights.

SEISMIC ACTIVITY AND EARTH LIGHTS

In fact, seismic activity and earth lights are exactly the outcomes that Lori and her family encountered. She was at home with her children when, suddenly, the house shook 'with a sonic-like boom'. She began to worry that a gas main had exploded, although, on calling her husband at his place of work a couple of blocks away, she learned that he had heard nothing. On another occasion, the whole family witnessed three or four orange/red lights (a typical earth-light colour) just above the fields at the back of their house. These glowed brilliantly before fading out. These are an indicator of elevated field levels and the 'sonic boom' is a typical example of geosound; the latter occurs during tectonic activity in masses of highly stressed strata, and often has an oddly local-ized aspect to it. Also, such raised field levels and power surges have implications for experiencers, who are, of course, EH.

CONSCIOUSNESS EFFECTS

Two nights after the appearance of the light phenomena, Lori began to have a vivid dream which featured UFOs with light beams coming from them. Such UFO/alien-theme dreams are typical precursors to visions with the same thematic content, and there are periods when the experi-encer has difficulty distinguishing between what is a dream and what is 'real', i.e. a vision (which is, in effect, an 'upgraded dream'). Suddenly, she was 'bolted upright' and saw a dark shadowy figure at the end of her bed, and began to grapple with it, terrified, thinking that it must be an alien. Her own screaming snapped her out of this hallucinatory state, which was an epileptiform seizure. The EM stimulation of a number of brain areas would be involved in the tactile sensation of grappling with a shadowy intruder, which, incidently, is a commonly reported hallucina-tion among experiencers. Anomalous firing of the neurons in the primary tactile area (the *kinaesthetic strip*) and in the parietal lobe can induce the tactile sensation of grabbing something or, in this case, someone.

About 15 minutes later, Wayne, one of Lori's sons, awoke and ran up the stairs to her room to ask her what the loud noise was; he was some-what perturbed as it virtually shook the house but Lori had heard nothing. This phenomenon of differential hearing may be due to the fact that some auditory effects are entirely subjective, being produced by the stimulation of the auditory centres in the brain. As consultant neurologist Dr Peter Nathan relates:

> *From the stimulation of the brains of conscious patients by Penfield and his successors, we have learned that the parts of the hemispheres that produce obvious responses are ... the back of the occipital lobe ... [where] visual hallucinations occur, and temporal lobe auditory hallucinations ...*
> *[Nathan, 1988, p. 225]*

It would seem therefore that, while Lori was undergoing her seizures, during which she grappled with a shadowy figure, Wayne was experi-encing some of his own, in which a violent auditory effect was produced; both had produced dramatic and different experiential results, despite their common causative trigger. Lori's household was also subject to the usual electronic anomalies, where the phone would ring repeatedly but there would be no caller on the line. Also, on one occa-sion, the police were involved. They received a call on the emergency services number, which was traced to Lori's house, but nobody was at home. Such telecommunication anomalies are typical of hot-spot locations and, like so many of the factors that can be predicted in such cases, they are so commonly reported that we can take them for granted. We must remind ourselves of their significance: that they are reported consistently across populations of experiencers, independently of each other, and are indicators of hot-spot activity. In Chapter 4, I outlined how such light phenomena are the physical and luminous expression of the elevated field levels at hot-spot locations. Therefore, we can predict that such phenomena should occur in Lori's local area and, in fact, she reports:

> ... I found out that numerous people spotted a UFO near our home. Actually, police reports were filed in several townships that were in the path of this craft. A neighbor who lives a mile or so away watched it for about fifteen minutes. She said it was the size of a small blimp and seemed to be multi-colored. It shone down a beam of light. She said it followed the high tension tower [pylon] lines toward our house (we have a tower at the back of our property).

In the light of the evidence on the generation of electric fireballs (p.175), the significance of the association of a 'UFO' with power lines should not be lost, especially as a pylon stands so close to Lori's house.

OTHER FAMILY MEMBERS: THE 'UPGRADING' OF DREAMS

Lori also had a daughter called Chelsea and two sons, Paul and Pete, aged 8, 12 and 14 respectively. All of them have had vivid alien/UFO dreams throughout their lives or they dream of odd interactions with fairytale/other-wordly figures; typically, they report that some of these experiences are not dreams, i.e. they have a feeling of waking reality. This is a common pattern, in which a progression can be traced. It begins when themes of UFOs and aliens dominate the dream life of experiencers and continues to the stage where such dreams begin to feel real although there is still a certain ambivalence. It culminates when the formed figures previously seen in dreams are seemingly encountered externally in the bedroom as emergent consciousness effects, otherwise known as 'visitations'. This is the pattern which Lori and her family experienced and it is indicative of the development of progressive epileptiform activity, where areas of the brain that are repeatedly kindled into activity by intruding fields give a super-real quality to imagery. However, before this stage is reached, it is evident that, in the commonest pattern, the experiencer is irradiated by magnetic fields during the critical period of REM sleep. The presence of these fields registers in the brain and begins to influence the actual dream content in terms of themes and imagery. This intriguing concept is currently under investigation by the small team with which I am involved, as the exploration of such a process, using a graduated series of magnets on sleeping volunteers, is relatively easy. Further irradiation could certainly stimulate the pineal gland, which contains magnetite deep inside the brain, to produce beta-carbolines; these have been linked chemically to psycho-active substances, further enhancing hallucinatory episodes.

The perceptions themselves were often fleeting glimpses of formed figures, which were described as being about 1–1.5m (3½–5ft) tall, with oval black eyes, a vestigial nose, a slit mouth and skin which is white, bluish-white or greyish-blue. (It should be recalled, however, that other cases disclose a wide range of other forms, including winged technological fairies, tall silver-suited spacemen – some with octagonal-shaped helmets – beings of pure light, garden gnomes, etc.) Pete reported nocturnal visitations from beings who peered into his bedroom window and stood at the top of the stairs, once holding a piece of paper and on another occasion holding an object that looked like a model of an upside-down house. Such elements are difficult to interpret in isolation and, just as dream imagery occurs in terms of the current preoccupations of the dreamer, such hallucinations are part of a wider scheme relating to environmental sensitivities. On another occasion, also during the night, Pete saw a white vapour, which appeared to be coming out of his sister's bedroom and moved towards him, apparently altered course and drifted out of the window. An example of 'electrical mist' was outlined in connection with the Aveley case (p. 141), and it would be only too easy to attribute such apparent avoidance behaviour to an intelligence instead of to a sudden alteration in electrical ambience induced by Pete's arrival. Pete was once awoken in the early hours by the sensation of someone feeling his face, and such tactile sensations have been previously identified as being epileptiform (see p. 22). This conclusion is supported by evidence showing a disturbance to the electricity supply on this occasion, as Pete saw that his digital clock had stopped and was flashing 4.03. His physical sensations during visitation experiences have included feeling tense, paralysed except for the eyes, uncontrollable sleepiness, a burning heaviness in the head and floating feelings. Some of these can be found in Persinger's work on temporal-lobe stimulation (Ruttan et al., 1990), and electrosleep has been mentioned on p. 218.

Lori's father also seems to have developed epileptiform symptoms, as Lori reports:

> He was working in the garage at his workbench and was in deep concentration. The next thing he knew he was in the living-room with two black people discussing something. Suddenly he is aware that he is back in the garage.

Readers will probably recognize this as a typical description of automatic behaviour.

SENSATIONS, SENSITIVITIES AND PERCEPTIONS

In Lori's case, a typical experiencer's profile is once more displayed. She has chemical sensitivities and cannot tolerate cigarette smoke or perfume, and caffeine can trigger panic attacks. She also has a tendency towards candida overgrowth, or thrush, and has to be aware of her sugar intake, which feeds this yeast/fungal infection. Candida overgrowth is one of the sensitivities-related conditions treated at the Breakspear Hospital. Her childhood photophobia still seems to be present, and she cannot tolerate full sunlight. She mentions that she sees small flickering lights, which, tellingly, 'usually seem to appear towards the upper part of my visual field'. This is a hallmark of magnetophosphenes, which are seen in the upper left quadrant of the visual field and are induced by the effect of magnetic fields on the temporal lobes. Lori mentions that anxiety attacks are often triggered in department stores lit with fluorescent tubes, which is an indication of their contribution to her load-phenomenon threshold.

Because of power surges, Lori's home has the usual range of hot-spot electrical malfunctions: the house-lights and television suddenly going off, although her neighbours enjoy normal services; the radio plays while unplugged; the timer on the microwave oven bleeps in the middle of the night. Power surges also induce systemic effects in Lori, such as bodily tingling (somesthesia), hair on the arms standing out (piloerection), and numbness (paresthesia) in the hands and legs, especially during her episodic anxiety attacks. She also experiences a sense of presence, usually during the night. Like so many experiencers, Lori spends much of her time writing and she always has 'a notebook full of my thoughts and theories'; she documents her dreams too. This is typical of hypergraphia. Also, as with others exposed to hot spots, she has developed heart-beat irregularities (*tachycardia*). Her anxiety attacks began at puberty, although her hormone levels are within the normal range, and, like so many of the apparently idiopathic conditions developed during hot-spot exposure, these attacks remain largely unexplainable to the medical profession.

Conclusion

From an examination of a map of the areas concerned, it is clear that Lori has lived in EM hot spots of one type or another for all her life. This lifelong irradiation was matched by a major electrical and magnetic event very early in her life and she has developed a sensitivity to fields since this period. Usually, EH is seen as a chronic end-state in patients in whom food allergies and chemical sensitivies develop beforehand. However, so exceptional were Lori's major events, in that she was so incredibly young (18 months and under 5 years old when they occurred), that an atypical reversal of the usual pattern of development of EH took place. I have predicted and found the cluster of signs, symptoms and sensitivities that typify alien-contact/abduction experiences and, as Lori has mentioned that her mission is to find out what has been going on with her and her family for so many years, I hope I have been of some use to her.

To conclude, I would like to register my thanks to Lori and her family for providing such well-documented information, tantamount to genuine data. Few experiencers have grasped the essential elements of the EM-pollution approach so quickly and completely as Lori, and it is my hope that other experiencers in the USA will also begin to recognize the aspects I describe here.

Until quite recently, the reactions I have received from American experiencers have all been negative, ranging from instant hostility and barely suppressed anger to patronizing tolerance, and seeing the approach described as just another attempt to explain away their contacts with ETs. This is slowly changing, however, and a sort of post-Hopkins/Mack/Jacobs era is developing, although experiencers sometimes keep one foot in both camps, e.g. Whitley Strieber, who recognizes the EH aspects but feels that his 'visitors' act autonomously. However, it should be remembered that such imagery originates in the unconscious, an aspect it shares with dreams, it should be realized how the action within our dreams also displays a vivid sense of being separate from us, with an independent life of its own, despite being a reflection of our innermost aspects.

INTERLUDE FOR NEUROSCIENCE

Before we continue to examine the fascinating contents of case files, we should be fully aware of the wide range of sensations and experiences that can be induced by the EM stimulation of the brain. The skull is entirely transparent to magnetic fields and it would appear that there has been an increase in temporal-lobe lability in the populations of industrialized countries generally, due to an acceleration in the amount of EM pollution. It would also appear that neurologists have not made the link between this increased temporal-lobe lability and EM pollution, as it would certainly seem that this tendency is far more widespread than the layman would realize. This partly explains why there has been an increase in psychical events generally over the past few years.

This statement must seem like just another conspiracy theory – 'we are all going to have bizarre psychical experiences soon, due to too many mobile phone networks' – and I do not want to overstate it. However, I was struck by a passage in *Seized*, LaPlante's book on temporal-lobe epilepsy (TLE). This echoes my own observations, and says:

> *Spiers and other TLE experts suspect that the contemporary fascination with mysticism and the paranormal – such as UFOs, alien sightings, out-of-body travel, ESP, past-life regressions and reincarnation – may be the result of mild, undiagnosed temporal lobe epilepsy (TLE) in the general population.* [LaPlante, 1993.]

From my own forays into the 'general population' who have such experiences and preoccupations, it is evident that any such population trend could be triggered and sustained by a generalized proliferation of EM hot spots. Also, depending on what it is that Spiers and other workers are referring to, such other-worldly mythologies could also be promoted by advertising and TV/film productions! However, from such generalizations, let us focus on specifics, as the point of this section is to examine the private experiences of individuals. Once the link has been made, it is not difficult to identify many of the odd perceptions reported at 'haunted' locations, and also sensations which occur during alien-encounter experiences, as being neurological in nature. For years I have collected reports of the same clusters of perceptual events in many different cases, but have been unable to place them in any known context. Now, by referring to the neurological textbooks (e.g. Simpson & Fitch, 1988), I can find them all in great detail.

People in 'haunted' locations often report ghostly physical contacts, which are really their brushes with EM fields sweeping through the room. Such contact sensations can be induced by the stimulation of the receptors in the skin, there being specialized ones for touch, pressure, vibration and tickle. Combinations of these give sensations of wetness, smoothness, roughness, etc., when the mechanoreceptors are stimulated. An electrical stimulation of less than 40Hz gives a fluttering sensation on the skin, while one of 60–300Hz gives a sensation of vibration, as receptors in the Pacuinian corpuscles are stimulated. On looking back at my old case notes, taken during investigations of hauntings, it is very difficult not to smile at the reports of phantom invisible birds which flutter through the ubiquitous haunted 'blue room' and are vividly felt by the witnesses as they brush against them in their transparent flight. It is also very worrying to see that a long-dead 'keeper of the doves' was quite spuriously recalled, after apparently passing away in mysterious and tragic circumstances. Investigators should be wary of mistaking folklore for data. Similarly, there is no doubt that many people have felt 'the vibrations of spirits on the other side'.

Stimulation of the somatosensory areas of the brain induces a wide range of sensations. 'Abductees' have reported how, during their medical examination by aliens, various intimate intrusions were felt. In somatosensory area I, stimulation of the lowest nerve roots on the medial surface of the gyrus will induce sensations in the genitals, bladder and rectum. Remembering that these physical sensations can be felt during these visionary episodes, it is easy to see how they could be incorporated as aliens operating on the body, especially as, in effect, the fields *are* aliens in terms of how they are apprehended by the body. Similarly, bodily feelings of warmth, tingling and numbness can be obtained by the stimulation of somatosensory area II. The parietal lobe has already been mentioned in relation to the destabilization of the body image (p. 111) and there are countless reports of how witnesses have been 'floated out of the room' or 'levitated into the spaceship', etc.

This can, of course, be extended to many other areas and functions of the brain, although we are more concerned with sensation, perception and memory when we match up reports of apparent anomalies with focal seizures. However, the whole point and central message of this approach is that everything we perceive as reality is either 'hard-wired' or encoded in the brain; it is all there, waiting to be brought forth into consciousness by electricity. A transient reality that is certainly acceptable to us in terms of its stability can be produced by our interaction with such energies; in the light of the fantastic realities that have been reported with complete sincerity, this is clearly highly relevant. Critics of the EM-pollution approach have expressed doubts about the feasibility of reproducing extended periods of action, behaviour and experiences by such electrical stimulation. That is to say, they doubt that any sort of convincing reality can be induced in this way. However, they clearly underestimate the scope and versatility of this brain/electricity interaction, and it is pioneer neurologist Wilder Penfield who reminds us how real such hallucinatory realities can be:

> *The record of the stream of consciousness may be activated as though it were a strip of cinematograph film, recording the sight and sound, the movement and the meaning which belonged to each successive period of time. [Nathan, 1988.]*

Interestingly, an 'abductee' recently related to me what it was like to experience a 'visitation', and actually described it as 'like you are watching a film'.

MAKING SENSE OF IT ALL

In the early to mid-1980s, while the alien-abduction scene in the USA seemed to be gripped by hypnotic regression and 'extraterrestrial fever', certain groups of investigators in the UK were searching for an alternative. While battling with essentially the same enigmas, they became aware of an intrinsically subjective aspect to the phenomena, although it could not honestly be denied that there was also an *external physical factor* that seemed to intrude and act as a medium into which the thoughts and imagery of witnesses were somehow implemented. I was one of these ufologists and, over the years, became acutely aware of just what was needed to fulfil this criterion which bridged the gap between the human mind and a physical 'UFO reality'. This mysterious 'something' had to fulfil a rigorous battery of conditions which included both psychical and physical features.

It must seemingly do the impossible and bridge the gap between subjective and objective realities as well as being able to induce a number of other effects. These include: inducing a large globe of light which hovers; causing a car to stall; taking over the consciousness of the driver; making aliens appear; erasing the driver's memory; inducing the battery to go flat; decolourizing the paintwork; stopping the clock or possibly causing the mileometer to run backwards; inducing psychical abilities as an after-effect; causing flashbacks of an alien realm; inducing electrical equipment to malfunction in the experiencers' presence; causing burn-like marks and reddening to the skin; inducing a radical change in outlook so that experiencers become more spiritual, artistic or creative, as well as developing an acute awareness of their health and the environment; triggering poltergeist and other psychical happenings in experiencers' homes.

This is the idiosyncratic cluster of effects which investigators found repeatedly in the course of their examinations of many UFO/alien-related cases. The 'reality' which fulfils all these criteria, and more, is the interaction of the human body and the environment with electromagnetic energy, in all its many forms. This is because electromagnetic energy physically affects not only the environment but also the organ which is the seat of our subjective realities: the brain. Electromagnetic energy does indeed bridge the gap between outer and inner realities and, when this energy is carried by luminous globes which descend from the sky, it is little wonder that it should become the basis of the modern ETH mythology.

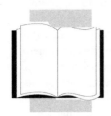

Case 4

The Norfolk Girl (TNG)

Location(s): Norfolk, UK and Arkansas, USA
Timeframe: 1978 to the present day.

Introduction

'Abductees' manage their health with varying degrees of success, although it is a truism to say that present experiencers who are having on-going 'visitations' are unwell on a more or less permanent basis, as their sensitivities are established and they may be irradiated daily. Others may no longer be experiencers, but they still have disabilities due to prolonged exposure in the past. They manage these and they may be having treatment for an idiopathic condition that 'the doctors are baffled by'. Their state of health depends on a number of factors, such as: how well they have recognized and responded to the 'welfare messages' implicit in their experience; how much of a make-or-break situation, physiologically speaking, the experience has induced; whether, by pure chance, they have moved house away from the hot spot. However, I was not ready for the range of disabilities of the young lady who, in deep shadow, told of her 'alien encounter' for a Birmingham TV station on which was I was appearing. She was 30 years old and so fragile, because of recurring inflammation of the pancreas and liver, that she was dependent on a wheelchair.

Such details and other information on the health of the witness are not usually emphasized by 'abductologists' as the relevance of it is never realized. For me, reading most accounts provides the equivalent of two or three still snapshots out of a long movie film on the abduction-experience event. All the health and environmental effects, which are reeled off with such robust consistency when one really looks into these cases, are absent.

Description

LIGHT PHENOMENA AND LIGHTNING:
MAJOR ELECTRICAL EVENTS

TNG's story could be said to date from when she was about 14 years old and out walking alone one evening, close to an army base in Arkansas, USA. As she came to the brow of a hill, on a road leading from the base, she was suddenly 'transfixed' by a luminous sphere, hovering low down in the sky and made up of bright bands of colour. A strange atmospheric silence suddenly descended and all the ambient sounds, such as birdsong and insect noises, vanished. She watched the UFO for about 5 minutes, or so she thought, standing directly underneath it, overcome by a tingling sensation. Her next memory is of arriving home, with no sense of transition, only to learn that her parents were beginning to get worried about her because she had been gone for over 2 hours. This mystery, however, was overshadowed by her battle with an intense migraine attack. (Many years later, hypnotic regression, initiated by English investigator Tony Dodd, produced an alien-abduction experience. Accepting this on face value, it should be remembered of course, that a purely subjective event was described.)

Shortly after this UFO encounter, she was in her father's car, which was parked beside a row of corrugated-iron farm buildings, during a thunderstorm. Lightning struck the next but one building and the physical force of it made the car rock. TNG felt a sharp pain in her finger as an electric spark came up through the floor, striking a ring she was wearing. Six months later, aged 15, she was caught up in the fringes of a tornado and, as she watched it from close by, she could see small lightning bolts discharging inside the funnel.

Other events

When she was 14, soon after she saw the light phenomenon near the Arkansas military base, her parents were arranging their Christmas-tree lights and were amazed to see them flicker and stay on for a few moments as she came near them. They were not plugged in. For some reason, TNG then recalls that they all fell asleep and, when they awoke, they were surprised to find the lights plugged in, twinkling beautifully. Soon after this, she began to experience poltergeist cluster effects, including her mattress lifting spontaneously and the appearance of 'three-dimensional shadows'.

At the age of 24, when she was married to a serviceman and living on a military base, she was sometimes awoken by a dazzling white light in the early hours of the morning. Also around this age, she developed gall-stones, which puzzled the doctors as she was so young to have this condition. Soon after this she awoke to find that she was paralysed down one side of her body, her face was swollen, her eyes watering and her speech slurred. This lasted 6 weeks before subsiding completely and was diagnosed as Hodgkinson's disease.

Observations

If we pause at this point in the catalogue of events, we can see once again how the same robust pattern emerges. Multiple MEEs have precipitated degenerative processes in major organs and systems, which have accelerated to anomalous degrees. The incidence of gall-stones at the age of 24 is just the type of baffling idiopathic health anomaly that occurs with these subjects and, once again, we find the stroke-like attack common to so many experiencers' histories. With such an accelerated deterioration of functions, it is little wonder that the body and mind work together to produce powerful visions and belief systems which influence the sufferer to take remedial action, and that this action is so often spontaneously holistic and naturopathic in its approach. TNG reminds me of 'Kathie Davis', an experiencer investigated by Budd Hopkins; she too had multiple and anomalous health problems, although the significance of this major aspect was never realized by Hopkins or any of the other investigators who adopted the same regression/alien-intelligence approach.

We again find a history of psychical experiences, and living in a military base greatly increases the risk of hot-spot exposure because of the powerful communication networks and radar installations. In fact, TNG has actually lived in and around such bases all her life. We also find typical effects of power surges, EH and automatic behaviour in the Christmas tree incidents, and the bright light of the 'exploding head syndrome'. Other typical epileptiform symptoms include experiencing sudden strongly floral and lavender odours.

TNG also experiences the electrical rippling sensation of fasciculation in the muscles just below the skin, which is so strong that others can also feel it by touching her. The skin beneath her stainless-steel ring becomes enflamed and scaly and she cannot wear watches as the shape of the watch-back 'burns' into the skin and peels like sunburn. As mentioned, she has an on-going pancreatic problem that results in diabetic tendencies – another predicted parameter. She was found to have a cyst on her ovaries just 4 days before she had her gall-bladder removed. She also has a kidney abnormality and a heart murmur. She has been advised to wear sunglasses by her doctor because of her photophobia and has bi-focals with UV filters. Sunlight is contra-indicated.

Due to the high rate of light-bulb burn-out, her husband has had long-life xenon bulbs fitted. She finds that the flickering they produce when coming on is extremely uncomfortable, if not intolerable. The odour of domestic gas makes her actually nauseous, and she cannot tolerate petrol or paint fumes, although she does fare better with cigarette smoke.

Electrical equipment malfunctions when she is under stress and she reports that she can make the big hand of the clock move backwards when she is angry. Stress triggers such electrical activity as it causes her load-phenomenon threshold to be exceeded by introducing hormones and neurotransmitters that are non-routine, such as adrenalin. This acts as an allergen or chemical that challenges the allergic system and reacts synergistically to promote EH symptoms, i.e. the emission of coherent personal fields. She is generally afraid of being electrocuted when handling plugs and appliances, etc., especially the microwave oven, and she readily gets shocks from metal. Television sets in her home lose their picture quickly and then malfunction completely. She and her husband are on their sixth set. The batteries in the remote control lose power and are changed constantly.

She was abused by her first husband and divorced when still quite young, re-marrying a man 30 years her senior; as mentioned, this is a recurring pattern with experiencers and is related to their traumatic psychological history. TNG is a typical, if not extreme, example of the environmental-sensitivities/psychical-experiences syndrome so far described. She accepts many of the identifications relating to the EM-pollution approach and shows an interest in and an understanding of them. Nevertheless, she still retains her belief that aliens abducted her when she was 14, as well as much of the associated mythology.

She is, however, involved with ETH/alien-orientated investigators as well as another 'abductee' who is violently opposed to my approach because of the threat it represents to her belief system. This, however, is somewhat ironic, as this other experiencer, whom I shall call 'Maria', lives close to high-voltage power lines, which loom over *both* sides of her house; she has taken photographs of balls of light in the rooms, as well as video-recordings of similar lights around the pylons close by. Interestingly, like TNG, 'Maria' has also chosen a partner many years her senior. As if this was not enough evidence of her conformity to the parameters predicted, she also answered in the affirmative to 'The 25 Questions' that embody the EM-pollution approach in the presence of the chairman of the British UFO Research Association! Readers may sense the ideological battles which rage between fundamentalist ETH believers and the scientific/clinical EM-pollution approach.

Case 5

Morgan of Swansea

Location: Near Swansea, Wales, UK

Time frame: 1956 to the present day

Introduction

Morgan, a Welsh lady in her late thirties at the time of writing, has had encounters with numerous bizarre formed figures, objects and environments over a period of decades, beginning in early adulthood. Morgan manages her experiences on a full-time basis. They have been so acutely disturbing at times that she has sought medical treatment, spiritual counselling, exorcism and hypnotherapy, as well as approaching numerous investigators and researchers over the years, basically seeking answers to the meaning of and reasons for her vivid and highly strange experiences.

Her own thinking on these events has varied considerably and has been influenced by individuals and groups who have imprinted their own belief systems on to the perceptions and sensations which Morgan reports, although she has now evolved to a point where she feels that rationality leads to a greater understanding. Readers can make their own judgments as to the validity of the identifications I have made, after coming on to the scene late in her experiential 'career'.

Morgan's time is taken up with caring for her elderly mother on a full-time basis, and the local social services support her in this, providing 'respite' days, when they take over care for short periods. She lives in a small Welsh village, where, externally, her life must appear routine and mundane.

Description

One morning in November 1994, I took a call from her and she related a weird incident that had taken place the previous evening. It was about 8 p.m. as it had been dark for a couple of hours, and she had been standing in her bedroom, looking out of a large picture window into her small back garden area, which is surrounded by a tall fence. Staring out into the blackness, thinking about her evening routine, she was suddenly alerted by a strong sense of impending arrival. This was quickly followed by the appearance of a man in a suit who emerged vertically from behind the fence a few yards in front of her. Startled, she saw that he seemed to be standing to attention with his arms by his sides, but she hardly had time to take anything else in before he flew into the air like a rocket and gracefully arced round in a loop before turning to swoop close to the window and dive silently away into the darkness. Morgan later recalled her shock at the flicker of recognition in the brief moment when their eyes met at the window-pane, as if he knew her well.

It soon became clear that, beneath the surface, Morgan leads an extraordinary covert life, punctuated with incidents of 'high strangeness', such as this one, as well as equally unpredictable struggles with emotions and sensations that descend without warning, shattering any sense of normality. This has been the private battle that Morgan has had to endure for decades and, somewhat understandably, on several occasions she has been at an extremely low ebb, wondering if life was worth living.

I have described this battle as private because, as far as anyone else is concerned in her small and close-knit village, she leads a perfectly normal life and is depended upon by her ailing parent, for whom she provides round-the-clock support. There is no doubt, despite her strange experiences, that Morgan functions well and does not display any of the erratic and disordered thinking of psychosis. Her hallucinations, like those of other experiencers, are the product of acquired environmental sensitivities due to an overly close relationship with electricity in her formative years.

Observations

THE EARLY YEARS

Between the ages of 3 and 5 years, Morgan lived with her parents in a converted bus, parked close to a large transformer, mounted about 2.4m (8ft) up on two telegraph poles. During the day, she and a friend used to play beneath it and Morgan can still recall the note it made as it continually hummed. In this rural area of Wales, the electricity supply to houses comes as low-voltage cables in ceramic insulators mounted on a series of posts, about 6m (20ft) from ground level, supplying the standard 240V. It is only when levels in the UK are compared with those in other countries (e.g. 110V in Canada) that one realizes how high they are. We have seen from other cases that such prolonged and regular daily irradiation during the very early formative years constitutes an effect comparable to an MEE and, as in Morgan's case, it is usually found that profound epileptiform reactivity is precipitated, predominantly in the temporal lobes. After the age of 5, Morgan moved house as it were, but only a short distance away, to a house on the other side of the road.

Although the actual living quarters were moved a little distance away from the transformer, and they were perhaps shielded from electrical fields by the protection of bricks and mortar, it is almost impossible to shield out magnetic fields and they would certainly have penetrated the house. In fact, some of the older houses enhance field levels, as cast-iron fireplaces re-radiate them; I have also found curiously high RF-field high points inside houses of such age. These occur on the corners of the chimney-stack, because these structures run the height of the house and form a substantial internal pillar down into the rooms. It would appear that it is these sooty hollows, sticking up high above the roofs, which act as wave guides to trap field emissions from RF transmitters. It is precisely this wave-guide function that attracts ball lightning in the atmosphere during storms, and it is well-documented how one of the commonest ways for fireballs to enter houses is down the chimney, from there to sail around the room. This is mentioned here because the general area around Morgan's locale has many 'mountains', as the locals refer to them, upon which are mounted numerous radio masts. There is also a burgeoning Citizens-Band (CB) radio-enthusiast network, which takes advantage of the altitudes and, although this may relate more to Morgan's present situation, there is also a prospering CB-radio shop in the village.

Morgan's second home would also have been irradiated to some degree, so her acquired sensitivity would have been enhanced further. Also, between the ages of 17 and 19, Morgan was hospitalized and treated for clinical depression with three electroconvulsive therapy (ECT) sessions. Again, these would have made her sensitivities worse, constituting three MEEs. It is therefore not surprising that Morgan is one of the most severe cases I have on my files.

HEALTH AND CONSCIOUSNESS EFFECTS

Morgan does not seem to have developed food or chemical sensitivities, although there have been a few isolated incidents which have triggered seizures. One of these involved an exposure to an aerosol fly-spray, although this seemed to have interfered with her breathing, causing her to overbreathe; this is a well-known trigger for TLE. In fact, Morgan is a typical field-triggered TLE sufferer, displaying many of the signs and symptoms, although a standard electroencephalogram (EEG) test did not disclose the condition. This is not unusual because a diagnosis requires either 'nasopharyngeal' electrodes to be placed at the back of the nose or, more effectively it appears, a magnetic resonance imaging (MRI) scan, which detects lesions. However, Morgan does seem to have experienced some spectacular hallucinations and the following was described to me as an example of a shared experience.

One day, when she was in her late twenties, she was walking with a friend, a girl slightly younger than her, on the shore of a beach in Sussex, and was startled to look up from beach-combing to see a huge ocean liner sailing very close to the shore, less than 20m (70ft) from the beach. The whole ship was lit up from bow to stern, with many brilliant lights in the cabins and on deck, and she could see people and hear the general hubbub of their conversation. As they stood there, Morgan had no reason to think that the vast ship was anything but real, although its relatively sudden appearance seemed a little strange. She also had no reason to suppose that her companion did not also see it, and assumed that she did, although for some reason they did not discuss it, and Morgan does not recall how she lost sight of the ship. Only when she was relating this incident to me recently, as an example of a shared experience, did she realize that it could have actually been entirely subjective and that the shared aspect was entirely assumed.

A DAY IN THE LIFE

Such outstanding visions are interspersed with what she regards as routine daily experiences, and what would be a typical day's entry in her diary gives us some idea as to how much of a strange ordeal life must be for such TLE sufferers.

After going to bed one night, Morgan awakes, or so she assumes, and becomes aware of 'things' approaching her from many different directions, giving her a claustrophobic feeling of 'being hemmed in'. This is a variant on the sense of presence and, from the positions of the various CB-radio transmitters in the locale, could be due to Morgan sensing their transmissions. This is certainly supported by another case, in which the 'haunted' subject told the investigator that 'a presence has just entered the room' and the investigator, on looking at his field-meter, noticed that the room was experiencing a power surge at precisely that moment. On looking to her right, Morgan sees a gargoyle face grinning malevolently on the wall, as if it was painted on it in luminous paint; this eventually fades in and out as if it were a pulsating light within the brickwork. The bedhead is under the window and, out of many presences, Morgan can sense one in particular behind her, getting nearer all the time – a definite feeling of something mysterious approaching from outside the window.

Sitting upright now, and alert, she is overcome with a sense of resigned calm. The hall light is on because she cannot sleep without its reassuring glow, and she briefly catches sight of an imp-like entity peeping in at the door, as if it was adding a humorous touch, to make her feel less afraid; in fact, it does have a calming effect as she waits for whatever is still approaching. Then, suddenly, a powerful presence sweeps into the room from the window and halts at the bedroom door. She sees a long, tall figure, dressed in robes, but instead of a head, it has a large open book resting on its shoulders. The pages show many question-marks as well as wavy lines and symbols she does not understand. It vanishes, and a sense of stillness fills the room, until a hand comes through the wall and grabs hers.

When the figure has gone, there is a red sore-looking wheal on her wrist. Such examples of skin trauma are indicative of field-induced electrical burns, and the synchronization of such field exposure (intersecting microwave beams, forming small transient areas of high field amplitudes) with appropriate imagery is typical. Morgan's description of 'presences' approaching from different directions is another clue that enables us to visualize the various transmitting antennae around her in the area. Situated on the sides of the mountains, their transmissions intersect to form potent RF hot spots within houses in the valley, and inside the rooms of her house, especially when they are in phase with each other. Therefore, we have a picture of energetic beams which flicker and intersect within the house, with higher field strengths at their points of intersection.

Sometimes Morgan awakes to find a stream of people walking through the walls of her bedroom, some of them acknowledging her as they pass through. Other visions have included three figures standing together, but with wolf's heads and laser-like beams of light coming from the eyes. She is, of course, terrified and finds it hard to differentiate between 'ordinary' fear and field-induced terror, although, to her, this is somewhat academic. She has also described very physical fights with shadowy figures, just as Lori reported, and, as would be expected, the same types of entity, such as the 'gray' on occasion, and clusters of symptoms and sensations. However, this consistency, which applies to many types of mental phenomena, is not indicative of encounters with real intruders or real physical aliens, as the ETH enthusiasts would have us believe, but simply shows that the human system reacts in the same ways to the same EM-field exposure.

REITER'S RESPONSE: THE TRUTH AT LAST

The aspect that has caused experiencers such as Morgan to feel that they may be dealing with denizens of another world is the sheer vivid reality of the experiences and, until fairly recently, although Morgan understood on an intellectual level that her perceptions were due to field exposure, she still had reservations because of the vivid impression of autonomy that her visions and entities displayed. Experience is evidently more convincing than rational analysis. However, after years of what can only really be called torment, Morgan has discovered something that she feels is a breakthrough. As with many experiencers in later life, her mission has been to find out why she is having these strange and frightening experiences and, as mentioned, she has turned to many different groups and 'experts' over the years, sometimes with humiliating results. However, just as her firsthand experience still produces a certain conviction for the physical reality of her entities, another experience has demonstrated how magnetic fields are the real stimulus behind such visions. This is Reiter's magnetic response (MR) test (see p. 88).

Morgan phones me in London from her village in Wales and provides updates on her latest experiences. In the course of these conversations I suggested that she test her responses to a small magnet placed on the sides of her head, close to the temporal lobes. Several months passed and I had forgotten our conversation until, one evening, Morgan called in an excited state; she had tried the MR test with a fridge magnet and had induced symptoms that were only too familiar to her. Summoning her courage, she relaxed on her bed and placed a magnet on the side of her head. There was a pop in her right ear and for 10 minutes nothing else happened. Then, suddenly, came a period of intense physical fear, complete with palpitations, the sense of presence, a pulling sensation on one side of her head and the overwhelming impression that one side of her body was twice as large as the other. There was a quick flash in her visual field, which illuminated a face with large eyes, jerking sensations in her body and a period when her room seemed to have a strange unfamiliar atmosphere (*jamais vu*). While this had been a somewhat unpleasant experience, she now knew for sure that such symptoms, which always accompanied her encounters with entities, could be brought on to order by a magnet. The period of waiting between placing the magnet and the sensations, the *latency period*, also occurred with Persinger's subjects. For Morgan, however, for the first time in her life, she felt that she had some degree of control over her sensations, i.e. she could bring them on whenever she wished. This period of exultation was quickly followed by anger:

> *My God, those people who go around telling people that they are being visited by aliens or are under psychic attack have a lot to answer for! All these years I have been led to believe that I have been singled out by evil entities in the spirit world, and have been terrified out of my wits. Or I have been scared that aliens are going to take me away for some kind of surgical operation ... Some of these investigators need to be shot!*

This test had been carried out using a small fridge magnet and Morgan reported back after I had sent her a stronger one from a speaker diaphragm. She told me that she felt as if there were explosions going off inside her head, especially at the back. Then she had the sensation of falling, a well-documented epileptiform effect, followed by a distorted sense of body image, whereby she felt that her head was facing the wrong way, around 180 degrees to one side.

THE SURROUNDING AREA: HOT SPOTS

Old Carmel is a mountainous area close to Morgan's village and it is well known for strange phenomena. The local inhabitants have seen many strange and unidentified lights meandering around the mountain. Also Morgan's friends recall an evening's excursion into the wild and untouched countryside on the sides of the mountains, which typifies the area, when they were extremely startled to see a huge luminous white horse galloping across their path, accompanied by the sounds of whiplash, especially when this shining majestic beast faded into the air as it moved away from them. The street-lights in the village often flicker and cut out for short periods, and another mountain in the same range has a chapel built on it, also haunted by floating lights and a local 'white lady' apparition. This area's hot spots combine natural tectonic activity, fields from the low-voltage cables mounted in threes about 9m (30ft) up on posts, transformers, both at ground level and at a height of about 4.5m (15ft), and a flourishing CB network and rural radio hams.

Conclusion

To conclude, therefore, once again, this case demonstrates the robust consistency of the EM-pollution approach by showing how early encounters with electricity followed by prolonged irradiation produce the same clusters of health, consciousness and environmental effects. The following case also demonstrates this, but has some extremely unusual features, including the perception of a complex UFO, complete with helmeted spaceman, coupled with EH so severe that the subject is disabled and housebound. Another atypical aspect is the identification of the subject, as his case has already been published in the specialist literature. This includes a version by myself, on which this entry is based, and which, of course, shows how it conforms to the parameters predicted.

Case 6

The Quantock Horror

Location: Quantock Hills, Somerset, UK

Time frame: 1988

Description

...in daylight on a sunny day in May 1988, Tony Burfield was taking photographs on the Quantock Hills north of Petherton, Somerset, England, when he observed an object flying towards him making a low noise. It reputedly flew directly over his head very low down, appearing to be the size of two fields and blocking the sun. In shape it was like two saucers with stacked decks and protruding wings in a fantastically complex shape. He took several close photographs as it passed directly above, including one in which an entity was seen standing on the rim. A wave of heat struck him from the object as it flew past, 'burning the negatives' ... Tony also developed very serious ill effects (at one stage believing he was dying). He claimed weakness, inability to eat solid foods, extreme sensitivity to electrical equipment, a metallic taste in his mouth and much else. He received medical and protracted psychiatric treatment ... [Phillips/Jaafar, 1993.]

This was the report that appeared in *Northern UFO News* and is typical of its kind. It appears to be a mysterious and spectacular event which drew considerable attention from many investigators, researchers and experiencers alike, and was highly publicized in the UFO-study periodicals. However, none of the robust parameters of the EM-pollution approach were identified, despite the fact that they virtually scream from the account: extreme sensitivity to electrical equipment, a metallic taste, extreme weakness, nutritional problems, etc. Before any analysis of the event, let us consider the background parameters, as these will enable us to understand how this report came to be made. This information comes from a mixture of sources, including extensive reports from such investigators as the late Ken Phillips (who explored the case extensively with Judith Jaafar) and Robert Moore (who lives in the area), as well as reference sources from the British Geological Survey and BBC TV Engineering Information. I also corresponded directly with Tony Burfield, who has now moved house and whose health has improved considerably, the reason for which will become evident. I published an extensive article on the case in the *The Ley Hunter* (Budden 1994/5), then edited by earth-lights pioneer, Paul Devereux.

Artist's impression of experiencer Tony Burfield undergoing his close encounter on the Quantock Hills, Somerset, UK. (Graham Fletcher)

Background

HOT SPOTS: ARTIFICIAL AND NATURAL

The experiencer himself lived in a terraced house barely 100m (110yd) from high-voltage power lines, whose pylons loomed over his home in the East Bower district of the town of Bridgewater, Somerset, UK. The experience itself, however, took place in a pasture on the nearby Quantock Hills, when the subject was equidistant between two rows of intersecting high-voltage power lines of the National Grid, which were at a distance of about 200m (220yd) either side of him. This site in the Quantock Hills consists of Carboniferous and Devonian strata which is extensively faulted, the Cothelstone Fault being the largest. A British Geological Survey publication on the area relates:

> ... *most of the displacement between the Devonian Rocks of the Quantock Hills and those of the Brendons was accounted for by the Cothelstone Fault, which defines the Quantock Hills on their south-western side. [Edmonds & Williams, 1985.]*

Although this would indicate geomagnetic and geoelectric fields in this central area, these would only provide ambient fields for the site where the witness had his experience, which was much closer to a tight cluster of smaller unnamed faults, about 300m (330yd) away from where he lay on the grass taking photographs. It should be remembered that such natural fields would include radio frequencies.

MAJOR ELECTRICAL EVENT

In July 1994 I wrote to Tony Burfield to ask him about this. His reply confirmed the pattern already established regarding the consistency of major MEs in samples of experiencers. He wrote:

Yes, I have had a big electrical accident in the past, and I know I can't die.

What other predicted parameters were in place?

ELECTRICAL HYPERSENSITIVITY

It is useful here to quote from my *Ley Hunter* article, which tells us:

As the term implies, EH individuals are sensitive to electromagnetic fields considerably below normal thresholds, and exposure induces adverse symptoms. It is significant, therefore, that in a transcript of an interview with the witness and his wife, she states: 'The only time you weren't in pain was when the electric run out ... We had no electricity the other night and you had no pain at all ...' [Budden, 1994/5.]

PHOTOPHOBIA

The experience itself took place between two rows of intersecting power lines in bright sunlight. This is an acute exposure to an additional source of non-ionizing radiation – ultra-violet (UV) and infra-red – and would have added considerably to Tony's load-phenomenon threshold. So this apparent UFO encounter took place when he was exposed to fields from two sets of high-voltage power lines either side of him, in the burning sunshine of an unusual heatwave. Before this experience, he evidently found sunlight bearable, but subsequently his photophobia became so acute that even night-time excursions had a devastating effect. Tony related:

I haven't been out (at night) for ages ... I come in with car-lights burnt on me ...

And, from a letter dated 30 October 1992:

I went out last night for a walk [and] I wish I did not ... car-lights pushed my head and then I had a very severe pain inside the back of my head. [In Budden, 1994/5.]

It is the posterior part of the brain that contains visual functions.

Taste anomalies

Tony complained of a strong metallic taste and, as with many other cases, this was due to the effect of electrical fields on saliva and the tin/mercury amalgam of tooth fillings producing electrolysis, during which the metal amalgam breaks down and fills the mouth with mercury vapour.

Food allergies

Typically, Tony is especially sensitive to gluten in wheat products (coeliac disease) and his description of how his body reacts has its own eloquent authenticity:

> I have had Weetabix, and it makes my arms where the muscles are go big and it feels like my arms are ripping apart.

Also, a paramedic who became familiar with the case, Mark Gulliver, reported that Tony's symptoms were indicative of a 'total allergy syndrome', which is absolutely correct. However, this was totally ignored by the host of investigators, researchers and experiencers who visited Tony and explored the case over the years.

Psychical experiences/hallucinations

As we have seen, such experiencers have a history of psychical events and Tony is no different. On one occasion he actually saw 'little men' who shot electrical bolts at him, which he felt. We must remember that this was in the hot-spot location of his home. Once again we can identify how physical field effects and imagery come together to produce a vivid but ludicrous reality, with the typical elements of absurdity that mark these cases, which the ETH fraternity must filter out. Interestingly, Tony also heard a mental voice which told him to shoot them back, which he did by making a gun with his fingers and doing just that! However, this makes me think of the way in which language is used by the unconscious in dreams and, colloquially, when something is eradicated with some force, you 'get shot of it', which Tony was, in effect, told to do by his mental voice.

Other hallucinations included a swarm of locusts which was perceived to have come through the window-glass into the room before vanishing. Again, interestingly, it would seem that this was an actual *visual representation* of how EM fields physically enter the house and 'swarm' through the rooms. This is entirely consistent with the form of many hallucinations perceived by EH-status individuals. That is to say, the physical form of the fields and the field source is transposed into imagery, which is superimposed upon them; for example, in many cases, an unexplained atmospheric phenomenon (UAP), when it is close enough, forms the physical basis for a hallucination, appearing as a structured craft. This is a key concept that cannot be emphasized enough. It demonstrates how multiple witnesses may see a UAP, the witness in close proximity perceives as a hallucination of a spacecraft. Subsequently investigators are sometimes able to find physical traces, in the form of thermal effects and EM disturbance.

HYPERAESTHESIA

This generalized sensitivity to the noise, vibration, light and chemical stimuli of the environment is frequently so stressful for EH-status individuals that they become housebound. This certainly applied to Tony, who states:

> I used to go along the Quantocks (a hilly rural area) and come back and feel a bit better ... everytime I get up there now I get worse, because everything around me affects me now ... I haven't been out for ages ... if I go out I'll be six times worse.

His wife states flatly:

> ...and he can't do a lot of things that he used to. He's sort of housebound.

GENERALIZED MEMORY LOSS

EH sufferers report that their memory becomes enfeebled and are aware of material that they can no longer recall in detail. This appears to be a side-effect of their developing epileptiform condition, and Tony has made several references to this, e.g.:

> I can remember what happened to me, and then my memory goes ... There's still a lot of stuff at the back of my mind that I can't remember anymore ...

OTHER SENSATIONS

Transcripts of Tony's and his wife's conversations with investigators reveal a number of other aspects that are consistent with the EM approach:

> I've had it ever so bad ... I'm getting cold in bed, I shiver in bed ... My nose is blocked off with skin [in the sinus region] and it shouldn't be like that ... [feels a constricting feeling high in the nose] ... the passage to my head squeezes and squeezes ...

Inexplicable temperature extremes are commonly reported by experiencers, and are generally due to disturbances to the hypothalamus. The feeling of pressure, or 'knots' in the sinuses, as they have been called by Strieber [In LaPlante, 1993], is produced by gyromagnetic effects on the layers of magnetite in the thin bones of the sinuses, as detected by the Manchester zoologists (Baker *et al.*, 1983). Such magnetic disturbances have been 'identified' as alien nasal implants (see p. 86).

THE CLOSE-ENCOUNTER EVENT

It is against this backdrop of EH and hot-spot exposure that Tony Burfield, in bright sunlight, while lying in the grass of a pasture on the side of the heavily faulted Quantock Hills, in between two rows of power lines barely a hundred metres (a few hundred feet) either side of him, had his close encounter experience. This is what he described:

> *I was going to take some photos of the scenery when in the distance there was a very deep noise and there was a black object coming towards me. It had bat-like wings with decks, and was the shape of a saucer, with like wings in the middle. I managed to take a photo of it as it was coming towards me. Then in came over and hovered for about five minutes. In that time, I saw it had two decks with a dome on top. Also, there was a person up inside the ship — he was smallish — he put a helmet on his head for talking — I have got a photo of him in the ship. As I had to lay down to take the photos, I felt my clothes get hot. The ship took up two fields and blocked out the sun when it came over.*

Remembering that Tony is hypersensitive to environmental fields, we can begin to present some identifications of the perceptions he reported. The 'very deep noise' could have been externally produced geosound and is a typical description of this electrical/mechanical activity, in which subterranean rock faces grind together on a massive scale to produce auditory effects and piezoelectric/piezomagnetic fields. Alternatively, the 'noise' could have been internally stimulated by the action of these fields upon the brain. Dr Peter Nathan, in his neurological textbook, *The Nervous System*, tells us:

> *When the areas surrounding the primary receptive areas are stimulated, the patient reports a change … In the case of hearing, when the primary auditory area is stimulated, the patient hears … **rumbling** or … rushing sounds. [Nathan, 1988, p. 228. My emphasis.]*

When considering the apparent blocking out of the sun by a huge craft, I have seen several cases in which EH individuals subjected to ELF fields from power lines reported that their visual field went dark. One of these stated:

> *… For myself, it was an almost indescribable episode in which the light seemed to go black (although I could still see) and I was completely disorientated. [Smith & Best, 1989.]*

Other experiencers have described this darkening of the upper area of the visual field as 'like a curtain drawn across the sky', and such 'curtains' have been reported as being roughly octagonal. This has been associated with the stimulation of the superior temporal lobes, an effect known as *hemianopia*.

Also, it must be remembered that Tony Burfield whole-heartedly believes in the 'space people', as we can tell from the sentiments in the letter telling us of his major electrocution (p. 248). This belief system would, of course, colour his perceptions and, instead of the huge complex craft he describes, one of the photographs he took shows a small dark object while another shows a simple light. Significantly, the investigator who lives in the area, Robert Moore, related how there is a microlight aircraft centre in the area, as well as hang-gliding enthusiasts. There is little doubt that Tony's perceptions of this spectacular craft were hallucinatory, although one photograph does show something quite small which passed over where he lay. In another UFO report that Tony made, photograph shows the unmistakable image of a hang-glider and, although there is an absence of required information, it would seem that his Quantock Hills sighting features the same object. But how could such a relatively small object be the basis for such an expansive hallucinatory image?

To answer this question, we must remember that the space above the site where Tony lay was saturated with EM fields from numerous high-voltage power lines and from piezoelectric and piezomagnetic geological sources.

It should also be mentioned that the area would have elevated ambient levels due to the massive 500kW TV transmitter on the nearby Mendip Hills. A microlight aircraft flying into this EM concentrate would have been subject to electric-field enhancement:

> As soon as an object is placed within an electric field, the field behaves rather like a curtain and drapes itself in close folds over the object, leaving a clear space beneath. The field so folded can reach values up to a hundred times that of the ambient unperturbed field. [Smith & Best, 1989, p.137.]

Conclusion

Was it a one-manned microlight craft flying into an EM 'soup' that acted as the core for the build-up of a massive electric wave form which formed the physical basis for Tony's hallucination? After all, his other hallucinations (e.g. the swarm of locusts which flew through window-glass, just as EM fields would penetrate it) also transformed actual physical wave forms into imagery. Also, I have repeatedly noticed how UFO witnesses who get close to electric fireballs report how such simple lights become structured craft, sometimes with absurd embellishments, such as propellers or ski-runners. After examining many such cases over an extended period I have reached the seemingly inescapable conclusion that the EH-perceptual system can apprehend physical field sources and wave forms as imagery based upon their actual structure, e.g. a magnetic vortex as a spinning disc. Such an identification also explains why a small aerial object registered on the film that Tony exposed.

An alternative identification may not have involved a microlight/hang-glider, although it could still have been there, and the light which the second photograph shows may have been an earth light, as geosound does imply tectonic activity. This has been associated with such geologically originating fireballs and proximity to this could have induced unconsciousness and the UFO vision. Again, this UAP could also have acted as the physical basis on to which the hallucinatory craft was imposed, as it must be remembered that no other witnesses to the massive craft that Tony describes have come forward. However, whatever happened exactly, the point here is that *any realistic identification is in EH/hot-spot terms*, not in any of the exotic 'explanations' offered by the ETH. Nor are any of the psychosocial approaches, based on the concept of urban myth, appropriate, because clinical parameters and measurable field levels are involved.

Case 7:

June of Coventry: caught in the net currents

Location: Coventry, UK

Time frame: 1971 to the present day

Introduction

This experiencer, in her late thirties at the time of writing, is another example of someone who underwent an MEE in her formative years (at the age of 17) and then went on to have psychical experiences followed by alien-abduction events on an episodic basis.

Like so many EH-status individuals, the number of her experiences that can be classified as strange or anomalous is high, and happen on an almost routine basis. As a result we get a picture of an individual's life so at odds with what is regarded as the norm that it is clear that her relationship to mundane reality is very different from that of the majority of people. Because of the frequency of these weird events and perceptions, there is little surprise on her part and such things as electrical oddities and the strange consequences of automatic behaviour (this was the experiencer who awoke to find potatoes around the edge of the bath) are just accepted as normal. Also, she strongly feels that she is 'a psychic', and has self-reported ESP on a regular basis, where she feels that she can become aware of future events, known as *precognition*.

Description

An alien-abduction experience

June's diary relates:

> *Evening and the children had gone to bed. It was dark outside and my husband and myself heard an aeroplane fly over. Following this, a stationary humming noise could be heard. We looked through the curtains and saw lights darting all over the sky. Neither of us has seen anything like this before and we called the children to come and look. These lights also made musical notes but not a tune. The children pulled the curtains right back and put the light on but I was not happy with this and told them to turn the light off. The next minute we saw an 'alien'*

about three feet high with a large rounded head, small eyes and bright attractive coloured clothes coming up the drive towards the house. I panicked and ran to lock the doors screaming to the children not to let it in even though it looked friendly.

Very soon into this description we are faced with typical absurdities, which should ring alarm bells with researchers as to the internal nature of this sequence. However, I am constantly surprised as to how blind many are to the humour in such descriptions, noticing that it is always those who are keen to regard such reports as evidence of real physical aliens who seem oblivious to such absurdities. For example, June, when confronted with an unwelcome alien at the door, simply told it to go away, which is probably standard procedure under such circumstances:

The 'alien' stood at the front door and as I told it to go away it duplicated itself and another one appeared inside [on the other side of the door].

This hallucination of passing through the door by duplication has appeared in other reports, notably the Betty Andreasson case in the USA:

The four entities that had passed by the window now entered the house by going through the kitchen door … they passed through its solid wood as if it were nonexistent … They came in like follow-the-leader … They are starting to come through the door now … right through the wood, one after the other … [Fowler, 1980.]

In many other cases, there are reports of entities which pass through walls and doors, echoing the popular image of ghosts. Tony Burfield (p. 249) saw a swarm of locusts pass through window–glass, and this was noted as being precisely the manner in which EM fields would enter a room, suggesting that the hallucination was superimposed on the actual physical field presence and movement. Assuming that June's hallucinatory formed figure was superimposed on, and represented, a pulsed wave form from the environment, the door would have offered less effective shielding than the brickwork; although it would have screened out much of the electric field, the magnetic component would not have been absorbed and would, in fact, have passed through, just as the figure was perceived to do. While this way of regarding the perceptions of EH subjects has not been tested experimentally, it does offer a usefully consistent perspective as a way of understanding the relationship between hallucination and field in case after case, i.e. the field presence forms the physical basis for the hallucination. June continues, relating an aspect which also occurred in the Andreasson case:

I looked to my family and saw that they were in some kind of trance-like state.

At this point, it can be revealed that, when examining these seemingly external events in retrospect, it transpired that June's family were away from home visiting relatives and were not there at all. Instead, such depictions are typical strategies implemented by the brain during its efforts to present a convincing version of reality. That is to say, the brain takes the simplest route by depicting the family members as immobile, because the provision of so many formed figure images behaving normally is too complex a construction for it to undertake in its creation of a vision which also incorporates the home environment. Such an authentic reality replacement would involve conversation and movement for example, and the depiction of the family as still and silent avoids this complexity while at the same time including them as both witnesses and participants. The context of a visit by aliens provides a certain creative licence for the mental 'producer' to exploit (see Note 18), and such usually incongruous depictions as an immobile family are certainly within the repertoire of feats that science-fiction aliens display. This management of the elements of the vision was evidently successful, as the experience seemed absolutely real to June at the time. Commenting now, she relates:

> For quite some time I had believed this experience had actually happened!

As this event was entirely subjective, albeit appearing as a vividly real vision, we should of course begin to wonder about the reality status of other accounts that have become 'classic' cases, complete with family members as witnesses. *When it is realized what is possible in terms of the replacement of normal reality by visionary realities, the true nature of these experiences becomes evident*, but this is only possible when one opts out of the belief system that surrounds them and considers alternatives. However, at the time, as June stresses, things seemed to be really happening, and the family seemed to have been there, complying with the aliens' wishes:

> We went with them, following one another in a single line. The next moment we were in a spacecraft which was oblong like a coach, and there were other humans there too. Everyone sat in rows, one behind the other and in front of us were tables, but these were circular and coloured red and orange with glass that had a lot of depth at the centre, similar to a bar-code scanner in the supermarkets. We were told that we were being taken to another planet and to look into the glass. I refused to do this, as I was not in the same trance-like state as the others. We were also asked to look out of the windows, but I made an excuse saying I did not like heights.

> *When we were told that we were at the other side of the moon I looked and was surprised to see lights and buildings of some kind. We then moved on and within seconds were at our destination. I thought we had been conned as it looked like the earth to me, except for the complexes. Then we were in one.*

The 'complexes' which June refers to, and in which she then found herself, were a sort of enclosed world, rather like a shopping mall. Throughout the account, I noticed that June had not given any description of what the aliens looked like and, when I asked, I realized why she may have been reluctant to mention this aspect.

'They were like garden gnomes,' she somewhat sheepishly informed me. In other words, like so many aspects of these experiences that many ETH-orientated investigators must filter out of their reports, they were absurd. Of the enclosed world of the 'complex', June tells us:

> *The complex had everything to support life including leisure centres, and was clean and unpolluted. All the people living there were young – there were no children or old people – and they were happy. I wondered where the aliens lived, but nobody seemed to know for sure, except that it was outside of the complex. This looked like a wilderness – a sandy desert, where life could not survive.*

While there does not seem to have been any explicit 'welfare message' in this vision, it does seem to have shown an idealized, happy, regulated and pollution-free environment set within a hostile wilderness. This symbolism could even be called heavy-handed and, in environmental terms, does seem to have been a metaphor for a healthy body state. This is supported by the issue of where the aliens lived, as they were clearly identified with the wilderness. It is difficult not to notice that a kind of suburban Garden-of-Eden scenario was expressed in this abduction vision, although humankind's original and natural state had been replaced with a more accessible idealization, with all the modern new-town facilities and, appropriately, an equally contemporary town-garden and nature-spirit guide – the garden gnome.

June's 'return' was abrupt, unpleasant and salutary. At one point she was looking out at the alien wilderness, then she found herself waking up in this same desert, lying on her back in the sand. Then the vision of the wilderness dissolved away and she was in bed on her back in a state of paralysis, which lasted for some time.

About 3 weeks later, she had a vivid dream in which she looked out of the window of her home and saw several large electrical generators nearby. She comments:

I was surprised as they did not belong to us. There were a lot of police and military men and tall people who I knew to be alien. They came to my door in single file, gave me a gold ring and apologised for frightening me earlier.

Again, the symbolism of this – a warning about the effects of environmental fields – may seem laboured, but it must be remembered that it was a dream in isolation with none of the relevant context outlined here. Around this time, June had another dream which also seems to have contained the environmental-fields theme:

A helicopter was chasing me. On the side was written either GEC Telecomminications or British Telecommunications. When the searchlight landed on me the helicopter changed into a UFO.

The details of this are also unusually significant, especially as it is dream imagery which often precedes abduction scenarios (these can be usefully regarded as electrically 'upgraded' versions of dreams), and an EM-pollution theme also dominates this helicopter dream.

Background

HOT-SPOT ASPECTS

If these dreams were an indicator of irradiation from the environment, just what sources were there exactly? I actually field-surveyed June's home with instrumentation (a Coghill Fieldmouse and TriField Meter) on two separate occasions, about 2 years apart; at both times I found elevated magnetic-field levels, well off the scale, i.e. over 100mGs. These emanated from the bedroom walls and floor, as well as from the architraves and floors of doorways downstairs; interestingly the *length* of the front garden path, extending from the underground mains cables and junction box in the street, was especially 'hot', electromagnetically speaking. It should be remembered that the alien first approached the house by dashing up the front path …

A report by Powerwatch also emphasizes the EM hazards of underground power cables:

According to research, including some carried out by National Grid, most domestic ambient EMFs [electromagnetic fields] are caused by underground low voltage distribution cables. Fields well over 0.2 microteslas can be found in many houses due to such underground cables, and Powerwatch has found fields of up to ten microtesla. These are usually due to what are termed 'net' currents. These are 'stray' currents either flowing through the earth, or more usually through the wrong piece of cable or metal pipework. These net currents can be due to equipment or installation faults and could be prevented relatively easily if the electricity supply industry chose to tackle the problem ... A number of houses and flats can have fields exceeding 1000 nT due to underground cables ... [Philips, 1996.]

It would certainly appear that such 'net currents' due to underground cables proliferate in June's home, judging from the field surveys carried out. Hot spots tend to vary in their potency, as transmitters can be switched off or redirected, and previously active locations can become 'quiet' or 'cool'. It would appear, therefore, that June's home is constantly subject to high ambient field levels, due to 'net currents' from subterranean power cables. There are also periods of additional and overlying irradiation in the form of a RF/microwave near-field emanating from a phased array of transmitters situated about 800m (875yd) away on the roof of a high-rise block housing police trainees, beside a police training centre. These were measured as between 0.1 and $0.3 mW/cm^2$ and are time-varying. There is also a Victorian substation at the end of her road, about 100m (110yd) away, from which the underground cables that eventually run to her house can be traced. This is too far away to affect her directly, although of course it is the cables from this which bring power and 'net currents' to her home.

MAJOR ELECTRICAL EVENTS

When June was 17 years old, she was a passenger in a car which, from her description, seems to have been subject to a form of *sheet lightning*. This is the term given to lightning-induced illumination, usually of clouds, which causes a sheet-like section to become luminous. As the vehicle came to the top of a hill, it was suddenly engulfed in a bright white light, causing it to malfunction and bringing it to a stop. The interior was so brilliantly lit that 'everything seemed like a negative'. This may also have been a type of geologically induced light phenomenon, but the event happened so long ago that June cannot recall any other details.

Also, much later in her life, June received a massive electric shock which threw her across the room. This occurred when she was in her late twenties and handled a plug in a mains socket with wet hands. Usually, the average domestic electric shock would not really qualify as an MEE, but this electrocution seems to have been somewhat above average because she was unconscious for a short period of time.

PHYSICAL TRAUMA

In an examination of an experiencer's 'electrical history', as it could usefully be called, we look for events which would induce a permanent altered reactivity, such as prolonged exposure to a close-field source, or an MEE. However, as implied in the 'Ian of Peckham' case (p. 204), head injury can also induce brain lesions, and even head injuries that are of a minor nature, involving only limited neurological damage, may have far-reaching effects in terms of the occurrence of unusual sensations.

Returning to the dream described by June, in which she encountered a helicopter, a closely similar event involving a car accident actually occurred a few weeks afterwards (recorded as being 18 March 1994). The dream seemed to indicate confusion between a helicopter and a UFO and, the day before the accident, June had been curious about an unusual light in the sky near her home, which she observed for some time from her car and which, at one point, hovered low over it. In fact, the area of Coventry where June lives is well known for the occurrence of all manner of Fortean phenomena, including unexplained columns of smoke or mist, falls of straw from the sky and odd lights in the sky. On this occasion, June eventually came to the conclusion that the light was a helicopter, although she was puzzled by the absence of any sound. However, whether it was a helicopter or a UAP of some kind, it seems that she was sensitive to the fields it emitted and became completely disorientated, driving around the usually familiar streets for some time in a daze, completely lost, before eventually finding her way home via an extremely circuitous route.

The following day, when out driving in the town, she was hit by another car from behind and suffered a whiplash effect and hit her head. This injury affected her memory and speech, as well as her ability to read and write for a short period afterwards; she is currently under treatment by a neurosurgeon. It is precisely this order of head trauma that should be noted by investigators, especially in combination with electrical trauma, because it could clearly influence perception and this, after all, is a central aspect under examination in these cases. Any form of acquired physical lesion of the brain will affect the stability of its electrical activity and influence the formation of focal seizures.

The curious interweaving of dreams and subsequent events is an aspect that is extremely common among experiencers, most of whom are convinced that they have a precognitive ability. They may be correct in this, as experiments by Dr Shallis [In Smith & Best, 1989], who tested ESP faculties of EH subjects, do tend to confirm the tendency for such sensitives to have a higher than average ability in this area. Therefore, once again, with an almost monotonous regularity, we find that the usual parameters are outlined. June's answers to 'The 25 Questions' reveal the following:

- Photophobia and an intolerance to fluorescent light;

- Short life of light-bulbs in June's home, which should last 1000 hours but actually last about half this period;

- Spontaneous activation of electrical equipment due to power surges, although this is not a constant phenomenon, but is described as occurring 'at times';

- An inability to wear a watch because it malfunctions but, again, not all the time;

- Sensitivity to domestic gas and some volatile substances;

- No apparent food allergies;

- Sense of presence on occasion;

- Amnesiac periods, probably due to automatic behaviour (she once found that she had decorated her bathroom with potatoes during the night!)

- Fasciculation as painful rippling sensations under the skin;

- Significantly, childhood abuse.

It should also be added that June has had 'visitor' experiences episodically, usually at night. She describes the regular appearance of small thin entities that she calls 'bendy men' as they remind her of the plastic figurines which can be bent into different postures and which were popular when she was a child. In fact, so common were these episodes that she eventually regarded them as a nuisance, as they would wake her up during the night 'to ramble on about crystals and things' and she would ignore them, being more concerned with getting a good night's sleep! This reflects the normalization that occurs when EH subjects experience unusual events so frequently, and as an investigator I have been struck by the almost blasé attitude that develops. In fact, it is only when an outside party reflects their situation back to them, that they realize how bizarre their life-style has become, and how insidious the acceptance of these perceptions can be.

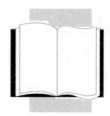

Case 8

Maureen Puddy

Location: Australia

Time frame: February 1973

Introduction

Although I have not investigated this case personally, it is included here because of one unique feature. Two investigators were present while the experiencer was undergoing an alien-abduction experience, but they saw and heard nothing except her trance state and verbal description. This is precisely what Dr Jean Monro, Director of the Breakspear Hospital, described to me – that sometimes her EH patients are able to describe what they are seeing as they experience it.

Description

The event occurred in February 1973 and involved two Australian investigators – Judith Magee and Paul Norman – who had arranged to meet Puddy at a particular location which, for her, involved a fairly long car journey. During the drive, Puddy saw a 'spaceman' in her car, who appeared to be dressed from head to foot in gold foil. This apparent materialization only lasted for a few seconds and soon vanished. When she arrived at the meeting place, Magee and Norman were already there waiting for her and, on seeing her, went over and got into her vehicle to interview her, as she was regarded as a 'repeater', i.e. someone who had experienced repeated UFO sightings and 'alien' encounters. However, as Magee touched the bodywork of Puddy's car, she was startled to feel a strong electric shock, as if a static charge was earthing itself through her, and this is probably exactly what occurred. Working backwards this time, we are now in a position to state with confidence that, as an experiencer, Puddy was EH, and it has been shown that such individuals emit fields as a whole-body effect. In fact, they really re-radiate ambient fields and produce a coherent form (see p. 81). Puddy would have been subjected to unearthed fields from the vehicle during the journey, as cars are prevented from earthing because their rubber tyres are in contact with the ground. As an indicator of the possible field levels present, consider the following:

> ... the metering of fields within the family car indicated the presence of unexpectedly high magnetic fields in the space occupied by the front seats,

which were no doubt created by the alternator. A field strength of 40 to 50 milligauss was found around the leg room areas, 30 milligauss around the lower trunk, and 2.5 milligauss at head level. [Anon., 1993c.]

In an EH individual, this could certainly trigger symptoms, especially as it is likely that a driver would have been sensitized to the specific frequencies present due to the lengthy car journeys involved in travel in Australia. This is what seems to have occurred, judging from the perception of the hallucinatory spaceman by Puddy, but more spectacular effects were to follow. As she told the investigators of her weird experience, she suddenly broke off and exclaimed: 'There he is! Can't you see him? He's in the same clothes.'

Neither investigator could see anything. Puddy then went on to describe how the figure had been walking towards the car and had stopped in front of it. Norman then got out and also walked to the front of the car where Puddy said the 'spaceman' was, and she told them how it had moved back to let Norman pass by. Interestingly, we have noted earlier how hallucinatory apparitions have been seen to behave in terms of their immediate environment, by moving around furniture, through doorways, etc., reflecting how the unconscious supplies realistic detail to its hallucinatory productions in order to make them convincing to the conscious mind.

Puddy then saw the 'spaceman' beckoning to her but, when she did not move, it seemed to melt away into some bushes. The next moment she was screaming that she had been abducted. The two investigators present were able to witness her reactions and hear the details of the interior of the flying saucer – in which there were no doors or windows – but, of course, they saw nothing. Puddy went on to describe how there was a large structure in the middle of the craft, rather like a giant mushroom with a transparent dome through which a jelly-like substance could be seen moving about. Such details from the investigators' report certainly conform with those obtained from Dr Jean Monro, who related how EH patients sometimes describe their visions as they experience them, frequently with their eyes open. However, an inwardly directed attention would be more efficient when sensory noise and light from their immediate surroundings is shut out. Interestingly, Puddy then related that 'He wants me to close my eyes ...' before falling into an immobile state and continuing her description of the interior of the saucer as she saw it.

It is just such allergic trance states which occur with all alien-abduction/contact experiences, the uncommon aspect in this case being the fortuitous presence of the investigators. The manner in which Puddy did this was reminiscent of how regression hypnosis is able to relay information about periods of time for which experiencers cannot account (the so-called 'missing time' aspect), but, of course, Puddy had not been hypnotized. However, the point should be made that experiencers may indeed describe what they see, feel and hear during these regression periods, but they are describing an internal subjective experience.

Eventually, Puddy simply said 'He's gone. I can tell. It feels different' and returned to her normal state. This case is important as it demonstrates the internal nature of these experiences, although those wishing to retain their belief in real aliens and real saucers have conveniently forgotten its significance because it undermines their strongly held views.

OTHER EXPERIENCES

Experiencers undergo multiple encounters, some clearly psychic in nature and others with more obviously 'alien' overtones, although such categorization reflects the limited horizons of these involved in such study areas, as such anomalous experiences shade into each others' territory, blurring any apparent distinctions. Puddy, true to the way that EH subjects have on-going experiences, was classified by the investigators as a 'repeater', which seemed suspicious even to the ETH enthusiasts who studied her, such as Australian investigator Judith Magee. To their credit, they suspected that some external agency was inducing the sort of trance state just described:

> Many of the case histories show that eyewitnesses could be deep-trance subjects, and it may well turn out that there is a high percentage of these. If there is something 'out there' or for that matter 'down here' which exerts a subtle control, then it is possible that the chosen 'contactees' could be sensitive to hypnotic control, and on a continuing basis. [Magee, 1977.]

This unspoken 'something' was never identified as electromagnetism, however, although it does echo the conclusions of many researchers around the world who, in their search for any definitive ground rules that apply to the UFO-alien-contact phenomenon, recognize that there is an external and objective component to these experiences, but have been unable to identify it. For such pioneering individuals the EM-pollution approach offers them the way out of this impasse, if they are really searching for answers to these enigmas rather than gathering knowledge which they feel confirms what they would like the answer to be: ETs. Also, returning to the Puddy case specifically, it must be remembered that the source material from which the following accounts are taken appeared in *Flying Saucer Review*, an established periodical which upholds the belief in the activities of alien intelligences on Earth. Nevertheless, their existence does show a recurring feature of EH-status individuals: on-going experiences. Puddy related that she was driving home late one night along Mooraduc Road, between Frankston and

Dromana, some 55km (35 miles) southeast of Melbourne. Investigator Judith Magee continues with the account:

> *Her attention was drawn to a blue light which seemed to be coming from above and behind her car ... She stopped the car and got out to take a look: she wasn't prepared for what she saw! A huge object was hovering above and completely overlapping the road on both sides, at an altitude of just two telegraph poles. This made possible an estimate of the size of the object ... Mrs Puddy feels that the UFO was at least 100 feet [30 metres] in diameter ... The UFO was shaped like two huge saucers, one inverted on top of the other, with a smooth surface, no joins, welds, seams or rivets, no windows, doors or portholes, and no wheels. And this great object was radiating a brilliant blue light all around, not in beams, but in an intense glow ...'* [Magee, 1977.]

The account continues with Puddy returning to the car and driving it for some miles, followed for about 15km (8 miles) by the saucer, until it suddenly streaked away. The report dates this incident as taking place on 5 July 1972. Twenty days later, another encounter was reported very close to the same time and place she had experienced the first. This account reveals that Puddy kept driving on this occasion and, as the saucer paced her car, she received some mental communications, in the form of a voice intruding into her consciousness. This voice said 'All your tests will be negative', followed by 'Tell the media, do not panic, we mean no harm'. At the onset of the period when Puddy's car first encountered the UFO, she describes an unusual 'vacuum' effect which interfered with her control of the vehicle. However, the last words she 'heard' were 'You now have control' and the car returned to normal.

Analysis

THE INTERNAL/EXTERNAL FACTORS

Of course, the problem with all accounts like this is that there is no way of showing whether it had any external reality at all. If another EH sufferer could spend 3 days in a seaside hotel under the impression that he was fighting with his army unit in the Falklands, we can safely assume, in the light of such visionary realism, that this too was a somewhat typical late-at-night, remote-road, single-witness event, which was entirely hallucinatory. One of the first requirements that should be put to any witness who presents such a report is:

> *Convince me as to why this could not have been entirely hallucinatory. Is there any other evidence apart from your testimony that could show that this event had some external reality?*

Puddy's account was published in the *Australasian Post* on 24 August 1972, and this did seem to provide another witness:

> *At about 10 o'clock on the night of July 25 ... a young man came out into the street ... about three quarters of an hour after Mrs Puddy says what happened ... He was Maris Ezergailis ... a qualified air pilot licenced to fly commercially ... And what did he see on July 25? Something that didn't quite make sense to him. A flash of blue light from the sky, and when he looked up, a meteor trail, but an unusually broad one traveling horizontally! Just a streak of light and it was gone, but it left him wondering ... Mrs Puddy reacted strongly when told about what the witness saw, relating – 'That's the way it looked when it took off the first time I saw it ... a wide streak of light and then nothing.'* [Magee, 1997]

THE UNEXPLAINED ATMOSPHERIC PHENOMENON OPTION

From such evidence it certainly seems that there was a UAP involved in Puddy's encounters. It should be remembered how EH witnesses seem to apprehend an electric fireball in close proximity. When irradiated by its fields, their perceptual system seems to respond by superimposing appropriate imagery on it, and Puddy's encounter does seem to have involved just such a process. The simplicity of the shape of the 'saucer' is just the type of abbreviated form, free of detail, which the brain could cope with in terms of imagery. Puddy's 'craft', with its minimalist stripped-down appearance, is typical of the range of hallucinatory imagery reported for such realities. Also, its dual appearance on the same stretch of road around the same time is suggestive of a response to an RF transmission to which Puddy is sensitized, or perhaps to geomagnetic energies, or to both as an intermodulation effect. It is unlikely, however, for her to have encountered the same UAP twice, one would have thought, but I am willing to leave this issue open, as I have been repeatedly surprised by the phenomena which I have studied over the past 17 years or so. Alternatively, the observations by Ezergailis may have been quite spurious, and the whole encounter may have been a journey through inner space for Puddy.

THE NATURE OF EVIDENCE – AGAIN!

It must be realized that, in considering these accounts, we are not following any sort of scientific criteria. There is little about them which can offer us information that can be tested. However, a clinical survey of Maureen Puddy's state of health at the time of her encounters, a field survey of her home, and information on her 'electrical history' would show us the extent to which she conforms (or otherwise) to the EM-pollution/environmental health model I have outlined here. There are small tantalizing details in the published accounts on her experiences, not the least being the fact that she was a 'repeater'. For me, this alone is enough to indicate that she has developed the EH/sensitivities syndrome. Passing remarks alluding to the electric shocks which the investigators felt as they touched the bodywork of her car when getting into it are also interesting and relevant. This case has been included because it shows how two investigators witnessed an experiencer undergoing an alien-abduction experience *as it happened*. However, like so many 'classic' cases that have gone into the history of ufology, it is difficult to investigate due to the amount of time that has elapsed. Many accounts which make up the mythology of the ufological movement are untouchable because of this time factor, but they are now preserved in amber for the collectors who regard them as fact.

I was struck by the similarity of the events that Puddy reported to those described by the witness/investigator mentioned on p. 16-7; in this incident, it was claimed that a huge metal flying saucer descended upon a car and hovered above it, but subsequent investigation showed no correlations with official documentation. Even small details are identical, for example: how the saucer hovered exactly over the road, overlapping it on either side; how a car was involved and how it malfunctioned; how both Puddy and the narrator of this tale had recently contacted a doctor about their children's health, etc. From such a comparison I am strongly reminded of how modern folktales draw from a common stock of images and themes, and the subculture of ufology has, as its currency, reports compiled by people with well-developed belief-systems. It is not difficult to detect the formation of 'factual accounts' as they occur within such a hot-house climate. I am constantly appalled by what is identified as sure-fire evidence by 'researchers' who seem unable to distinguish between the clashing methodologies of what is required to establish a case/debate in a courtroom, and what is required by science in order to establish criteria which can actually *predict* outcomes of witness/environment investigations.

The 'communications' that Puddy tells us she received are ambiguous. 'All your tests will be negative' could become meaningful seen against Puddy's life-situation in terms of her sensitivities at the time of her experience. Like the symbology in dreams, which needs to be linked to the dreamer's personal conditions in order to make any sense, this is clearly a statement looking for a context.

Conclusion

To conclude, this case not only serves to confirm the internal nature of such experiences, but also provides clear evidence of adverse health effects due to EM exposure. Despite the presence of the investigators, Puddy was clearly extremely disturbed by her experience, and both Magee and Norman were actively involved in calming her in the hours after the event. It is easy to overlook the fact that, in many instances, being subjected to painful and disorientating physical sensations, coupled with what feels like a new weird reality involving entities intent upon performing some kind of surgical procedure on you, has been terrifyingly traumatic for many experiencers around the world.

List of abbreviations

5-HT	5-hydro-tetramine
AM	amplitude modulation
ANSI	American National Standards Institute
APRO	Aerial Phenomena Research Organisation
APW	Ally-Pally Woman (case file)
ASSAP	Association for the Study of Anomalous Phenomena
ATC	air traffic controller
BL	ball lightning
BUFORA	British UFO Research Association
CAT	computerized axial tomography (scan)
CB	Citizens' Band (radio)
CE4	close encounters of the fourth kind
CNS	central nervous system
DMT	dimethoxy-tryptamine
ECT	electroconvulsive therapy
EEG	electroencephalogram
EH	electromagnetic hypersensitivity
ELF	extremely low frequency
EM	electromagnetic
EMF	electromagnetic field
EMP	electromagnetic pulse
ESP	extrasensory perception
ET	extraterrestrial
ETH	extraterrestrial hypothesis
FDA	Food and Drug Administration
FM	frequency modulation
GEC	General Electric Company
IBS	irritable bowel syndrome
ICS	intracellular space
IEE	Institution of Electrical Engineers
IEEE	Institute of Electrical and Electronic Engineers
ION	Institute of Optimum Nutrition
KP	kryptopyrrhole
LED	light-emitting diode
LITS	lights in the sky
ME	myalgic encephalomyelitis
MEE	major electrical event

MEM   magnetic event marker
MIR   magnetic implant response
MR   magnetic response
MRI   magnetic resonance imaging
MUFON   Mutual UFO Network
MW   microwave
NERC   National Environmental Research Council
OBE   out-of-body experience
PK   psychokinetic, psychokinesis
REM   rapid eye movement
RF   radio frequency
SAR   specific absorption rate
SLI   street light interference
SPR   Society for Psychical Research
SQUID   superconducting quantum interference detector
TLE   temporal-lobe epilepsy
TNG   The Norfolk Girl (case file)
TVI   television interference
UAP   unclassified atmospheric phenomena
UFO   unidentified flying object
UFORIC   UFO Research Institute of Canada
UHF   ultra-high frequency
ULF   ultra-low frequency
USAF   United States Air Force
USSR   (former) Union of Soviet Socialist Republics
UV   ultra-violet
WHO   World Health Organization

UNITS:

A .... Amp
Gs .... Gauss
Hz .... Hertz
T .... Tesla
V .... Volt
W .... Watt
n .... nano
μ .... micro
m .... milli
k .... kilo
M .... mega
G .... giga

Notes

1. *Magonia* can be contacted through the editor, John Rimmer, at John Dee Cottage, 5 St James Terrace, Mortlake Churchyard, LONDON SW14 8HB, UK.

2. Both Dr Jean Monro and Dr C W Smith, who treat and work with EH patients, report that such individuals typically have a history of 'paranormal' experiences.

3. The Powerwatch Network, who publish a regular newsletter on EM pollution, can be contacted at 2 Tower Road, Sutton, ELY, Cambridgeshire CB6 2QA, UK.

4. A circulated report on the operation of the Hutchison device (*Vancouver Experiment Observations*, August 1985) was compiled by Jack Houck, an electrical engineer who was employed by McDonnell Douglas Aerospace. The device was also investigated by the Los Alamos National Laboratory, USA, using four cameras, one of which was trained on Hutchison throughout their visit. The results of their findings are now classified, even to Hutchison himself, although they can be applied for under the Freedom of Information Act in the USA. The Max Planck Institute, Germany, analysed Hutchison's metal samples.

5. Dr Anthony Barker (in 'Electricity, magnetism and the body: some uses and abuses', a paper/lecture delivered at the IEE, London, on 28 October 1993) relates:

   The energy output from a defibrillator is impressively large, as can be demonstrated by discharging it into a 5mm air gap between two ordinary pencil leads, resulting in a large flash of light and a considerable bang.

6. Unpublished article/paper by Reiter, written in February 1994, entitled 'The magnetic event: a new clue to an enigma'. The succeeding extracts are also from this.

7. For data on the Aveley case, author Andrew Collins can be contacted at PO Box 189, LEIGH-ON-SEA, Essex, SS9 1JF, UK. His original report 'The Aveley Abduction' was available from Independent UFO Network, UK, which has now disbanded. However, the British UFO Research Association (BUFORA) has research and investigation sections and can be contacted by writing to: BM BUFORA, LONDON WC1 3XX, UK.

8. 'Hidden scars', an article by Madhustee Mukerjee in *Scientific American* (October 1995, p. 10), reports new discoveries regarding the role of stress in the formative years of children. It relates:

> *The brain responds to intense stress by causing adrenaline, noradrenaline, cortisols, opiates and several other hormones to be released into the blood-stream. The chemicals alter neuronal connections and seem to mediate psychological reactions: enhanced noradrenaline levels cause post-traumatic stress disorder sufferers to experience flashbacks. The hippocampus is particularly sensitive to high levels of cortisols, which circulate for hours or days after stress.*

The implications for the consciousness effects being considered, e.g. alien-abduction experiences, are far reaching. Both myself and Professor Kenneth Ring found histories of childhood abuse in the backgrounds of experiencers, and the article goes on to outline the formation of permanent physical changes to the hippocampus of sufferers. That is to say, those experiencers with this developmental trait *have differences in brain structure from the rest of the population*. The findings also provide us with an understanding of how stress precipitates hallucinatory periods, as this is precisely what flashbacks are. Therefore it certainly appears that the developmental traumas of experiencers have equipped them with enhanced facilities for visionary hallucinations.

9. Highly relevant is a letter published in *Nature* (1995, vol. 374, p. 123) which supports my own conclusions regarding the implication of endogenous materials in the human system in EH:

> *Magnetite particles, 100nm in diameter, either naked or coated with bovine serum albumin are readily taken up by human white blood cells … Because the ferromagnetic particles interact strongly with magnetic fields, their presence in cell structures at a density far higher than that of the cells may provide a simple mechanism to account for the links between EMF exposure and in vitro biological effects.*

> *Atsuko K. Kobayashi and Joseph L. Kirschvink. Division of Geological and Planetary Science, California Institute of Technology, Pasadena, CA, USA. Also Michael H. Nesson, Department of Biochemistry and Biophysics, Oregon State University, Corvallis, OR, USA.*

10. I recall approaching experiencer Maria Ward at Central TV, Birmingham, UK, in 1994 and, in the presence of a BUFORA council member, asking her 'The 25 Questions'. She answered in the affirmative to over 20 of them, unaware of how revealing her answers were of her environmental sensitivities.

11. See the Rowley Regis/Jean Hingley case in my previous book (Budden, 1995a), from which the succeeding extracts are taken.

12. For information on microwave and radio-frequency emissions from geological sources see:

Zhizhen, Z (1991). *Advances in Geophysical Research*. Pergamon Press. 1991.

Massinon, B., Bernard, P., Caristan, Y (1993) 'Quelques precurseurs des seismes.'

CHOCS Revue Scientifique et Technique de la Direction des Applications Militaires No. 7.

13. US researcher Linda Moulton-Howe ('Animal mutilations: the unsolved mystery.' *Nexus* 1997, February/March) stated:

... as long as those orange balls of light were around, they had [animal] mutilations in Elizabeth, Colorado. When people stopped reporting these glowing balls of light, the mutilations stopped. The link between the lights and the mutilations was something I had heard everywhere I went.

14. UK experiencer Linda Jones encountered a UAP at close range, along with her daughters. However, what UK investigators do not generally realize about this well-known case is that Linda was also very close to a lightning strike during her early years, the location being near to where the close-encounter experience occurred. A geological analysis of the area shows that it has a high magnetic ambience, is prone to lightning strikes and, it would seem, other electrical phenomena. Such areas are known as 'lightning nests'. Interestingly, Jones's close encounter (like the Pascagonla case, USA) has undergone a revisionist make-over. The early reports describe a 'gondola-shaped light', but a recent conversation with Linda provides the object she saw with her daughter with structured legs on which it landed!

15. In my first book (Budden, 1994) I described 'The Plumstead Common Case' where a woman was hospitalized after a large ball of light came down and settled on the grass near where she was sitting, about 100m (110yd) away. She hallucinated two bizarre entitities who emerged from the light dressed like chauffeurs, and then, on turning, she saw her father sitting on the grass close by, dressed in a suit. He had been dead for 6 years. She was found unconscious by her family and immediately hospitalized for systemic shock and loss of sight, which lasted for 3 months.

16. Science magazine *OMNI* (1984, vol. 16, no. 6) reported that, in the mid-1980s, Christie Dennis from Phoenix, AZ, USA, reported a vivid abduction experience to US investigator Dr Leo Sprinkle, who was so impressed that he recruited her for a 1981 conference for 'abductees' and she went on to meet UFO Contact Centre International. *OMNI's* Robert Sheaffer relates: 'she rocked the nation's UFO establishment by admitting that her dramatic "UFO abduction" was a hoax.'

17. In 'Hidden scars: sexual and other abuse may alter a brain region.' (*Scientific American* 1995, October: p.10), on the role of stress in formative years resulting in changes in the development of the hippocampus in the child, Madhustee Mukerjee relates:

> *Murray B. Stein of the University of California ... compared 22 women who reported severe childhood abuse with 21 control subjects and detected an average volume reduction of 5 percent of the left hippocampus.*

This alerts us to a factor in experiencer populations which indicates that such individuals are further delineated from non-experiencers in that their adult brain structure may have altered physical aspects. See also Note 7.

18. This important and underrated concept was first introduced by Hilary Evans in his seminal work *Visions, Apparitions, Alien Visitors*, published by Aquarian Press in 1984. Evans argued that the mind/brain has an extraordinary creative faculty that functions autonomously with tremendous speed to produce hallucinatory/visionary presentaions for the experiencer. He called this faculty 'the producer'.

References

Anon. (1976a) *APRO Bulletin* 25 (1): 6.

Anon. (1976b) *APRO Bulletin* 25 (2): 1–3.

Anon. (1984a) *Northern UFO News* November/December: 110

Anon. (1984b) *Northern UFO News* May/June: 107

Anon. (1993a) 'Leukaemia death No. 2 in meter boy street.' *Mail on Sunday* 29 August.

Anon. (1993b) 'Uncontrolled wheelchair movements.' *Microwave News* July/August.

Anon. (1993c) 'Under the 'fluence.' *Pharmaceutical Journal* 27 March: 404.

Anon. (1993d) 'Gamida', *UFO Afrinews* January: 7

Anon. (1995) *Nature* 374 (9 March).

Anon. (1996) *ASSAP News* May: 59

Adey, W.R. (1993) 'Whispering between cells: electromagnetic fields and regulatory mechanism in tissue.' *Frontier Perspectives* 3 (2). Center for Frontier Sciences, Temple University, USA.

Bach. E. (1992) 'Volcanic ball lightnings.' *Electric Spacecraft Journal* No. 7.

Baker, R.R., Mather, J. & Kennaugh, J. (1983) 'Magnetic bones in human sinuses.' *Nature* 301 (6 January).

Ballone, P. (1993) 'Molecular dynamics reveals more hydrogen surprises.' *Physics World*.

Blackmore, S. (1994) 'Alien abduction: the inside story.' *New Scientist* 19 November: 31.

Blakeslee, S. (1996) 'Pulsing magnets offer new method of mapping the brain.' *New York Times* 21 May.

Braithwaite, J. (1996) 'Northern blanket.' *ASSAP News* No. 59 (May).

Breakspear Hospital (1994) *Environmental Illness.* [Information sheet.] Breakspear Hospital, Belswain Lane, Hemel Hempstead, Hertfordshire, UK.

Breakspear Hospital (1994) *The Load Phenomenon.* [Information sheet.] Breakspear Hospital, Belswain Lane, Hemel Hempstead, Hertfordshire, UK.

Brodeur, P. (1977) 'The zapping of America: microwaves, their deadly risk and the cover-up.' *Microwave News*.

Budden, A. (1994a) *Allergies and Aliens: The Visitation Experience – An Environmental Health Issue.* Discovery Times Press.

Budden, A. (1994b) 'An Allergy at the Inn'. *Anomaly* May

Budden, A. (1994/95) 'The "Quantock Horror" revisited.' *The Ley Hunter* No. 122.

Budden, A. (1995) *UFOS – Psychic Close Encounters: The Electromagnetic Indictment.* Blandford, UK.

Budden, A. (1995b) 'Aliens, electricity and allergies.' *MUFON Journal* No. 322 (February).

Budden, A. (1996) 'Poltergeist' *Fortean Times* 92: November p.23.

Budden, A. (1996/97a) 'The poltergeist machine.' *Nexus* 4 (1).

Budden, A. (1996/97b) *The Poltergeist Machine. The Hutchison Effect: A Lift and Disruption System.* Limited edition. Discovery Times Press.

Bullard, T.E. (1987) *UFO Abductions: The Measure of a Mystery.* 1. *Comparative Study of Abduction Cases.* 2. *Catalogue of Cases.* 2 volumes. Fund for UFO Research, Bloomington, Indiana, USA.

Burke, H.E. (1986) *Handbook of Magnetic Phenomena.* Van Nostrand Reinhold, New York, USA. [An essential text for the identification of environmental effects, despite its high cost.]

Choy, R., Monro, J. & Smith, C.W. (1986) 'Electrical sensitivities in allergy patients.' *Clinical Ecology* 4 (3).

Coghill, R. (1992) *Electrohealing.* Thorson.

Collins, A. (1974) *The Aveley Abduction.* [See also Note 9.]

Concar, D. (1995) 'Happiness is a magnet.' *New Scientist* 5 August.

Corum, K.L. & Corum, J.F. (1988) 'The missing Chapter 34. Colorado Spring Notes.' *Tesla Coil Builders' Association News* 7 (3).

Corum, K. & Corum, J. (1989) 'Tesla's production of electric fireballs.' *Tesla Coil Builders' Association News* 8 (3).

Corum, K.L. & Corum, J.F. (1990) 'Nikola Tesla and the laboratory generation of ball lightning.' *PACE Newsletter* 6 (1): 21–2.

Corum, K.L. & Corum, J.F. (1992) 'RF high voltage fireball experiments and electrochemical fractal clusters.' *International Committee on Ball Lightning.* Article Series No. 1992 (1).

Corum, K.L. & Corum, J.F. (1993a) 'Nikola Tesla and the laboratory generation of ball lightning.' Ph.D. submission to the 1993 Tesla Symposium, Novi Sad, Serbia.

Corum, K.L. & Corum, J.F. (1993b) 'High voltage RF experiments: slow-wave resonators, Tesla coils and ball lightning.' Ph.D. submission to the 1993 Tesla Symposium, Novi Sad, Serbia.

Corum, J.F., Edwards, D.J. & Corum, K.L. (1989) *'Tesla Coils': 1890–1990 – 100 Years of Cavity Resonator Development.* Corum & Associates Inc.

Corum, J.F., Green, R.J. & Pinzone, B.F. (1996) 'ANSI standards for MW radiation.' In: *An Introduction to Earth Station Engineering Considerations.* American National Standards Institute.

Dayton, L. (1993) 'Secrets of a bolt from the blue.' *New Scientist* 18 December: 16.

Demarne, C. (1991) *The London Blitz: A Fireman's Tale*. Battle of Britain Prints International Ltd.

Devereux, P. and McCartney, P. (1982) *Earth Lights*. Turnstone.

Devereux, P., Roberts, A. & Clarke, D. (1989) *Earth Lights Revelation*. Blandford.

Dimbylow, P.J. (1990) *Hot Heads?* National Radiological Protection Board, Chilton, UK.

Edmonds, E.A. & Williams, B.J. (1985) *Geology of the Country around Taunton and the Quantock Hills*. British Geological Survey, National Environmental Research Council, UK.

Egely, G. (1994) *Hungarian Ball Lightning Observations*. Publishing Associates of the Hungarian Academy of Sciences.

Eidelman, W.S. (1995) 'The bio-energy revolution.' In: *You are a Healer*. Self-published. [Booklet and video.]

Evans, H. (1984) *Visions, Apparitions, Alien Visitors*. Aquarian Press. [This important and underrated concept was first introduced in this seminal work.]

Falla, G., compiler (1979) *Vehicle Interference Project*. Case No. 422. [Edited by Lockwood, C.F. & Price, A.R.] British UFO Research Organisation, London, UK.

Finkelstein, D. & Rubinstein, J. (1970) 'Ball lightning.' *American Scientist* 58: 262–80.

Forrest, S.R. & Witten T.A.(1979) 'Longe range Correlations in Smoke-Particle Aggregates' *Physics Journal* 12(5) pp.109–17

Fowler, R.E. (1980) *The Andreasson Affair*. Bantam, UK.

Frey & Wesler (1990) 'Interaction of psychoactive drugs with exposure to EMF.' *Journal of Biochemistry* 9 (2): 187–196.

Gilroy, J. (1990) *Basic Neurology*. Pergamon Press, Oxford, UK.

Goddard, G.V. (1967) 'Development of epileptic seizures through brain stimulation at low intensity.' *Nature* 214: 1020–1021.

Goddard, G.V., McIntyre, D.C. & Leech, C.K. (1969) 'A permanent change in brain function resulting from daily electrical stimulation.' *Experimental Neurology* 25: 295–330.

Goldfader, L. (1993) 'Power-grids and abductions: is there a link?' *Flying Saucer Review* 38 (3).

Goldstein, K. (1995) *The Organism*. Zone Books.

Gotlib, D. (1994) *Bulletin of Anomalous Experience* 5 (4).

Grosse, M. (1995) [Correspondence.] *Anomaly* 17 (November): 28.

Halgren, E., Walter, R.D., Cherlow, D.D. & Crandall, P.H. (1978) 'Mental phenomena evoked by electrical stimulation of the human hippocampal formation and amygdala.' *Brain* 101: 83–117. [*Déjà vu* is specifically covered on pp. 105 and 109.] [14]

Hathaway, G. & Hutchison, J. (1992) 'The Hutchison effect.' *Electric Spacecraft Journal* No. 4 (April).

Hind, C. ed. (1993) 'Gamida' Case No. 48. *UFO Afrinews* No. 7.

Holford, I. (1977) *The Guinness Book of Weather Facts and Feats.* Guinness Superlatives Ltd.

Holt, J. (1996) 'Asthma rise is blamed on radio frequencies.' *The Times* 30 April: 5.

Hopkins, B. (1987) *Intruders.* Sphere Books, Random House.

Huxley A. (1963a) *Heaven and Hell.* Penguin. [Republication.]

Huxley, A. (1963b) *The Doors of Perception.* Penguin. [Republication.]

IEE (1991) 'The possible effects of low-frequency electromagnetic fields.' *Public Affairs Board Report* No. 10 (July): 5. Institution of Electrical Engineers, London, UK.

Kobayashi, A.K, Kirschvink, J.L. & Nesson, M.H. (1995) [Correspondence.] *Nature* 374 (9 March): 123.

Kravs, D. (1991) 'Antennas and radiation.' In *Electromagnetics.* Chapter 6. [For technical details.]

Kuster, N., Wieser, H.G. & Dobson, J. (1993/94) 'Iron biomineralization in the human brain and the effect of magnetic fields on the EEG-recorded brain wave activity.' ETHZ.ETH and Swiss National Foundation and Department of Neurology, UHZ, Institute for Geophysik, ETH, Zurich, Switzerland.

LaPlante, E. (1993) *Seized.* HarperCollins.

Le Fanu, J. (1994) 'May I examine your dream?' *The Times* 13 January. London.

Lin, J. (1977) 'On microwave-induced hearing sensation.' *Trans. of Microwave Theory Tech.* MTT-25: 605–13.

Little, G.L. (1994) *Grand Illusions.* White Buffalo Books, USA.

Lockwood C. F. & Price A. R. Eds. (1979) Vehicle Interference Project, compiled by G. Falla. BUFORA Case No. 422.

Lynn, P.A. (1987) *Radar Systems.* Macmillan Education. [For technical information.]

Magee, J. (1977) 'UFO Over the MoorAduc road. [Encounter cases from *Flying Saucer Review.*] Edited by C. Bowen. Signet Books. New American Library/Times Mirror, New York, USA.

Marincic, A.A. ed. (1978) Compilation based on the *Colorado Springs Notes.* Nolit, Beograd.

Massinon, B., Bernard, P,. & Caristan, Y. (1993) 'Quelques precurseurs des seismes.' *CHOCS Revue scientifique et technique de la direction des applications militaires* No. 7 (April). [For information on microwave and radio-frequency emissions from geological sources.]

McClure, K. (1995) 'Getting carried away: assessing the reliability of research into alien abductions.' *Psi Researcher* No. 17 (May): 5.

Moulton-Howe, L. (1997) 'Animal mutilations: the unsolved mystery.' *Nexus* (February/March).

Mukerjee, M. (1995) 'Hidden scars: sexual and other abuse may alter a brain region.' *Scientific American* October: 10–12.

Nathan, P. (1988) *The Nervous System*. 3rd edition. Oxford University Press, Oxford, UK.

Ornstein, R. (1991) *The Evolution of Consciousness*. Prentice Hall.

Oscar, K.J. (1972) Analysis of microwaves for barrier warfare. US Army Mobile Equipment Research and Development Center.

Parkin, J. (1990) *General Practitioner* 11 May: 42.

Persinger, M. & Cameron, R.A. (1986) 'Are earth faults at fault in some poltergeist-like episodes?' *Journal of the American Society for Psychical Research* 80 (1): 49–73.

Philips. A. (1996) 'Electricity, power lines and health.' *EMF Notes: 6. [Obtainable from Powerwatch. See Note 3.]*

Phillips, K. & Jaafar, J., *Northern UFO News* September: 162

Pickering (1993) *International Journal of Alternative and Complementary Medicine* October.

Playfair, G.L. (1981) *This House is Haunted*. Sphere.

Poole, I.D. (1992) *An Introduction to Scanners and Scanning* Bernard Baban Ltd.

Randles, J. ed. (1993) 'Quantock update.' *Northern UFO News* No. 162 (September): 19.

Randles, J., ed. (1984a) 'Case histories: An unexpected visit to the toilet!' [Pagless, M., Hart, S. & Mortimer, WYUFORG Report, March 1979.] *Northern UFO News* May/June.

Randles, J., ed. (1984b) 'The intruder on runway 27.' [Investigated by Johnson & Warrington.] *Northern UFO News* No. 110 (November/December): 11.

Rapp, D.J. (1979) *Allergies and the Hyperactive Child*. Thorson. [Contains photographs (pp. 60–65) of both children and adults with the distinctive 'allergic look' of masked food allergies, frequently seen in experiencers.]

Reeve, B. & Reeve, H. (1957) *Flying Saucer Pilgrimage*. Amherst Press, USA.

Reiter, N. (1994) 'The magnetic event: a new clue to an enigma.' Unpublished.

RFI Shielding Ltd (1995) *Material Design Manual*. Appendix II: 257.

Rhine (1974) *Phantoms: Experiences and Investigations*. David & Charles.

Richey, D. (1994) 'Elephantology: the science of limiting perception to a single aspect of a large object. Parts 1 and 2.' *Bulletin of*

Anomalous Experience 5 (6).

Rimmer, J. (1997) 'Mr Hutchinson's [sic] amazing machine.' Magonia 58.

Ring, K. (1992) *The Omega Project*. William Morrow, USA.

Roney-Dougal, S. (1991) *Where Science and Magic Meet*. Element, Shaftesbury, UK.

Rothera, E. (1991) *Encyclopedia of Allergy and Environmental Illness*. David & Charles.

Ruttan, L.A., Persinger, M.A. & Koren, S. (1990) 'Enhancement of temporal lobe-related experiences during brief exposures to milli-gauss intensity extremely low frequency magnetic fields.' *Journal of Bioelectricity* 9 (1): 33–54.

Scarfe, C. (1997) *Pyoluria: A Stress-induced Disorder*. Institute of Optimum Nutrition, London, UK.

Sheaffer, R. (1984) 'Anti-matter-UFO update.' *OMNI* 16 (6)

Silk, A. (1996) 'Of bells, smells and cells: the normality of the para-normal.' 20th International Conference of the Society for Psychical Research, London.

Simpson & Fitch (1988) *Applied Neurophysiology*. Butterworth.

Smith, C.W. & Best, S. (1989) *Electromagnetic Man; Health and Hazard in the Electrical Environment*. Dent. [This work is the most important published in the UK and is an essential text for researchers in the fields under study.] [6]

Smith, C.W., Choy, R. & Monro, J. (1986) 'The diagnosis and therapy of electrical sensitivities.' *Clinical Ecology* (6) 4.

Steiner, S. (1994) *The Curse of Electricity*. Times Group Newspapers, UK.

Strand, E. (1984) *Project Hessdalen*. Final technical report. Part 1.

Strieber, W. (1995) [Correspondence.] *MUFON Journal*. No. 324 (April): 18.

Taylor, J. (1975) *Superminds: An Enquiry into the Paranormal*. Macmillan.

Tesla, N. (1897) *Electrical World and Engineer* 5 March.

Thompson, R. (1976) *Progress in Psycho-biology*. Freeman.

Uman, M.A. (1969) *Lightning*. McGraw-Hill.

Vallée, J. (1970) *Passport to Magonia*. Sphere books

Van der Castle (1984) *OMNI* 6(6).

Veacock, C. (1994) 'Skidbrook church – a case of magick?' *Psi Researcher* No. 14.

Weaver, J.C. (1995) 'Electroporation in cells and tissues: a biophysical phenomenon due to electromagnetic fields.' *Radio Science* 30 (1): 205–21.

Wells, A. (1994) 'The White Hart Inn.' *Anomaly* 14 (November).

WHO (1993) 'Electromagnetic fields 300Hz–300GHz.' *Environmental Health Criteria* 137. World Health Organization, Geneva. [20]

Zhizhen, Z. (1991) *Advances in Geophysical Research*. Vol. 2. Geosound and Nanoearthquake. Pergamon Press. [179]

Index

Page numbers in *italic* refer to the illustrations in the text